CHILTON'S Repair and Tune-Up Guide

Audi

ILLUSTRATED

Prepared by the

Automotive Editorial Department

Chilton Book Company

Chilton Way

Radnor, Pa. 19089

215–687-8200

editor-in-chief **JOHN D. KELLY;** managing editor **JOHN H. WEISE, S.A.E.;** assistant managing editor **PETER J. MEYER;** technical editors **David P. Galluccio, William J. Jones, John M. McGuigan, Ronald L. Sessions, N Banks Spence Jr**

CHILTON BOOK COMPANY RADNOR, PENNSYLVANIA

First Edition

Published in Radnor, Pa. by Chilton Book Company
and simultaneously in Ontario, Canada,
by Thomas Nelson & Sons, Ltd.
Manufactured in the United States of America

Library of Congress Cataloging in Publication Data

Chilton Book Company. Automotive Editorial Dept.
Chilton's repair and tune-up guide for the Audi.

1. Audi automobile. I. Title. II. Title:
Repair and tune-up guide for the Audi.
TL215.A8C48 1973 629.28'7'22 73-11010
ISBN 0-8019-5864-4
ISBN 0-8019-5902-0 (pbk.)

Chilton Book Company expresses appreciation
to the following for their generous assistance:

Porsche-Audi Division of Volkswagen of America, Inc.

Although information in this guide is based on industry sources and is as complete as possible at the time of publication, the possibility exists that the manufacturer made later changes which could not be included here. While striving for total accuracy, Chilton Book Company can not assume responsibility for any errors, changes, or omissions that may occur in the compilation of this data.

Contents

Chapter One

General Information and Maintenance

Introduction

The Audi is produced by Auto Union of Germany and distributed in the United States by the Porsche Audi division of Volkswagen of America. It has been available in the United States since 1970 in three models: the Super 90, Super 90 station wagon (Variant), and the 100 LS. They were initially imported with a 1,760 cc slanted four-cylinder, OHV engine. Displacement has since been increased to 1,871 cc.

The Audi uses a transaxle behind the forward mounted engine to transmit power to the front drive axle, while a dead axle is used at the rear. Regular features are inboard mounted front disc brakes, rear drum brakes, and rack and pinion steering. A four-speed transmission is standard and a three-speed automatic is optional.

The Super 90 model was dropped in 1972, after 4,500 were sold. It was replaced by the 100 as a lower cost alternative to the 100 LS. The top of the line 100 GL, with automatic transmission as standard equipment, was added in 1973.

All models imported into the United States are described in this book with procedures specifically labeled as to model and year (whenever there is a significant difference). The troubleshooting section is specially designed to enable the owner to diagnose and correct minor motoring ills before they require major repair jobs. Each chapter contains the maintenance, repair, and overhaul procedures related to a particular component or system.

This book covers maintenance and repair procedures that the owner or repair shop will be able to perform without special tools or equipment. The few jobs that absolutely require special factory tools, such as automatic transmission overhaul, are best left to an authorized Audi dealer. It is assumed that the person using this book for repair or maintenance operations will have access to a basic mechanic's tool kit. In addition, most overhaul operations do require a torque wrench for best results and safety.

It is hoped that this book will also prove valuable as a reference for those owners who merely wish to understand their cars, or possibly their mechanics, better. In this case, no tools at all are required.

Super 90

100 LS, the 100 and 100 GL differ only in trim

Serial Number Identification

VEHICLE

SUPER 90

The chassis number is on a plate on top of the instrument panel, clearly visible through the driver's side of the windshield. It is also stamped into the crossmember behind the battery, in the engine compartment. The vehicle identification plate is mounted on the right side of the engine compartment. The chassis number follows the words "Fahrgest.-Nr." on this plate.

Super 90 vehicle identification (a) is the vehicle identification plate (b) is the chassis number, and (c) is the emission control information sticker

100, 100 LS, 100 GL

The chassis number is on a plate on top of the instrument panel, clearly visible through the driver's side of the windshield. It is also stamped into the upper right corner of the firewall. The vehicle identification plate is mounted on the support directly behind the engine, except on 1973 models. On these it is on the right wheel housing. The chassis number follows the words "Fahrgest.-Nr." on this plate.

100, 100 LS, 100 GL vehicle identification (a) is the chassis number (b) is the vehicle identification plate

ENGINE

SUPER 90

Up to chassis numbers 6842 025 559, 6843 018 078, and 6834 000 156, the engine number is stamped on the engine block above the fuel pump. After these chassis numbers, the engine number is located on the left side of the engine block.

Super 90 engine number location for current models

An engine code number indicating the exact cylinder bore of the particular engine is stamped on the starter end of the engine block, just below the cylinder head.

(e) is the engine number location for 100, 100 LS, and 100 GL

100, 100 LS, 100 GL

The engine number is stamped on the left side of the engine block (clutch housing).

An engine code number is also stamped

Engine code number location

on the starter end of the engine block, just below the cylinder head. This number indicates the exact cylinder bore of the particular engine.

Routine Maintenance

The service intervals specified are for 1972 models. Consult the owner's handbook for exact recommendations for each year.

AIR CLEANER

The air cleaner has a paper element which should be cleaned every 6,000 miles and replaced every 12,000. There is a single hose from the air cleaner which must be rigged to receive outside air in the summer and warm air from the exhaust manifold in the winter. On the 100, 100 LS, and 100 GL, starting in 1972, this is done automatically by a thermostatic valve.

To clean or replace the filter element:

1. Release the six spring clips. Remove the cover.
2. Lift out the paper filter element, being careful not to drop any dirt down the carburetor throat.
3. Gently shake the element or tap it lightly on a clean, flat table top to remove loose dirt.
4. Wipe the housing out carefully.
5. Position the new or cleaned element in the housing.
6. Replace the top.

FLUID LEVEL CHECKS

Engine Oil

The engine oil level should be checked on a regular basis, at least at every gas stop, and more often under severe usage such as continuous high speeds, extreme temperatures, or trailer towing. If the check is made at a gas stop, wait until the gas tank has been filled. If the level is checked immediately after stopping, a false low reading will be obtained. The proper level is between the upper (maximum) and lower (minimum) level marks on the dipstick.

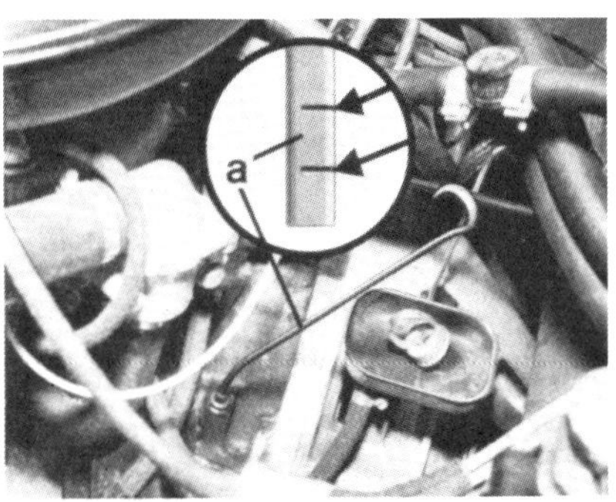

(A) is the engine oil dipstick on the 100, 100 LS, and 100 GL. The dipstick to the right in the illustration is the final drive dipstick on automatic transmission models and the transmission dipstick on manual transmission models

1. Pull out the dipstick. It is between the radiator and the ignition distributor on the front left side of the Super 90 engine, and on the rear left side on 100, 100 LS, and 100 GL engines. Do not take a reading yet, unless the engine has not been run for several hours.
2. Wipe the dipstick off with a clean rag.
3. Replace the dipstick, count slowly to ten, and remove it. Check the level on the dipstick.
4. If the level is at or below the lower mark, add enough oil to bring the level to the upper mark. The oil is added through the capped opening at the front of the valve cover. If the level is between the two marks, there is sufficient oil. See "Oil and Fuel Recommendations" for the proper oils.

Transmission

MANUAL

The transmission level should be checked every 6,000 miles. The proper lubricant is SAE 80 hypoid transmission lubricant. The 100, 100 LS, and 100 GL may have a transmission dipstick located behind the engine dipstick. The level should be between the two marks on the dipstick. If the level is at or below the lower mark, add enough lubricant through the dipstick tube to bring it to the upper mark. The Super 90 does not have a dipstick. The level is checked by removing the filler plug in the right side of the transmission case. The level should be at or very near the filler plug opening. Any lubricant required can be pumped in with a suction gun.

NOTE: *The 100, 100 LS, and 100 GL also have a filler plug in the right side of the transmission case.*

Super 90 manual transmission filler plug

Automatic

The transmission level should be checked every 6,000 miles. The proper transmission fluid is Dexron with the prefix letter B. With the transmission at normal operating temperature, proceed as follows:

1. Park on level surface. Shift into Neutral. Apply the parking brake. Allow the engine to idle.
2. Pull the dipstick from its tube at the rear of the engine compartment. Wipe it off with a clean rag.
3. Replace the dipstick and push it all the way in until the cap seats.
4. Pull the dipstick out after ten seconds and take a reading. The level should be between the two marks on the dipstick.
5. If the level is at or below the lower mark, add enough to bring the level between the marks. Be very careful not to overfill the transmission.

Brake Master Cylinder

The master cylinder is in the left rear of the engine compartment, on the firewall. The cap need not be removed to check the

Automatic transmission dipstick and filler tube (d)

level, since it can be seen through the translucent reservoir. The level should be between the MIN and MAX marks. If the level is at or below the MIN mark, proceed as follows:

Brake master cylinder reservoir

1. Clean off the area around the cap. Very small particles of dirt can cause serious difficulties in the brake system.
2. Remove the cap. Add fluid to the twin reservoirs to bring the level to the MAX mark.
3. Replace the cap.

NOTE: *Use only high-quality brake fluid specifically designated for disc brake systems. Ordinary fluid will boil during heavy braking, causing complete loss of braking power.*

Coolant

Since the cooling system is pressurized, the radiator cap should not be removed unless the engine has cooled. If you remove the cap while hot, you run the risk of being scalded by steam.

To check the coolant level:

1. Allow the engine to cool.
2. Turn the cap to the first catch.
3. If there is still pressure in the system, it will make a hissing sound as it escapes.
4. When there is no further hissing, completely remove the cap.
5. The coolant level should just reach the full mark (the small opening at the bottom of the filler neck). Do not overfill or coolant will be lost.

The coolant level should be up to the arrow

6. If the coolant needs to be replenished, refer to the Anti-Freeze Charts in the Appendix and to the Capacities Chart in this chapter to determine the proper amounts of anti-freeze and water to add to maintain the proper coolant mix.

NOTE: *Even in summer, the coolant mixture should provide anti-freeze protection. This is required to prevent rust.*

Final Drive

The final drive lubricant should be checked, on automatic transmission models, every 6,000 miles. On manual transmission models, the final drive is combined with the transmission and the two components share a common lubricant supply. The proper lubricant is SAE 90 hypoid lubricant, SAE 80 for arctic climates. If the level is at or below the lower mark, add enough lubricant through the dipstick tube to bring it to the upper mark. If the level is more than ½ in. above the upper mark, check for leakage from the automatic transmission.

Steering Gear

The level of the steering gear box, located at the rear of the engine compartment, should be checked periodically. The proper lubricant is liquid transmission grease.

Battery

The battery electrolyte level should be checked at least every four weeks. The Super 90 battery is under the hood. On the 100, 100 LS, and 100 GL, the battery is under the right side of the rear seat. The correct level should be at the bottom of the well inside each cell opening. Only colorless, odorless water should be added. It is a good idea to add the water with a squeeze bulb device to avoid having the sulfuric acid electrolyte splash out, as often happens when attempting to pour in water. If water is frequently needed, the most likely cause is overcharging. This is most often caused by an incorrect voltage regulator setting. If any acid should escape or spill, it can be neutralized with a baking soda and water solution. When replacing a battery, it is important that the re-

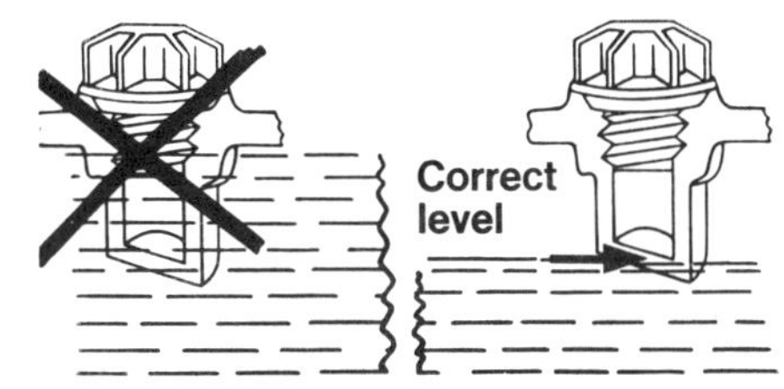

Correct battery electrolyte level

Capacities

Model	Engine Crankcase (qts)		Transaxle (pts)		Drive Axle (pts) ①	Gasoline Tank (gals)	Cooling System (qts)
	With Filter	Without Filter	Manual	Automatic			
All	4.3	N.A.	4.2	12.5 fill, 6 change	3	15	8

① Only with automatic transmission.

placement unit have an output rating equal to or greater than the original equipment.

TIRES AND WHEELS

It is a good idea to have an accurate tire pressure gauge on hand and to check tire pressures weekly. Not all servic station air pump gauges are reliable. If the car is used for high-speed driving rather than around town use, the pressure should be increased 3 psi. Do not exceed the maximum pressure marked on the tire sidewall. Snow tires should not be used at steady speeds over 75 mph, since their heavy tread builds up excessive heat. All four tires should be the same type; do not mix radial, bias, or bias-belted tires. Serious handling difficulties can result from mixing tires of different construction.

To obtain maximum tire wear, switch the tires from front to rear every 3,000 miles. Do not reverse a tire's direction of rotation; that is, do not rotate the tires from one side to the other. This is particularly important in the case of studded snow tires, as a change in the direction of rotation may cause loss of studs.

Tire Inflation Chart

(psi—Front/Rear)

Model	*2 Persons*	*Maximum Load*
Super 90 sedan	24/24	28/28
Super 90 sedan, radial tires	28/28	28/28
Super 90 wagon	24/24	28/32
Super 90 wagon, radial tires	28/28	28/32
100, 100 LS, 100 GL; radial tires	26/26	26/26

NOTE: *These pressures apply only to standard size tires: 6.45-13 or 165-13 for the Super 90, and 165-14 for the 100, 100 LS, and 100 GL.*

FUEL FILTER

The filter screen in the fuel pump should be cleaned every 6,000 miles. To do this:

1. Wipe the outside of the fuel pump clean. The fuel pump is on the left side of the engine block.

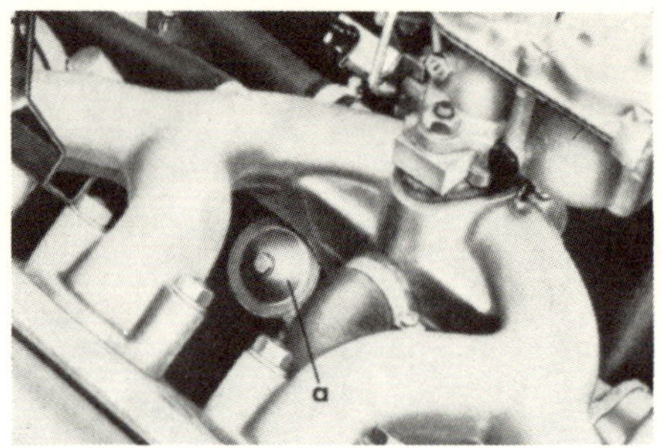

Fuel pump location—Super 90 shown

2. Remove the attaching bolt and the cover.
3. Remove the filter screen. Clean it in a safe solvent and air dry.
4. Replace the screen carefully. Use a new screen if the old one was damaged.
5. Replace and tighten the cover.
6. Start the engine and check for leaks.

Most models also have an in-line fuel filter in the line to the fuel pump. This should be replaced every 6,000 miles.

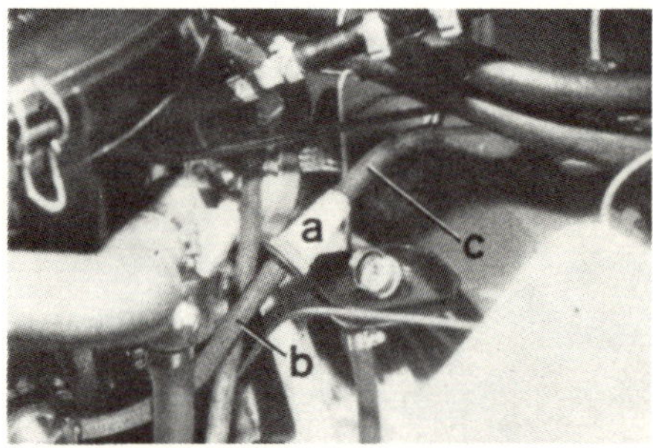

In-line fuel filter (a), (b), and (c) are connecting lines

Lubrication

OIL AND FUEL RECOMMENDATIONS

The factor which regulates the type of fuel needed is the engine compression ratio. Audi engines through 1971 have a high, 10.2:1, compression ratio and must use premium fuels. 1972 and later engines have a lower, 8.2:1, compression ratio and may subsist on regular, low-lead, or lead-free gasoline. If the engine pings while accelerating or runs on after the ignition is switched off, a better grade of fuel should be used.

Only oils labeled SE should be used. No additives are recommended. Recommended viscosities are as follows

Season or Location	*Temperature Range (deg F)*	*Viscosity*
Year round	+50 to −13	10W–20 10W–30 10W–40
Summer	+50 to +85	20W–20 20W–40
Winter	below +32	10W
Tropical	above +85	30
Arctic	below −13	5W 5W–20 5W–30

OIL CHANGES

Engine

The oil should be changed every 6,000 miles after the initial break-in period. This interval should be halved under city usage. During the break-in period, the oil should be changed at 600; 3,000; and 6,000 miles.

The oil filter should be replaced at each oil change. It is mounted on the engine block, near the alternator.

To change the oil and filter:

1. Operate the car until the engine is at normal operating temperature. If this is not done, most of the contaminants will remain in the engine. Stop the engine.
2. Slide a pan of at least five quarts capacity under the oil pan.
3. Remove the drain plug from the rear end of the oil pan, after wiping the area clean.

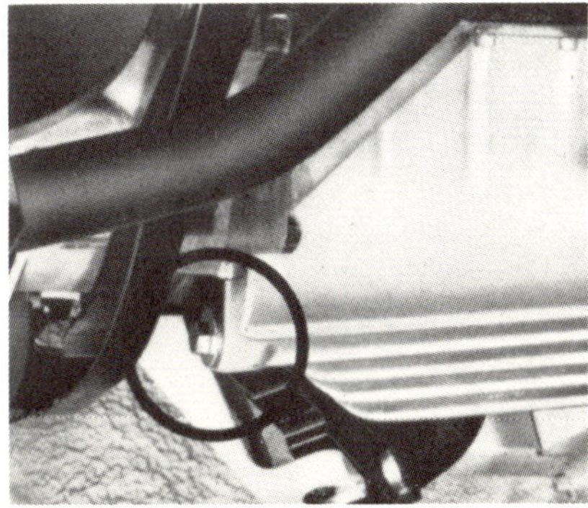

Engine oil pan drain plug

4. Allow the oil to drain into the pan. Do not replace the plug before the oil has completely stopped draining.
5. Clean off the plug, particularly the threads, and replace it.
6. Loosen the filter, using an oil filter wrench. These are available, often for less than a dollar, at discount and auto supply stores. Unscrew and discard the old filter after wiping the area clean.
7. Occasionally an overtightened filter will collapse when the filter wrench is used. The only remedy for this is to drive a long punch through the filter cartridge near the base and use this as a lever to unscrew the filter.
8. Smear a few drops of clean engine oil on the new filter gasket.
9. Screw the filter on by hand until the gasket makes contact. Then tighten the filter about one turn. If the filter is overtightened, it will be extremely difficult to remove.
10. Remove the filler cap on the front of the valve cover after wiping the area clean.
11. Add the amount of oil specified in the "Capacities Chart." Replace the cap.
12. Check the oil level on the dipstick. Start the engine and look for leaks around the drain plug and the filter.
13. Stop the engine and recheck the oil level.

Transmission

Manual

The lubricant should be changed every 18,000 miles after the initial break-in period. During the break-in period, it should be changed at 600 and 18,000 miles. The proper lubricant is SAE 80 hypoid transmission lubricant. To change the lubricant:

1. Operate the car until the transmission is at normal operating temperature.
2. Slide a pan of at least five pints capacity under the transmission.
3. Remove the drain plug from the bottom of the housing after wiping the area clean. The plug is located between the axle shafts.
4. Allow the lubricant to drain into the pan. Do not replace the plug before the lubricant has completely stopped draining.
5. Clean off the plug, particularly the threads, and replace it.

Manual transmission drain plug

6. Add lubricant either through the dipstick tube or through the filler plug opening in the right side of the transmission case on 100, 100 LS, and 100 GL models. On the Super 90, there is no dipstick. The level should be to the filler hole or to the upper mark on the dipstick. Use a suction gun to add lubricant through the filler plug opening.

Automatic

The automatic transmission fluid should be changed and the pan cleaned out every 18,000 miles. The interval should be shortened to 12,000 miles under severe use such as city driving or trailer towing.

To change the fluid:

1. Run the engine in Neutral for a minute or two.
2. Make sure that the vehicle is parked on level ground. Stop the engine.
3. Place a pan of at least four quarts capacity under the transmission.
4. Remove the plug from the transmission bottom pan, after wiping the area clean.

Automatic transmission drain plug (a), pan mounting bolts (x)

5. Remove the starter. See Chapter Three for details.
6. Remove and clean out the pan.
7. Replace the pan, using a new gasket. Torque the bolts to 7 ft lbs. Wait ten minutes and retorque the bolts.
8. Clean off the plug, particularly the threads, and replace it.
9. Replace the starter.
10. Pour in five pints of fluid through the dipstick filler tube. The proper transmission fluid is Dexron with the prefix letter B.
11. Start the engine and shift through all the lever positions.
12. The level should reach the tip of the dipstick. Add fluid until the level reaches this point.
13. Take a short test drive. Fill the transmission until the level is between the marks on the dipstick. See "Transmission Fluid Level Check" for details. Retorque the bolts.

NOTE: *If the transmission is overfilled, the excess must be drained.*

Final Drive

The final drive lubricant should be changed, on automatic transmission models, every 18,000 miles. On manual transmission models, the final drive lubricant is changed along with the transmission lubricant, since the two components share a common lubricant supply. The proper lubricant is SAE 90 hypoid lubricant, SAE 80 for arctic climates.

To change the lubricant:

1. Operate the car until the final drive is at normal operating temperature.
2. Slide a pan of at least four pints capacity under the final drive.
3. Remove the plug, after wiping the area clean.

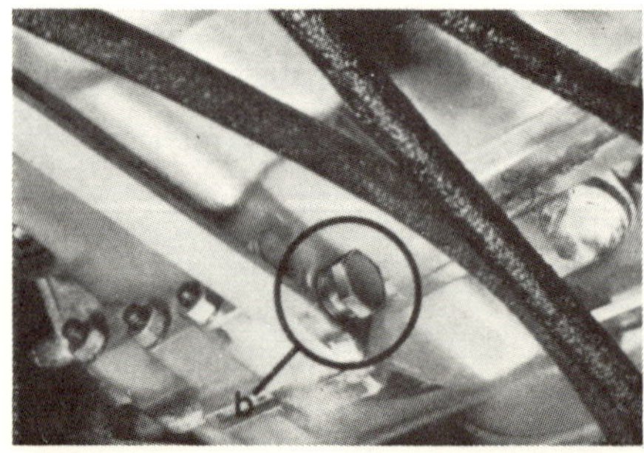

Final drive drain plug (b) on automatic transmission models

4. Allow the lubricant to drain into the pan. Do not replace the plug before the lubricant has stopped draining.
5. Clean off the plug, particularly the threads, and replace it.

6. Add enough lubricant through the dipstick tube to bring the level to the upper mark on the dipstick.

WHEEL BEARINGS

Once a year, the grease cap should be removed from each rear wheel bearing and ten grams of multi-purpose grease added.

Pushing, Towing, and Jump Starting

Cars equipped with automatic transmission may not be started by pushing. Manual transmission cars may be started by pushing. The car need not be pushed to high speed to start.

To push start a car with manual transmission:

1. Make sure that the bumpers of the two vehicles align so as not to damage either one.
2. Turn on the ignition switch in the pushed car. Place the transmission in second or third gear and hold down the clutch pedal.
3. Have the car pushed to a speed of 10–15 mph.
4. Ease up on the clutch and press down on the accelerator slightly. If the clutch is engaged abruptly, damage to the push vehicle may result.

The car should not be towed to start, since there is a chance of the towed vehicle ramming the tow car. Automatic transmission models should not be towed further than 30 miles or faster than 30 mph. The Super 90 has towing eyes on the left and right of the gas tank, under the car. Use the right eye for towing, if possible. To tow the car, place the tow line around the front torsion bar behind the bearings.

Attachment of tow line to the front of Super 90

The 100, 100 LS, and 100 GL have towing eyes under each side of the body, at the rear. Front towing eyes are provided at the pivot point of each side of the front suspension.

Jump starting is the only way to start an automatic transmission car with a weak battery, and the best method for a manual transmission car.

NOTE: *Do not attempt this procedure on a frozen battery. It will very likely explode.*

1. Turn off all electrical equipment. Place the automatic transmission in Park and the manual unit in Neutral. Set the handbrake.
2. Make sure that the two vehicles are not contacting each other. It is a good idea to keep the engine running in the booster vehicle.
3. Remove all caps from both batteries and cover the openings with cloths.
4. Attach one end of a jumper cable to the positive (+) terminal of the booster battery. The red cable is usually positive. Attach the other end to the positive terminal of the discharged battery.
5. Attach one end of the other cable (the black one) to the negative (−) terminal of the booster battery. Attach the other end to a ground point on the engine of the car being started. Do not connect it to the battery.

   NOTE: *Be careful not to lean over the battery while making this last connection.*
6. If the engine will not start, disconnect the batteries as soon as possible. If this is not done, the two batteries will soon reach a state of equilibrium, with both too weak to start an engine. This should be no problem if the engine of the booster vehicle is running fast enough to keep up the charge. Lengthy cranking can also damage the starter.
7. Reverse the procedure exactly to remove the jumper cables. Discard the rags, because they may have acid on them.

Jacking and Hoisting

The jack supplied with the car should never be used for any service operation other than tire changing. NEVER get under the car while it is supported only by the jack. If the jack should slip or tip over, as they occasionally do, it would be exceedingly difficult to raise the car again while pinned underneath. Always block the wheels when changing tires.

Some of the service operations in this book require that one or both ends of the car be raised and supported safely. The best arrangement is a grease pit or a vehicle hoist. A hydraulic floor jack may also be used. It is realized that these items are not often found in the home garage, but there are reasonable and safe substitutes. Small hydraulic, screw, or scissors jacks are satisfactory for raising the car. Safe jacking points on the car are on the floor pan behind the front wheel openings and in front of the rear wheel openings. It is also possible to use a jack under the rear axle assembly cross tube. This is located ahead of the rear axle tube.

NOTE: *Never use a jack under the rear axle tube (the tube connecting the wheels). It will be bent out of alignment.*

Heavy wooden blocks or adjustable jackstands should be used to support the car while it is being worked on. Drive-on trestles, or ramps, are also a handy and safe way to raise the car. These can be bought or constructed from suitable heavy timbers or steel.

In any case, it is always best to spend a little extra time to make sure that the car is lifted and supported safely.

NOTE: *Concrete blocks are not recommended. They may break if the load is not evenly distributed.*

Chapter Two
Tune-Up and Troubleshooting

Tune-Up Procedures

The following are specific procedures to be used in performing each tune-up step. For a more general discussion, see the tune-up section at the end of this chapter.

The manufacturer recommends that a tune-up be carried out at specified intervals. Naturally, this interval should be shortened if the vehicle is subjected to severe conditions or if starting or running deficiencies are noted. It is assumed that the routine maintenance described in Chapter One has been kept up, as this will have an effect on the results of the tune-up. All the tune-up steps should be followed, as each adjustment complements the effects of the others. If the tune-up (emission control) sticker in the engine compartment disagrees with the preceding Tune-Up Specifications Chart, the sticker figures must be followed. The sticker often reflects running changes made in production.

SPARK PLUGS

1. Disconnect each spark plug wire by pulling on the rubber cap, not on the wire.
2. Wipe the wires clean with a cloth dampened in kerosene and wipe them dry. If the wires appear to be cracked, they should be replaced.
3. Blow or brush the dirt away from each of the spark plugs. Sometimes this is done by loosening the plugs and cranking the engine with the starter.
4. Remove each spark plug with a spark plug socket. Make sure that the socket is all the way down on the plug to prevent it from slipping and cracking the porcelain insulator.
5. Refer to the "Troubleshooting" section at the end of this chapter for details on evaluating the condition of the plugs. In general, a tan or medium gray color on the business end of the plug indicates normal combustion conditions. A spark plug's useful life is about 12,000 miles. Thus it would be expedient to discard the plugs if it has been 12,000 miles or more since the last tune-up. Refer to the "Tune-Up Specifications Chart" for the proper spark plug type.
6. If the plugs are to be reused, file the center and side electrodes with a small, fine file. It is often suggested that plugs be tested and cleaned on a service station sandblasting machine; however, this piece of equipment is becoming rare. Check the gap between the two electrodes with a spark plug gap gauge. The round wire type is the most accurate. If the gap is not as specified, use the adjusting de-

Tune-Up Specifications

When analyzing compression test results, look for uniformity among cylinders, rather than specific pressures.

Year and Model	Engine Cu in. Displacement	Spark Plugs		Distributor		Ignition Timing (deg)		Intake Valve Opens (deg)	Fuel Pump Pressure (psi)	Idle Speed (rpm)		Valve Clearance (in.) ①	
		Type	Gap (in.)	Point Dwell (deg)	Point Gap (in.)	MT	AT			MT	AT	In	Ex
1970–1971 Super 90	107.5 (1,760 cc)	Ch N3	0.016–0.020	47–53	0.016	9A @ 950 rpm ②	—	6B	3.0	950	—	0.006	0.012
1972 Super 90	107.5 (1,760 cc)	Ch N8Y	0.024–0.030	47–53	0.016	9A @ 950 rpm ②	—	5B	3.0	950	—	0.008	0.016
1970–1971 100 LS	107.5 (1,760 cc)	Ch N7Y	0.023–0.029	47–53	0.016	9A @ 950 rpm ③	9A @ 950 rpm ③	5B	3.6	850–1000	850–1000	0.008	0.016
1972 100, 100 LS	114.2 (1,871 cc)	Ch N8Y	0.024–0.030 ④	47–53	0.016	8A @ idle ③	8A @ idle ③	5B	3.6	850–1000	850–1000	0.008	0.016
1973 100, 100 LS, 100 GL	114.2 (1,871 cc)	Ch N7Y	0.036–0.039	47–53	0.016	8A @ idle ⑤	8A @ idle ⑤	5B	3.6	850–1000	850–1000	0.008	0.016

A After Top Dead Center
① Set warm
② 18B @ 2,500 with vacuum hose disconnected
③ 27B @ 2,500 with vacuum hose disconnected
④ 0.036–0.040 with optional capacitive discharge ignition system
⑤ 30B @ 2,750 with vacuum hose disconnected

NOTE: *Emission control requires a very precise approach to tune-up. Timing and idle speed are peculiar to the engine and its application, rather than to the engine alone. Data for the particular application is on a sticker in the engine compartment on all late models. If the sticker disagrees with this chart, use the sticker figures. The result of any adjustments or modifications should be checked with a CO meter. The percentage of CO in the exhaust gases at idle should be 1.0 for all 100, 100 LS, and 100 GL, 1.5 for 1970–1971 Super 90, and 1.0 for 1972 Super 90.*

vice on the gap gauge to bend the outside electrode to correct. Be careful not to bend the electrode too far, because excessive bending may cause it to weaken and possibly fall off into the engine. This would require cylinder head removal to reach the broken piece, and could result in cylinder wall and ring damage.

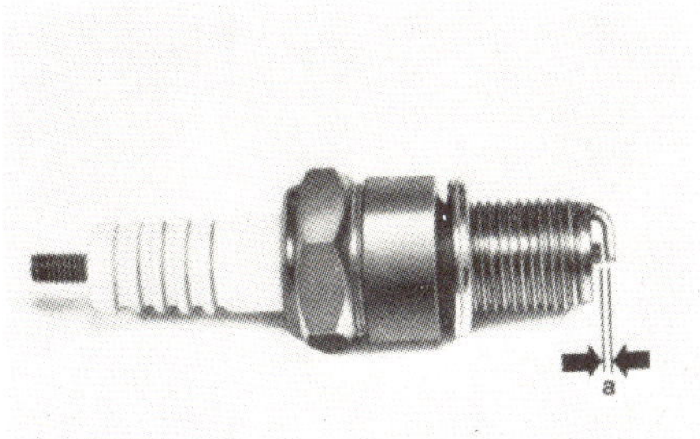

(a) is the spark plug gap

7. Clean the plug threads with a wire brush. Crank the engine with the starter to blow out any dirt particles from the cylinder head threads.

8. Screw the plugs in finger tight. Tighten them with the plug socket. If a torque wrench is available, tighten them to 22 ft lbs.

9. Reinstall the wires. If there is any doubt as to their proper locations, refer to the Firing Order Illustration in Chapter Three.

BREAKER POINTS AND CONDENSER

The condenser need not be replaced each time the points are replaced, since this item is not cheap and does not often give trouble. It should be replaced, however, if the points are severely burned. After every breaker point adjustment or replacement, the ignition timing must be checked and, if necessary, adjusted. No special equipment other than a feeler gauge is required for point replacement or adjustment, although a dwell meter should be used to ensure the accuracy of the adjustment.

1. Detach the two spring clips which secure the distributor cap. Remove the cap.

2. Clean the cap inside and out. Check for cracks and carbon paths. A carbon path shows up as a dark line, usually from one of the cap sockets or inside terminals to a ground. Check the condition of the button inside the center of the cap and the four inside terminals. Replace the cap if necessary.

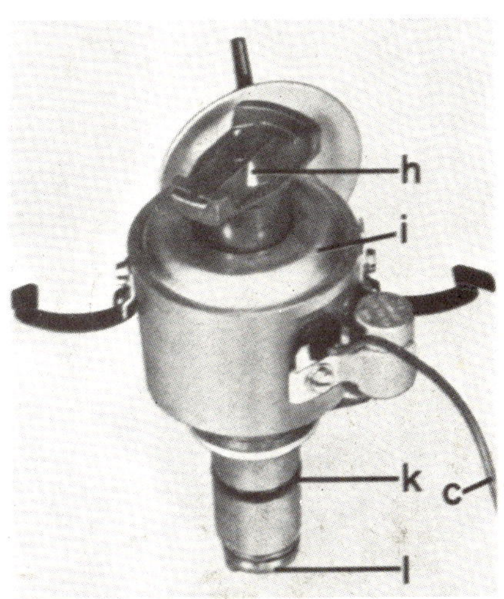

Distributor with cap removed

c Lead to coil
h Rotor
i Dust cap
k Seal
l Drive connection

3. Pull the rotor up and off the shaft. Clean off the metal end if it is burned or corroded. Replace the rotor if necessary. Remove the dust cap.

4. The manufacturer states that the points must be replaced, not reconditioned. Experience also shows that it is more economical and reliable in the long run to replace the point set while the distributor is open, than to have to do this at a later (and possibly more inconvenient) time.

5. Pull off the flat plug wire terminal from the point set. Remove the point set hold-down screw, being very careful not to drop it into the inside of the distributor. If this happens, the distributor will probably have to be removed to get at the screw. If the screw is lost elsewhere, it must be replaced with one that is no longer than the original to avoid interference with distributor workings. Remove the point set.

6. Remove the condenser by removing the clamp screw and pulling the assembly out. Detach the condenser lead from the coil. The condenser, wire, flat plug connection, and plastic sealing boot are a single assembly.

7. Apply a small amount of high-temperature grease to the pivot side of the point set rubbing block.

8. Replace the point set and tighten the screw lightly. Replace the flat plug terminal.

Breaker point installation

c Lead to coil
g Vacuum line connection
m Flat plug wire terminal
n Raised lugs
o Screwdriver slot
p Hold-down screw

9. Make sure that the contacts meet squarely. If they do not, bend the tab which supports the fixed contact.

10. Turn the engine until a high point on the cam (that opens the points) contacts the rubbing block on the point arm. The engine turns easier if the spark plugs have been removed. A manual transmission car can be pushed slowly forward in fourth gear to turn the engine. On an automatic transmission car, you can use a large screwdriver to turn the flywheel.

11. There is a screwdriver slot and two raised lugs near the contacts. Insert a screwdriver and lever the points open or closed until they appear to be open to the correct gap as specified in the chart.

12. Insert the correct size feeler gauge and adjust the gap with the screwdriver until you can push the gauge in and out between the contacts with a slight drag but without moving the point arm. This operation requires a bit of experience to obtain the proper feel. If there is any doubt, have an experienced mechanic check the setting. Another check is to try the feeler gauge blades 0.001–0.002 in. larger and smaller than the setting size. The larger one should disturb the point arm, whereas the smaller one should not drag at all. Tighten the point set hold-down screw snugly. Recheck the gap, because it often changes when the screw is tightened.

14. After all the point adjustments are complete, pull a white business card through (between) the contacts to remove any traces of oil. Oil will cause rapid point burning.

15. Replace the dust cap.

16. Push the rotor firmly down into place. It will only go on one way. If it is not installed properly, it will probably break when the starter is operated.

17. Replace the distributor cap and install the spring clips.

18. Check the dwell. The dwell meter hookup is shown in the "Troubleshooting" section. Dwell can be checked with the engine running or cranking. Decrease dwell by increasing the point gap; increase by decreasing the gap. Dwell angle is simply the number of degrees of distributor shaft rotation during which the points stay closed. Theoretically, if the point gap is correct, the dwell should also be correct or nearly so. If dwell varies more than 3 degrees from idle speed to 2,500 engine rpm, the distributor is worn.

19. Start the engine. If it won't start, make sure:

a. that all the spark plug wires are in place

b. that the rotor has been installed

c. that the wire inside the distributor is connected

d. that the points open and close when the engine turns

e. that the gap is correct and the hold-down screw is tight

f. that the condenser lead is attached to the coil

20. After the first 200 miles on a new set of points, the point gap often closes up due to initial rubbing block wear. For best performance, recheck the gap at this time.

21. Since changing the point gap affects the ignition timing setting, the timing should be checked and adjusted if necessary after each point replacement or adjustment.

IGNITION TIMING

Timing should be checked at each tune-up and any time the points are adjusted or replaced. The timing marks are located on the crankshaft pulley and the front of the engine. A stroboscopic flash (dynamic) timing light should be used, as a static light is too inaccurate for emission controlled engines. Basic timing can be set, however, with a static light. Final timing should be set with the stroboscopic light.

There are three types of stroboscopic timing lights. The first is a simple neon bulb with two wire connections. One wire connects to the spark plug terminal and the other plugs into the end of the spark plug wire for No. 1 cylinder, thus connecting the light in series with the spark plug. This type of light is rather dim and must be held very close to the timing marks to be seen. Sometimes a dark corner must be sought in order to see the flash at all. This type is very inexpensive. The second type operates from the car battery——two alligator clips connect to the battery terminals, while an adapter enables a third clip to be connected to the No. 1 spark plug wire. This type is a bit more expensive but provides a much more visible flash. It is the type most commonly used by professionals. The third type replaces the battery power source with 110 Volt current.

Basic Timing

This procedure is needed only after the distributor has been removed and replaced, or if timing must be checked when a stroboscopic light is unavailable.

1. Turn the engine until the basic ignition timing mark (the one specified for idle speed) is aligned with the ignition timing pointer on the timing cover and the distributor rotor points toward the No. 1 cylinder mark on the rim of the distributor body. A manual transmission car can be pushed slowly forward in Fourth gear to turn the engine. On an automatic transmission car, you can use a large screwdriver to turn the flywheel. This will put No. 1 cylinder at TDC (Top Dead Center of the compression stroke).
2. Connect a 12 Volt test lamp between the ignition coil terminal (terminal 1) connected to the distributor and a ground.
3. Loosen the distributor clamp screw at the base of the distributor. Turn the distributor body clockwise until the light goes out, indicating that the points have closed.
4. Turn the distributor body counterclockwise until the light goes on, indicating that the points are opening. Tighten the distributor clamp screw.
5. The ignition timing is now approximately set. As soon as possible, make a final timing adjustment with the stroboscopic light.

The distributor rotor (L) is aligned with the No. 1 cylinder mark (M) on the rim of the distributor body. The dust cap is removed here

Final Timing

This is the normal timing procedure.

1. Warm up the engine to normal operating temperature. Stop the engine and connect the timing light to the No. 1 (front) spark plug wire. Clean off the timing marks and mark them with chalk.
2. Connect a tachometer.
3. Loosen the distributor clamp screw at the base of the distributor until it is just possible to turn the distributor by hand.
4. Run the engine at the specified idle speed. Aim the timing light at the pointer. Be careful not to touch the fan or belts, because they may appear to be standing still. If the pointer does not appear to align with the timing mark specified for idle speed (refer to the "Tune-Up Specifications Chart"), the timing will have to be adjusted.
5. Turn the distributor body slowly to adjust. Turn it counterclockwise to advance the timing (toward Before Top Dead Center), and clockwise to retard it (toward After Top Dead Center).
6. Disconnect the vacuum hose(s) and check the timing at 2,500 rpm. Adjust as necessary.
7. Tighten the clamp screw. Stop the

engine and disconnect the timing light and tachometer.

NOTE: *Timing should always be checked both at idle and at 2,500 rpm.*

Timing marks for 100, 100 LS, and 100 GL. The Super 90 has a similar arrangement with different numbers. (M) is the timing cover pointer and (K) is the ignition timing mark used at 2,500 rpm

VALVE LASH

Valve lash adjustment should be checked at tune-up intervals and whenever there is excessive noise from the valve mechanism.

NOTE: *Do not set the valve lash closer than specified in an attempt to quiet the valve mechanism. This will result in burned valves.*

1. The engine must be at operating temperature.
2. Remove the air cleaner, valve cover, and distributor cap.
3. Set the engine at TDC on No. 1 cylinder by aligning the 0° T mark on the crankshaft pulley with the timing cover pointer and aligning the distributor rotor with the No. 1 cylinder mark on the rim of the distributor body. Turn the engine in the normal direction of rotation. On an automatic transmission car, you can use a large screwdriver to turn the flywheel. A manual transmission car can be pushed slowly forward in Fourth gear to turn the engine. This is made easier if the spark plugs are removed.
4. The valve clearances of cylinder No. 1 should be adjusted when the valves of No. 4 cylinder overlap, i.e., when both rocker arms move in opposite directions simultaneously. When this occurs, the exhaust valve is closing and the intake opening. The cylinders are numbered from front to rear. The intake and exhaust valves can be identified by the locations of the intake and exhaust manifolds on the engine. The intake valve is the front valve for each cylinder, and the exhaust valve is the rear one.

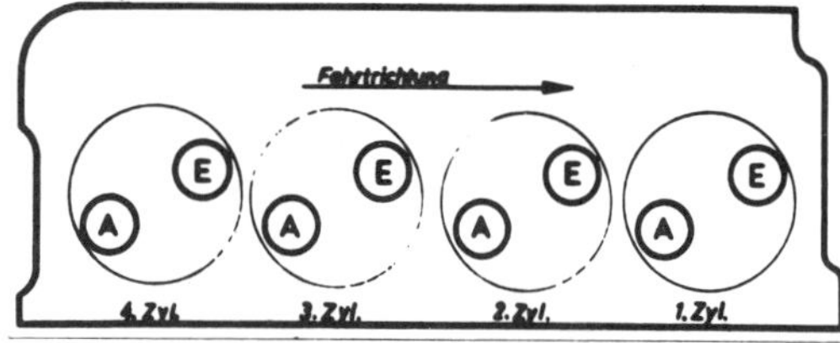

Exhaust valve location is indicated by (A) and intake valve by (E). The arrow points to the front

5. The lash is measured between the rocker arm and the end of the valve.
6. To check the lash, insert the correct size feeler gauge between the rocker arm and the valve. Press down lightly on the other end of the rocker arm. If the gauge cannot be inserted, loosen the self-locking adjustment nut on top of the rocker arm. Tighten the nut until the gauge can just be inserted and withdrawn without buckling.

Valve lash adjustment procedure

7. After both valves for No. 1 cylinder are adjusted, turn the engine in the normal direction of rotation until the distributor rotor has turned 90 degrees. Adjust the valves for cylinder No. 3 after making sure that the valves of cylinder No. 2 are overlapping.
8. Turn the rotor another 90 degrees. Adjust the valves for cylinder No. 4 after making sure that the valves of cylinder No. 1 are overlapping.
9. Turn the rotor another 90 degrees. Adjust the valves for cylinder No. 2 after making sure that the valves of cylinder No. 3 are overlapping.
10. The valves have all been adjusted in the sequence of the engine firing order, 1-3-4-2. Replace the items removed in Step

2. Start the engine and check for leaks around the valve cover.

CARBURETOR

Idle Speed and Mixture

The idle speed and mixture should be adjusted only after the engine has reached normal operating temperature. The air cleaner must be in place and the preheater hose from the exhaust manifold disconnected. The high-beam headlights must be on. The ignition system must be properly adjusted before any carburetor adjustments are attempted. The only accurate way to set the idle mixture is with a CO meter. The allowable percentage of CO in the exhaust gases is shown on the engine compartment emission control sticker.

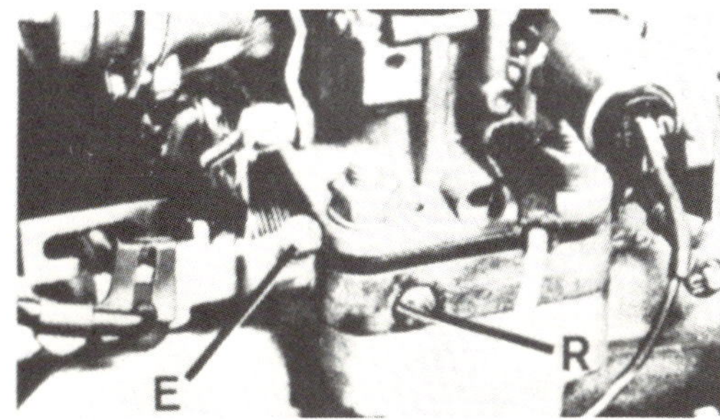

Standard carburetor adjustments. (E) is the idle speed adjusting screw and (R) is the idle mixture adjusting screw

Standard Carburetors

The carburetor has only two adjusting screws: one on the throttle linkage for idle speed and one in the carburetor body for idle mixture.

1. Set the idle speed with the idle speed adjusting screw.
2. Turn the mixture screw in until the engine just begins to slow down and run roughly. If turning this screw has no effect, the carburetor idle passages are probably clogged.
3. Back the mixture adjusting screw out ⅛–¼ turn. The engine should resume smooth operation.
4. Reset the idle speed if necessary.
5. Check the CO content of the exhaust gases. Reset the mixture screw if the allowable percentage is exceeded.
6. Complete the job by making a final adjustment of idle speed.

Idle air bypass carburetor adjustments. (3) is the idle mixture adjusting screw, (4) is the air control screw, and (7) is the sealed throttle plate adjusting screw

1. **Intake manifold**
2. **Retarded vacuum connection**
5. **Advanced vacuum connection**
6. **Electric fuel cutoff jet**

Idle Air Bypass Carburetors

The carburetor has three adjusting screws. The one on the throttle linkage controls the position of the throttle plate. This screw is sealed and is not to be adjusted. The fuel-air mixture bypasses around the throttle plate at idle. There is an idle mixture adjusting screw and an air control screw in the carburetor body.

1. Use the mixture adjusting screw to set the idle speed to specifications.
2. Gently tighten the air control screw all the way in. Back it out slightly less than a full turn.
3. Adjust the mixture adjusting screw to obtain the specified percentage of CO in the exhaust gases at idle.
4. If the idle speed is now too high, tighten the mixture adjusting screw to correct it. Then tighten the air control screw to get the proper CO content.

NOTE: *It is normal for idle speed to be low on new engines. This need not be adjusted unless the condition persists after break-in.*

Engine Tune-Up

Engine tune-up is a procedure performed to restore engine performance, deteriorated due to normal wear and loss of adjustment. The three major areas considered in a routine tune-up are compression, ignition, and carburetion, although valve adjustment may be included.

A tune-up is performed in three steps: *analysis*, in which it is determined whether normal wear is responsible for performance loss, and which parts require replacement or service; *parts replacement or service*; and *adjustment*, in which engine adjustments are returned to original specifications. Since the advent of emission control equipment, precision adjustment has become increasingly critical, in order to maintain pollutant emission levels.

Analysis

The procedures below are used to indicate where adjustments, parts service or replacement are necessary within the realm of a normal tune-up. If, following these tests, all systems appear to be functioning properly, proceed to the Troubleshooting Section for further diagnosis.

—Remove all spark plugs, noting the cylinder in which they were installed. Remove the air cleaner, and position the throttle and choke in the full open position. Disconnect the coil high tension lead from the coil and the distributor cap. Insert a compression gauge into the spark plug port of each cylinder, in succession, and crank the engine with the starter to obtain the highest possible reading. Record the readings, and compare the highest to the lowest on the compression pressure limit chart. If the difference exceeds the limits on the chart, or if all readings are excessively low, proceed to a wet compression check (see Troubleshooting Section).

Maxi. Press. Lbs. Sq. In.	*Min. Press. Lbs. Sq. In.*	*Max. Press. Lbs. Sq. In.*	*Min. Press. Lbs. Sq. In.*
134	101	188	141
136	102	190	142
138	104	192	144
140	105	194	145
142	107	196	147
146	110	198	148
148	111	200	150
150	113	202	151
152	114	204	153
154	115	206	154
156	117	208	156
158	118	210	157
160	120	212	158
162	121	214	160
164	123	216	162
166	124	218	163
168	126	220	165
170	127	222	166
172	129	224	168
174	131	226	169
176	132	228	171
178	133	230	172
180	135	232	174
182	136	234	175
184	138	236	177
186	140	238	178

Compression pressure limits
(© Buick Div. G.M. Corp.)

—Evaluate the spark plugs according to the spark plug chart in the Troubleshooting Section, and proceed as indicated in the chart.

—Remove the distributor cap, and inspect it inside and out for cracks and/or carbon tracks, and inside for excessive wear or burning of the rotor contacts. If any of these faults are evident, the cap must be replaced.

—Check the breaker points for burning, pitting or wear, and the contact heel resting on the distributor cam for excessive wear. If defects are noted, replace the entire breaker point set.

—Remove and inspect the rotor. If the contacts are burned or worn, or if the rotor is excessively loose on the distributor shaft (where applicable), the rotor must be replaced.

—Inspect the spark plug leads and the coil high tension lead for cracks or brittleness. If any of the wires appear defective, the entire set should be replaced.

—Check the air filter to ensure that it is functioning properly.

Parts Replacement and Service

The determination of whether to replace or service parts is at the mechanic's discretion; however, it is suggested that any parts in questionable condition be replaced rather than reused.

—Clean and regap, or replace, the spark plugs as needed. Lightly coat the threads with engine oil and install the plugs. CAUTION: *Do not over-torque taper-seat spark plugs, or plugs being installed in aluminum cylinder heads.*

SPARK PLUG TORQUE

Thread size	*Cast-Iron Heads*	*Aluminum Heads*
10 mm.	14	11
14 mm.	30	27
18 mm.	34*	32
7/8 in.—18	37	35

* 17 ft. lbs. for tapered plugs using no gaskets.

—If the distributor cap is to be reused, clean the inside with a dry rag, and remove corrosion from the rotor contact points with fine emery cloth. Remove the spark plug wires one by one, and clean the wire ends and the inside of the towers. If the boots are loose, they should be replaced.

If the cap is to be replaced, transfer the wires one by one, cleaning the wire ends and replacing the boots if necessary.

—If the original points are to remain in service, clean them lightly with emery cloth, lubricate the contact heel with grease specifically designed for this purpose. Rotate the crankshaft until the heel rests on a high point of the distributor cam, and adjust the point gap to specifications.

When replacing the points, remove the original points and condenser, and wipe out the inside of the distributor housing with a clean, dry rag. Lightly lubricate the contact heel and pivot point, and install the points and condenser. Rotate the crankshaft until the heel rests on a high point of the distributor cam, and adjust the point gap to specifications. NOTE: *Always replace the condenser when changing the points.*

—If the rotor is to be reused, clean the contacts with solvent. Do not alter the spring tension of the rotor center contact. Install the rotor and the distributor cap.

—Replace the coil high tension lead and/or the spark plug leads as necessary.

—Clean the carburetor using a spray solvent (e.g., Gumout Spray). Remove the varnish from the throttle bores, and clean the linkage. Disconnect and plug the fuel line, and run the engine until it runs out of fuel. Partially fill the float chamber with solvent, and reconnect the fuel line. In extreme cases, the jets can be pressure flushed by inserting a rubber plug into the float vent, running the spray nozzle through it, and spraying the solvent until it squirts out of the venturi fuel dump.

—Clean and tighten all wiring connections in the primary electrical circuit.

Additional Services

The following services *should* be performed in conjunction with a routine tune-up to ensure efficient performance.

—Inspect the battery and fill to the proper level with distilled water. Remove the cable clamps, clean clamps and posts thoroughly, coat the posts lightly with petroleum jelly, reinstall and tighten.

—Inspect all belts, replace and/or adjust as necessary.

—Test the PCV valve (if so equipped), and clean or replace as indicated. Clean all crankcase ventilation hoses, or replace if cracked or hardened.

—Adjust the valves (if necessary) to manufacturer's specifications.

Adjustments

—Connect a dwell-tachometer between the distributor primary lead and ground. Remove the distributor cap and rotor (unless equipped with Delco externally adjustable distributor). With the ignition off, crank the engine with a remote starter switch and measure the point dwell angle. Adjust the dwell angle to specifications. NOTE: *Increasing the gap decreases the dwell angle and vice-versa.* Install the rotor and distributor cap.

—Connect a timing light according to the manufacturer's specifications. Identify the proper timing marks with chalk or paint. NOTE: *Luminescent (day-glo) paint is excellent for this purpose.* Start the engine, and run it until it reaches operating temperature. Disconnect and plug any distributor vacuum lines, and adjust idle to the speed required to adjust timing, according to specifications. Loosen the distributor clamp and adjust timing to specifications by rotating the distributor in the engine. NOTE: *To advance timing, rotate distributor opposite normal direction of rotor rotation, and vice-versa.*

—Synchronize the throttles and mixture of multiple carburetors (if so equipped) according to procedures given in the individual car sections.

—Adjust the idle speed, mixture, and idle quality, as specified in the car sections. Final idle adjustments should be made with the air cleaner installed. CAUTION: *Due to strict emission control requirements on 1969 and later models, special test equipment (CO meter, SUN Tester) may be necessary to properly adjust idle mixture to specifications.*

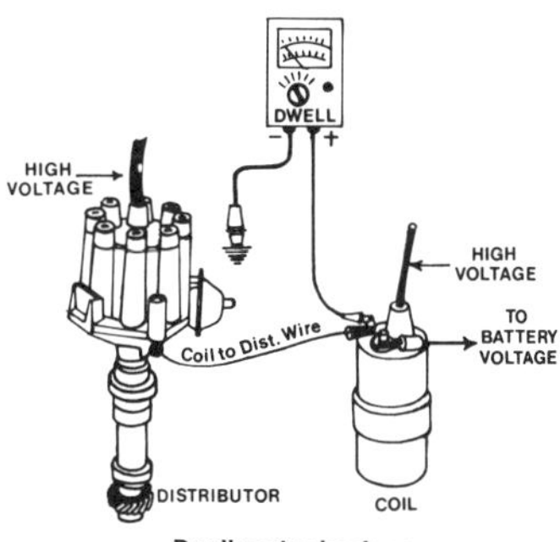

Dwell meter hook-up

Trouble-shooting

The following section is designed to aid in the rapid diagnosis of engine problems. The systematic format is used to diagnose problems ranging from engine starting difficulties to the need for engine overhaul. It is assumed that the user is equipped with basic hand tools and test equipment (tach-dwell meter, timing light, voltmeter, and ohmmeter).

Troubleshooting is divided into two sections. The first, *General Diagnosis*, is used to locate the problem area. In the second, *Specific Diagnosis*, the problem is systematically evaluated.

General Diagnosis

PROBLEM: Symptom	*Begin diagnosis at Section Two, Number ———*
Engine won't start:	
Starter doesn't turn	1.1, 2.1
Starter turns, engine doesn't	2.1
Starter turns engine very slowly	1.1, 2.4
Starter turns engine normally	3.1, 4.1
Starter turns engine very quickly	6.1
Engine fires intermittently	4.1
Engine fires consistently	5.1, 6.1
Engine runs poorly:	
Hard starting	3.1, 4.1, 5.1, 8.1
Rough idle	4.1, 5.1, 8.1
Stalling	3.1, 4.1, 5.1, 8.1
Engine dies at high speeds	4.1, 5.1
Hesitation (on acceleration from standing stop)	5.1, 8.1
Poor pickup	4.1, 5.1, 8.1
Lack of power	3.1, 4.1, 5.1, 8.1
Backfire through the carburetor	4.1, 8.1, 9.1
Backfire through the exhaust	4.1, 8.1, 9.1
Blue exhaust gases	6.1, 7.1
Black exhaust gases	5.1
Running on (after the ignition is shut off)	3.1, 8.1
Susceptible to moisture	4.1
Engine misfires under load	4.1, 7.1, 8.4, 9.1
Engine misfires at speed	4.1, 8.4
Engine misfires at idle	3.1, 4.1, 5.1, 7.1, 8.4

PROBLEM: Symptom	*Probable Cause*
Engine noises: ①	
Metallic grind while starting	Starter drive not engaging completely
Constant grind or rumble	*Starter drive not releasing, worn main bearings
Constant knock	Worn connecting rod bearings
Knock under load	Fuel octane too low, worn connecting rod bearings
Double knock	Loose piston pin
Metallic tap	*Collapsed or sticky valve lifter, excessive valve clearance, excessive end play in a rotating shaft
Scrape	*Fan belt contacting a stationary surface
Tick while starting	S.U. electric fuel pump (normal), starter brushes
Constant tick	*Generator brushes, shreaded fan belt
Squeal	*Improperly tensioned fan belt
Hiss or roar	*Steam escaping through a leak in the cooling system or the radiator overflow vent
Whistle	*Vacuum leak
Wheeze	Loose or cracked spark plug

①—It is extremely difficult to evaluate vehicle noises. While the above are general definitions of engine noises, those starred (*) should be considered as possibly originating elsewhere in the car. To aid diagnosis, the following list considers other potential sources of these sounds.

Metallic grind:
Throwout bearing; transmission gears, bearings, or synchronizers; differential bearings, gears; something metallic in contact with brake drum or disc.

Metallic tap:
U-joints; fan-to-radiator (or shroud) contact.

Scrape:
Brake shoe or pad dragging; tire to body contact; suspension contacting undercarriage or exhaust; something non-metallic contacting brake shoe or drum.

Tick:
Transmission gears; differential gears; lack of radio suppression; resonant vibration of body panels; windshield wiper motor or transmission; heater motor and blower.

Squeal:
Brake shoe or pad not fully releasing; tires (excessive wear, uneven wear, improper inflation); front or rear wheel alignment (most commonly due to improper toe-in).

Hiss or whistle:
Wind leaks (body or window); heater motor and blower fan.

Roar:
Wheel bearings; wind leaks (body and window).

Specific Diagnosis

This section is arranged so that following each test, instructions are given to proceed to another, until a problem is diagnosed.

INDEX

Group		Topic
1	*	Battery
2	*	Cranking system
3	*	Primary electrical system
4	*	Secondary electrical system
5	*	Fuel system
6	*	Engine compression
7	**	Engine vacuum
8	**	Secondary electrical system
9	**	Valve train
10	**	Exhaust system
11	**	Cooling system
12	**	Engine lubrication

*—The engine need not be running.
**—The engine must be running.

SAMPLE SECTION

Test and Procedure	Results and Indications	Proceed to
4.1—Check for spark: Hold each spark plug wire approximately ¼″ from ground with gloves or a heavy, dry rag. Crank the engine and observe the spark.	If no spark is evident:	4.2
	If spark is good in some cases:	4.3
	If spark is good in all cases:	4.6

DIAGNOSIS

Test and Procedure	Results and Indications	Proceed to
1.1—Inspect the battery visually for case condition (corrosion, cracks) and water level.	If case is cracked, replace battery:	1.4
	If the case is intact, remove corrosion with a solution of baking soda and water (CAUTION: *do not get the solution into the battery*), and fill with water:	1.2
1.2—Check the battery cable connections: Insert a screwdriver between the battery post and the cable clamp. Turn the headlights on high beam, and observe them as the screwdriver is gently twisted to ensure good metal to metal contact.	If the lights brighten, remove and clean the clamp and post; coat the post with petroleum jelly, install and tighten the clamp:	1.4
	If no improvement is noted:	1.3

Testing battery cable connections using a screwdriver

1.3—Test the state of charge of the battery using an individual cell tester or hydrometer.

Spec. Grav. Reading	*Charged Condition*
1.260-1.280	Fully Charged
1.230-1.250	Three Quarter Charged
1.200-1.220	One Half Charged
1.170-1.190	One Quarter Charged
1.140-1.160	Just About Flat
1.110-1.130	All The Way Down

State of battery charge

The effect of temperature on the specific gravity of battery electrolyte

If indicated, charge the battery. NOTE: *If no obvious reason exists for the low state of charge (i.e., battery age, prolonged storage), the charging system should be tested:* 1.4

Test and Procedure	*Results and Indications*	*Proceed to*
1.4—Visually inspect battery cables for cracking, bad connection to ground, or bad connection to starter.	If necessary, tighten connections or replace the cables:	2.1

Tests in Group 2 are performed with coil high tension lead disconnected to prevent accidental starting.

Test and Procedure	*Results and Indications*	*Proceed to*
2.1—Test the starter motor and solenoid: Connect a jumper from the battery post of the solenoid (or relay) to the starter post of the solenoid (or relay).	If starter turns the engine normally:	2.2
	If the starter buzzes, or turns the engine very slowly:	2.4
	If no response, replace the solenoid (or relay).	3.1
	If the starter turns, but the engine doesn't, ensure that the flywheel ring gear is intact. If the gear is undamaged, replace the starter drive.	3.1
2.2—Determine whether ignition override switches are functioning properly (clutch start switch, neutral safety switch), by connecting a jumper across the switch(es), and turning the ignition switch to "start".	If starter operates, adjust or replace switch:	3.1
	If the starter doesn't operate:	2.3
2.3—Check the ignition switch "start" position: Connect a 12V test lamp between the starter post of the solenoid (or relay) and ground. Turn the ignition switch to the "start" position, and jiggle the key.	If the lamp doesn't light when the switch is turned, check the ignition switch for loose connections, cracked insulation, or broken wires. Repair or replace as necessary:	3.1
	If the lamp flickers when the key is jiggled, replace the ignition switch.	3.3
2.4—Remove and bench test the starter, according to specifications in the car section.	If the starter does not meet specifications, repair or replace as needed:	3.1
	If the starter is operating properly:	2.5
2.5—Determine whether the engine can turn freely: Remove the spark plugs, and check for water in the cylinders. Check for water on the dipstick, or oil in the radiator. Attempt to turn the engine using an 18″ flex drive and socket on the crankshaft pulley nut or bolt.	If the engine will turn freely only with the spark plugs out, and hydrostatic lock (water in the cylinders) is ruled out, check valve timing:	9.2
	If engine will not turn freely, and it is known that the clutch and transmission are free, the engine must be disassembled for further evaluation:	Next Chapter

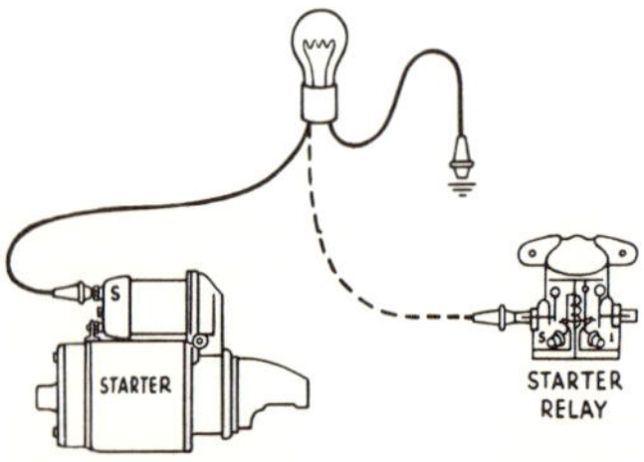

STARTER
STARTER RELAY

Checking the ignition switch "start" position

Tests and Procedures	*Results and Indications*	*Proceed to*
3.1—Check the ignition switch "on" position: Connect a jumper wire between the distributor side of the coil and ground, and a 12V test lamp between the switch side of the coil and ground. Remove the high tension lead from the coil. Turn the ignition switch on and jiggle the key.	If the lamp lights:	3.2
	If the lamp flickers when the key is jiggled, replace the ignition switch:	3.3
	If the lamp doesn't light, check for loose or open connections. If none are found, remove the ignition switch and check for continuity. If the switch is faulty, replace it:	3.3
Checking the ignition switch "on" position		
3.2—Check the ballast resistor or resistance wire for an open circuit, using an ohmmeter.	Replace the resistor or the resistance wire if the resistance is zero.	3.3
3.3—Visually inspect the breaker points for burning, pitting, or excessive wear. Gray coloring of the point contact surfaces is normal. Rotate the crankshaft until the contact heel rests on a high point of the distributor cam, and adjust the point gap to specifications.	If the breaker points are intact, clean the contact surfaces with fine emery cloth, and adjust the point gap to specifications. If pitted or worn, replace the points and condenser, and adjust the gap to specifications: NOTE: *Always lubricate the distributor cam according to manufacturer's recommendations when servicing the breaker points.*	3.4
3.4—Connect a dwell meter between the distributor primary lead and ground. Crank the engine and observe the point dwell angle.	If necessary, adjust the point dwell angle: NOTE: *Increasing the point gap decreases the dwell angle, and vice-versa.*	3.6
	If dwell meter shows little or no reading:	3.5
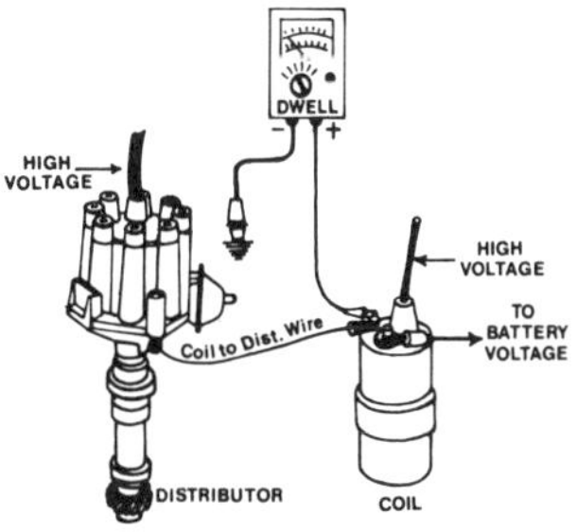 Dwell meter hook-up	Dwell angle	
3.5—Check the condenser for short: Connect an ohmmeter across the condenser body and the pigtail lead.	If any reading other than infinite resistance is noted, replace the condenser:	3.6
Checking the condenser for short		

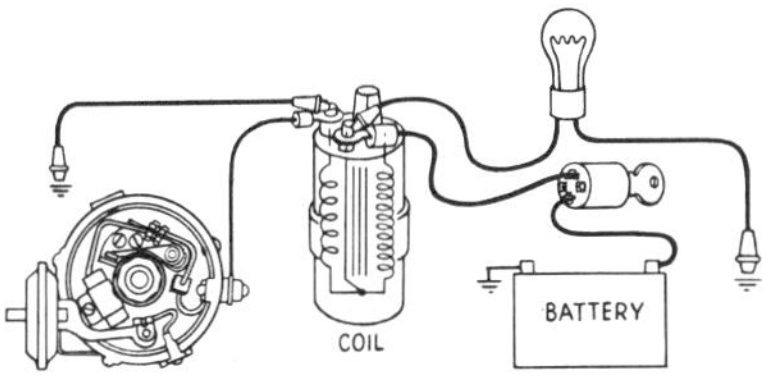

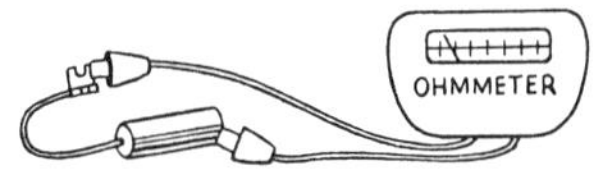

Test and Procedure	Results and Indications	Proceed to
3.6—Test the coil primary resistance: Connect an ohmmeter across the coil primary terminals, and read the resistance on the low scale. Note whether an external ballast resistor or resistance wire is utilized. Testing the coil primary resistance	Coils utilizing ballast resistors or resistance wires should have approximately 1.0Ω resistance; coils with internal resistors should have approximately 4.0Ω resistance. If values far from the above are noted, replace the coil:	4.1
4.1—Check for spark: Hold each spark plug wire approximately ¼″ from ground with gloves or a heavy, dry rag. Crank the engine, and observe the spark.	If no spark is evident:	4.2
	If spark is good in some cylinders:	4.3
	If spark is good in all cylinders:	4.6
4.2—Check for spark at the coil high tension lead: Remove the coil high tension lead from the distributor and position it approximately ¼″ from ground. Crank the engine and observe spark. CAUTION: *This test should not be performed on cars equipped with transistorized ignition.*	If the spark is good and consistent:	4.3
	If the spark is good but intermittent, test the primary electrical system starting at 3.3:	3.3
	If the spark is weak or non-existent, replace the coil high tension lead, clean and tighten all connections and retest. If no improvement is noted:	4.4
4.3—Visually inspect the distributor cap and rotor for burned or corroded contacts, cracks, carbon tracks, or moisture. Also check the fit of the rotor on the distributor shaft (where applicable).	If moisture is present, dry thoroughly, and retest per 4.1:	4.1
	If burned or excessively corroded contacts, cracks, or carbon tracks are noted, replace the defective part(s) and retest per 4.1:	4.1
	If the rotor and cap appear intact, or are only slightly corroded, clean the contacts thoroughly (including the cap towers and spark plug wire ends) and retest per 4.1:	
	If the spark is good in all cases:	4.6
	If the spark is poor in all cases:	4.5
4.4—Check the coil secondary resistance: Connect an ohmmeter across the distributor side of the coil and the coil tower. Read the resistance on the high scale of the ohmmeter. Testing the coil secondary resistance	The resistance of a satisfactory coil should be between 4KΩ and 10KΩ. If the resistance is considerably higher (i.e., 40KΩ) replace the coil, and retest per 4.1: NOTE: *This does not apply to high performance coils.*	4.1

Test and Procedure	*Results and Indications*	*Proceed to*
4.5—Visually inspect the spark plug wires for cracking or brittleness. Ensure that no two wires are positioned so as to cause induction firing (adjacent and parallel). Remove each wire, one by one, and check resistance with an ohmmeter.	Replace any cracked or brittle wires. If any of the wires are defective, replace the entire set. Replace any wires with excessive resistance (over 8000Ω per foot for suppression wire), and separate any wires that might cause induction firing.	4.6
4.6—Remove the spark plugs, noting the cylinders from which they were removed, and evaluate according to the chart below.	See below.	See below.

Condition	*Cause*	*Remedy*	*Proceed to*
Electrodes eroded, light brown deposits.	Normal wear. Normal wear is indicated by approximately .001″ wear per 1000 miles.	Clean and regap the spark plug if wear is not excessive: Replace the spark plug if excessively worn:	4.7
Carbon fouling (black, dry, fluffy deposits).	If present on one or two plugs:		
	Faulty high tension lead(s).	Test the high tension leads:	4.5
	Burnt or sticking valve(s).	Check the valve train: (Clean and regap the plugs in either case.)	9.1
	If present on most or all plugs: Overly rich fuel mixture, due to restricted air filter, improper carburetor adjustment, improper choke or heat riser adjustment or operation.	Check the fuel system:	5.1
Oil fouling (wet black deposits)	Worn engine components. NOTE: *Oil fouling may occur in new or recently rebuilt engines until broken in.*	Check engine vacuum and compression:	6.1
		Replace with new spark plug	
Lead fouling (gray, black, tan, or yellow deposits, which appear glazed or cinder-like).	Combustion by-products.	Clean and regap the plugs: (Use plugs of a different heat range if the problem recurs.)	4.7

Condition	Cause	Remedy	Proceed to
Gap bridging (deposits lodged between the electrodes).	Incomplete combustion, or transfer of deposits from the combustion chamber.	Replace the spark plugs:	4.7
Overheating (burnt electrodes, and extremely white insulator with small black spots).	Ignition timing advanced too far.	Adjust timing to specifications:	8.2
	Overly lean fuel mixture.	Check the fuel system:	5.1
	Spark plugs not seated properly.	Clean spark plug seat and install a new gasket washer: (Replace the spark plugs in all cases.)	4.7
Fused spot deposits on the insulator.	Combustion chamber blow-by.	Clean and regap the spark plugs:	4.7
Pre-ignition (melted or severely burned electrodes, blistered or cracked insulators, or metallic deposits on the insulator).	Incorrect spark plug heat range.	Replace with plugs of the proper heat range:	4.7
	Ignition timing advanced too far.	Adjust timing to specifications:	8.2
	Spark plugs not being cooled efficiently.	Clean the spark plug seat, and check the cooling system:	11.1
	Fuel mixture too lean.	Check the fuel system:	5.1
	Poor compression.	Check compression:	6.1
	Fuel grade too low.	Use higher octane fuel:	4.7

Test and Procedure	Results and Indications	Proceed to
4.7—Determine the static ignition timing: Using the flywheel or crankshaft pulley timing marks as a guide, locate top dead center on the *compression* stroke of the No. 1 cylinder. Remove the distributor cap.	Adjust the distributor so that the rotor points toward the No. 1 tower in the distributor cap, and the points are just opening:	4.8
4.8—Check coil polarity: Connect a voltmeter negative lead to the coil high tension lead, and the positive lead to ground (NOTE: *reverse the hook-up for positive ground cars*). Crank the engine momentarily. Checking coil polarity	If the voltmeter reads up-scale, the polarity is correct:	5.1
	If the voltmeter reads down-scale, reverse the coil polarity (switch the primary leads):	5.1

Test and Procedure	*Results and Indications*	*Proceed to*
5.1—Determine that the air filter is functioning efficiently: Hold paper elements up to a strong light, and attempt to see light through the filter.	Clean permanent air filters in gasoline (or manufacturer's recommendation), and allow to dry. Replace paper elements through which light cannot be seen:	5.2
5.2—Determine whether a flooding condition exists: Flooding is identified by a strong gasoline odor, and excessive gasoline present in the throttle bore(s) of the carburetor.	If flooding is not evident:	5.3
	If flooding is evident, permit the gasoline to dry for a few moments and restart.	
	If flooding doesn't recur:	5.6
	If flooding is persistant:	5.5
5.3—Check that fuel is reaching the carburetor: Detach the fuel line at the carburetor inlet. Hold the end of the line in a cup (not styrofoam), and crank the engine.	If fuel flows smoothly:	5.6
	If fuel doesn't flow (NOTE: *Make sure that there is fuel in the tank*), or flows erratically:	5.4
5.4—Test the fuel pump: Disconnect all fuel lines from the fuel pump. Hold a finger over the input fitting, crank the engine (with electric pump, turn the ignition or pump on); and feel for suction.	If suction is evident, blow out the fuel line to the tank with low pressure compressed air until bubbling is heard from the fuel filler neck. Also blow out the carburetor fuel line (both ends disconnected):	5.6
	If no suction is evident, replace or repair the fuel pump:	5.6
	NOTE: *Repeated oil fouling of the spark plugs, or a no-start condition, could be the result of a ruptured vacuum booster pump diaphragm, through which oil or gasoline is being drawn into the intake manifold (where applicable).*	
5.5—Check the needle and seat: Tap the carburetor in the area of the needle and seat.	If flooding stops, a gasoline additive (e.g., Gumout) will often cure the problem:	5.6
	If flooding continues, check the fuel pump for excessive pressure at the carburetor (according to specifications). If the pressure is normal, the needle and seat must be removed and checked, and/or the float level adjusted:	5.6
5.6—Test the accelerator pump by looking into the throttle bores while operating the throttle.	If the accelerator pump appears to be operating normally:	5.7
	If the accelerator pump is not operating, the pump must be reconditioned. Where possible, service the pump with the carburetor(s) installed on the engine. If necessary, remove the carburetor. Prior to removal:	5.7
5.7—Determine whether the carburetor main fuel system is functioning: Spray a commercial starting fluid into the carburetor while attempting to start the engine.	If the engine starts, runs for a few seconds, and dies:	5.8
	If the engine doesn't start:	6.1

Test and Procedures	*Results and Indications*	*Proceed to*
5.8—Uncommon fuel system malfunctions: See below:	If the problem is solved:	6.1
	If the problem remains, remove and recondition the carburetor.	

Condition	*Indication*	*Test*	*Usual Weather Conditions*	*Remedy*
Vapor lock	Car will not restart shortly after running.	Cool the components of the fuel system until the engine starts.	Hot to very hot	Ensure that the exhaust manifold heat control valve is operating. Check with the vehicle manufacturer for the recommended solution to vapor lock on the model in question.
Carburetor icing	Car will not idle, stalls at low speeds.	Visually inspect the throttle plate area of the throttle bores for frost.	High humidity, 32-40° F.	Ensure that the exhaust manifold heat control valve is operating, and that the intake manifold heat riser is not blocked.
Water in the fuel	Engine sputters and stalls; may not start.	Pump a small amount of fuel into a glass jar Allow to stand, and inspect for droplets or a layer of water.	High humidity, extreme temperature changes.	For droplets, use one or two cans of commercial gas dryer (Dry Gas) For a layer of water, the tank must be drained, and the fuel lines blown out with compressed air.

Test and Procedure	*Results and Indications*	*Proceed to*
6.1—Test engine compression: Remove all spark plugs. Insert a compression gauge into a spark plug port, crank the engine to obtain the maximum reading, and record.	If compression is within limits on all cylinders:	7.1
	If gauge reading is extremely low on all cylinders:	6.2
	If gauge reading is low on one or two cylinders:	6.2
	(If gauge readings are identical and low on two or more adjacent cylinders, the head gasket must be replaced.)	

Testing compression
(© Chevrolet Div. G.M. Corp.)

Maxi. Press. Lbs. Sq. In.	*Min. Press. Lbs. Sq. In.*	*Maxi. Press. Lbs. Sq. In.*	*Min. Press. Lbs. Sq. In.*	*Max. Press. Lbs. Sq. In.*	*Min. Press. Lbs. Sq. In.*	*Max. Press. Lbs. Sq. In.*	*Min. Press. Lbs. Sq. In.*
134	101	162	121	188	141	214	160
136	102	164	123	190	142	216	162
138	104	166	124	192	144	218	163
140	105	168	126	194	145	220	165
142	107	170	127	196	147	222	166
146	110	172	129	198	148	224	168
148	111	174	131	200	150	226	169
150	113	176	132	202	151	228	171
152	114	178	133	204	153	230	172
154	115	180	135	206	154	232	174
156	117	182	136	208	156	234	175
158	118	184	138	210	157	236	177
160	120	186	140	212	158	238	178

Compression pressure limits
(© Buick Div. G.M. Corp.)

Test and Procedure	Results and Indications	Proceed to
6.2—Test engine compression (wet): Squirt approximately 30 cc. of engine oil into each cylinder, and retest per 6.1.	If the readings improve, worn or cracked rings or broken pistons are indicated:	Next Chapter
	If the readings do not improve, burned or excessively carboned valves or a jumped timing chain are indicated: NOTE: *A jumped timing chain is often indicated by difficult cranking.*	7.1
7.1—Perform a vacuum check of the engine: Attach a vacuum gauge to the intake manifold beyond the throttle plate. Start the engine, and observe the action of the needle over the range of engine speeds.	See below.	See below

Reading	Indications	Proceed to
 Steady, from 17-22 in. Hg.	Normal.	8.1
 Low and steady.	Late ignition or valve timing, or low compression:	6.1
 Very low	Vacuum leak:	7.2
 Needle fluctuates as engine speed increases.	Ignition miss, blown cylinder head gasket, leaking valve or weak valve spring:	6.1, 8.3
 Gradual drop in reading at idle.	Excessive back pressure in the exhaust system:	10.1
 Intermittent fluctuation at idle.	Ignition miss, sticking valve:	8.3, 9.1
 Drifting needle.	Improper idle mixture adjustment, carburetors not synchronized (where applicable), or minor intake leak. Synchronize the carburetors, adjust the idle, and retest. If the condition persists:	7.2
 High and steady.	Early ignition timing:	8.2

Test and Procedure	Results and Indications	Proceed to
7.2—Attach a vacuum gauge per 7.1, and test for an intake manifold leak. Squirt a small amount of oil around the intake manifold gaskets, carburetor gaskets, plugs and fittings. Observe the action of the vacuum gauge.	If the reading improves, replace the indicated gasket, or seal the indicated fitting or plug:	8.1
	If the reading remains low:	7.3
7.3—Test all vacuum hoses and accessories for leaks as described in 7.2. Also check the carburetor body (dashpots, automatic choke mechanism, throttle shafts) for leaks in the same manner.	If the reading improves, service or replace the offending part(s):	8.1
	If the reading remains low:	6.1
8.1—Check the point dwell angle: Connect a dwell meter between the distributor primary wire and ground. Start the engine, and observe the dwell angle from idle to 3000 rpm.	If necessary, adjust the dwell angle. NOTE: *Increasing the point gap reduces the dwell angle and vice-versa.* If the dwell angle moves outside specifications as engine speed increases, the distributor should be removed and checked for cam accuracy, shaft endplay and concentricity, bushing wear, and adequate point arm tension (NOTE: *Most of these items may be checked with the distributor installed in the engine, using an oscilloscope*):	8.2
8.2—Connect a timing light (per manufacturer's recommendation) and check the dynamic ignition timing. Disconnect and plug the vacuum hose(s) to the distributor if specified, start the engine, and observe the timing marks at the specified engine speed.	If the timing is not correct, adjust to specifications by rotating the distributor in the engine: (Advance timing by rotating distributor opposite normal direction of rotor rotation, retard timing by rotating distributor in same direction as rotor rotation.)	8.3
8.3—Check the operation of the distributor advance mechanism(s): To test the mechanical advance, disconnect all but the mechanical advance, and observe the timing marks with a timing light as the engine speed is increased from idle. If the mark moves smoothly, without hesitation, it may be assumed that the mechanical advance is functioning properly. To test vacuum advance and/or retard systems, alternately crimp and release the vacuum line, and observe the timing mark for movement. If movement is noted, the system is operating.	If the systems are functioning:	8.4
	If the systems are not functioning, remove the distributor, and test on a distributor tester:	8.4
8.4—Locate an ignition miss: With the engine running, remove each spark plug wire, one by one, until one is found that doesn't cause the engine to roughen and slow down.	When the missing cylinder is identified:	4.1

Test and Procedure	*Results and Indications*	*Proceed to*
9.1—Evaluate the valve train: Remove the valve cover, and ensure that the valves are adjusted to specifications. A mechanic's stethoscope may be used to aid in the diagnosis of the valve train. By pushing the probe on or near push rods or rockers, valve noise often can be isolated. A timing light also may be used to diagnose valve problems. Connect the light according to manufacturer's recommendations, and start the engine. Vary the firing moment of the light by increasing the engine speed (and therefore the ignition advance), and moving the trigger from cylinder to cylinder. Observe the movement of each valve.	See below	See below

Observation	*Probable Cause*	*Remedy*	*Proceed to*
Metallic tap heard through the stethoscope.	Sticking hydraulic lifter or excessive valve clearance.	Adjust valve. If tap persists, remove and replace the lifter:	10.1
Metallic tap through the stethoscope, able to push the rocker arm (lifter side) down by hand.	Collapsed valve lifter.	Remove and replace the lifter:	10.1
Erratic, irregular motion of the valve stem.*	Sticking valve, burned valve.	Recondition the valve and/or valve guide:	Next Chapter
Eccentric motion of the pushrod at the rocker arm.*	Bent pushrod.	Replace the pushrod:	10.1
Valve retainer bounces as the valve closes.*	Weak valve spring or damper.	Remove and test the spring and damper. Replace if necessary:	10.1

*—When observed with a timing light.

Test and Procedure	*Results and Indications*	*Proceed to*
9.2—Check the valve timing: Locate top dead center of the No. 1 piston, and install a degree wheel or tape on the crankshaft pulley or damper with zero corresponding to an index mark on the engine. Rotate the crankshaft in its direction of rotation, and observe the opening of the No. 1 cylinder intake valve. The opening should correspond with the correct mark on the degree wheel according to specifications.	If the timing is not correct, the timing cover must be removed for further investigation:	

Test and Procedure	*Results and Indications*	*Proceed to*
10.1—Determine whether the exhaust manifold heat control valve is operating: Operate the valve by hand to determine whether it is free to move. If the valve is free, run the engine to operating temperature and observe the action of the valve, to ensure that it is opening.	If the valve sticks, spray it with a suitable solvent, open and close the valve to free it, and retest.	
	If the valve functions properly:	10.2
	If the valve does not free, or does not operate, replace the valve:	10.2
10.2—Ensure that there are no exhaust restrictions: Visually inspect the exhaust system for kinks, dents, or crushing. Also note that gasses are flowing freely from the tailpipe at all engine speeds, indicating no restriction in the muffler or resonator.	Replace any damaged portion of the system:	11.1
11.1—Visually inspect the fan belt for glazing, cracks, and fraying, and replace if necessary. Tighten the belt so that the longest span has approximately ½″ play at its midpoint under thumb pressure.	Replace or tighten the fan belt as necessary:	11.2
	Checking the fan belt tension (© Nissan Motor Co. Ltd.)	
11.2—Check the fluid level of the cooling system.	If full or slightly low, fill as necessary:	11.5
	If extremely low:	11.3
11.3—Visually inspect the external portions of the cooling system (radiator, radiator hoses, thermostat elbow, water pump seals, heater hoses, etc.) for leaks. If none are found, pressurize the cooling system to 14-15 psi.	If cooling system holds the pressure:	11.5
	If cooling system loses pressure rapidly, reinspect external parts of the system for leaks under pressure. If none are found, check dipstick for coolant in crankcase. If no coolant is present, but pressure loss continues:	11.4
	If coolant is evident in crankcase, remove cylinder head(s), and check gasket(s). If gaskets are intact, block and cylinder head(s) should be checked for cracks or holes.	
	If the gasket(s) is blown, replace, and purge the crankcase of coolant:	12.6
	NOTE: *Occasionally, due to atmospheric and driving conditions, condensation of water can occur in the crankcase. This causes the oil to appear milky white. To remedy, run the engine until hot, and change the oil and oil filter.*	

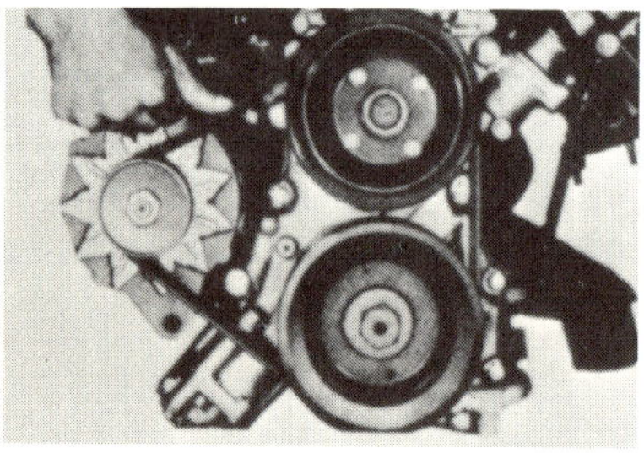

Test and Procedure	*Results and Indication*	*Proceed to*
11.4—Check for combustion leaks into the cooling system: Pressurize the cooling system as above. Start the engine, and observe the pressure gauge. If the needle fluctuates, remove each spark plug wire, one by one, noting which cylinder(s) reduce or eliminate the fluctuation.  Radiator pressure tester (© American Motors Corp.)	Cylinders which reduce or eliminate the fluctuation, when the spark plug wire is removed, are leaking into the cooling system. Replace the head gasket on the affected cylinder bank(s).	
11.5—Check the radiator pressure cap: Attach a radiator pressure tester to the radiator cap (wet the seal prior to installation). Quickly pump up the pressure, noting the point at which the cap releases. 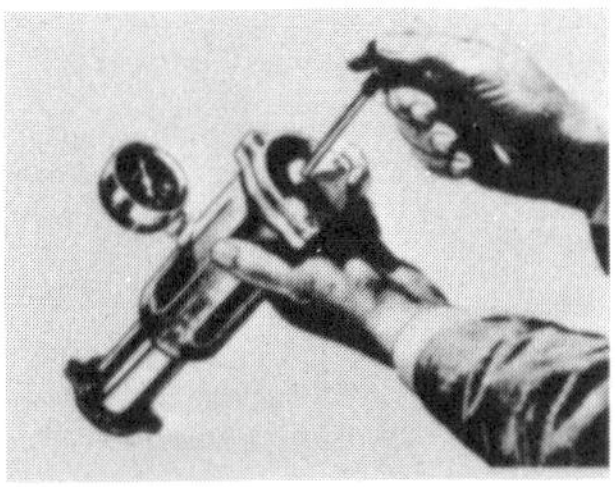 Testing the radiator pressure cap (© American Motors Corp.)	If the cap releases within ± 1 psi of the specified rating, it is operating properly:	11.6
	If the cap releases at more than ± 1 psi of the specified rating, it should be replaced:	11.6
11.6—Test the thermostat: Start the engine cold, remove the radiator cap, and insert a thermometer into the radiator. Allow the engine to idle. After a short while, there will be a sudden, rapid increase in coolant temperature. The temperature at which this sharp rise stops is the thermostat opening temperature.	If the thermostat opens at or about the specified temperature:	11.7
	If the temperature doesn't increase: (If the temperature increases slowly and gradually, replace the thermostat.)	11.7
11.7—Check the water pump: Remove the thermostat elbow and the thermostat, disconnect the coil high tension lead (to prevent starting), and crank the engine momentarily.	If coolant flows, replace the thermostat and retest per 11.6:	11.6
	If coolant doesn't flow, reverse flush the cooling system to alleviate any blockage that might exist. If system is not blocked, and coolant will not flow, recondition the water pump.	—
12.1—Check the oil pressure gauge or warning light: If the gauge shows low pressure, or the light is on, for no obvious reason, remove the oil pressure sender. Install an accurate oil pressure gauge and run the engine momentarily.	If oil pressure builds normally, run engine for a few moments to determine that it is functioning normally, and replace the sender.	—
	If the pressure remains low:	12.2
	If the pressure surges:	12.3
	If the oil pressure is zero:	12.3

Test and Procedure	*Results and Indications*	*Proceed to*
12.2—Visually inspect the oil: If the oil is watery or very thin, milky, or foamy, replace the oil and oil filter.	If the oil is normal: If after replacing oil the pressure remains low: If after replacing oil the pressure becomes normal:	12.3 12.3 —
12.3—Inspect the oil pressure relief valve and spring, to ensure that it is not sticking or stuck. Remove and thoroughly clean the valve, spring, and the valve body. **Oil pressure relief valve** (© British Leyland Motors)	If the oil pressure improves: If no improvement is noted:	— 12.4
12.4—Check to ensure that the oil pump is not cavitating (sucking air instead of oil): See that the crankcase is neither over nor underfull, and that the pickup in the sump is in the proper position and free from sludge.	Fill or drain the crankcase to the proper capacity, and clean the pickup screen in solvent if necessary. If no improvement is noted:	12.5
12.5—Inspect the oil pump drive and the oil pump:	If the pump drive or the oil pump appear to be defective, service as necessary and retest per 12.1: If the pump drive and pump appear to be operating normally, the engine should be disassembled to determine where blockage exists:	12.1 Next Chapter
12.6—Purge the engine of ethylene glycol coolant: Completely drain the crankcase and the oil filter. Obtain a commercial butyl cellosolve base solvent, designated for this purpose, and follow the instructions precisely. Following this, install a new oil filter and refill the crankcase with the proper weight oil. The next oil and filter change should follow shortly thereafter (1000 miles).		

Chapter Three

Engine and Engine Rebuilding

Engine Electrical

DISTRIBUTOR

Removal and Installation

1. Remove the air cleaner.
2. Pry back the retaining clips and remove the distributor cap. Mark the relationship between the distributor body and the engine block.
3. Disconnect the green condenser lead at the ignition coil. Detach the vacuum line, being careful not to damage the plastic tube.
4. Remove the bolt at the retaining clamp and pull the distributor from the housing. If the distributor is difficult to remove, the rubber seal is probably sticking. Carefully pry the distributor loose with a screwdriver if necessary.

To install the distributor:

5. Lubricate the distributor seal with a small amount of oil. Align the distributor locating marks made before removal and push the distributor into place. Turn the rotor until the distributor can drop into place. The projections on the bottom of the distributor driveshaft and the slots in the oil pump driveshaft, into which it fits, are off center. Thus the distributor will only fit in the correct way.

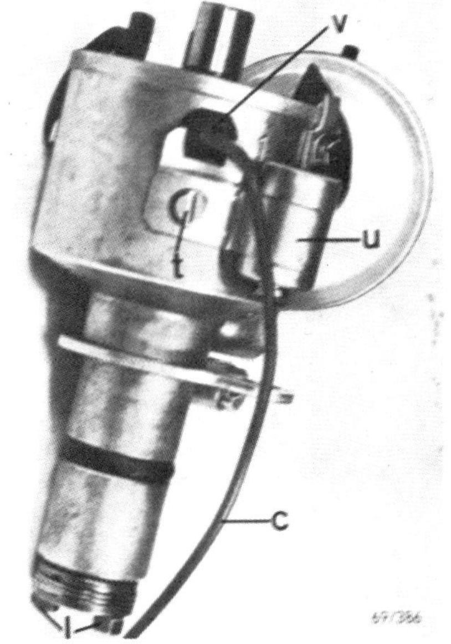

Distributor body removed from the engine. The projections (1) engage the slots in the oil pump driveshaft

c Green condenser lead
t Condenser clamp screw
u Condenser
v Plastic boot

6. After rechecking the alignment marks, install and tighten the bolt.
7. Replace the vacuum line, condenser lead, distributor cap, and air cleaner.
8. Check the ignition timing as de-

scribed in Chapter Two. Theoretically, this should not have changed if the distributor was reinstalled in its original position, but it is always best to make sure. If a new distributor is being installed, or if no marks were made in Step 2, it will be necessary to set basic ignition timing, then final timing.

Firing Order

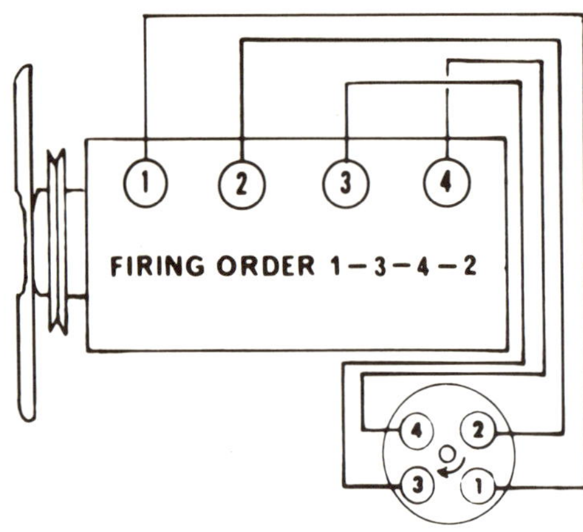

All models

ALTERNATOR

The alternator needs no lubrication or adjustments except for drive belt tension. Certain safety precautions should be observed concerning the alternator system.

1. Leads to any part of the charging circuit should be disconnected only after the engine has been switched off and has stopped turning.
2. When working on any part of the electrical system, always disconnect the lead from the negative battery terminal.
3. When performing any tests with the engine running, the battery must always be connected.
4. Temporary connections should never be made to the alternator. Always make firm connections.

The alternator warning light on the instrument panel should go out as soon as the engine reaches idle speed.

Removal and Installation

1. Disconnect the battery ground strap.
2. Disconnect all the leads to the alternator, after tagging them. Various arrangements of plug-in or bolt-on connections have been used. On some models the wiring may be unplugged from the back of the alternator; on others, it must be unplugged at the voltage regulator on the right front wheelhousing.

NOTE: *Current models have a voltage regulator built into the alternator.*

3. Remove the belt tensioning bolt from the slotted adjusting bracket.
4. Remove the drive belt.
5. Unbolt and remove the alternator.

To install the unit:

6. Install the hinge bolts, making sure that the head of the rear bolt is to the rear of the car.
7. Install the drive belt and the belt tensioning bolt.
8. Adjust the belt tension.
9. Replace all the electrical connections, making sure that they are installed in their original locations.
10. Connect the battery ground strap.

Belt Tension Adjustment

The alternator drive belt is correctly tensioned when the longest span of belt between pulleys can be depressed about ½ in. by moderate thumb pressure. To adjust, loosen the slotted adjusting bracket bolt, under the alternator. If the alternator hinge bolts are very tight, it may be necessary to loosen them slightly to move the alternator. Move the alternator in or out by hand to get the correct tension, then tighten the adjusting bolt.

NOTE: *Be careful not to overtighten the belt, as this may damage the alternator bearings.*

(c) is the alternator belt tension adjusting bolt as viewed from under the car

REGULATOR

If the voltage regulator is not on the right front wheelhousing in the engine compartment, it is built into the alternator.

Alternator and Regulator Specifications

Year	Alternator Part No. or Manufacturer	Alternator Output (amps.)	Regulator Part No. or Manufacturer	Regulator Volts
Early models	Bosch K1 14V 35A 20	35	Bosch AD 1/14V	13.9–14.8
Late models	Bosch K1 14V 55A 20	55	Bosch AD 1/14V	13.9–14.8

Note: A running change to a regulator built into the alternator took place during the 1971 model year. Previous to this, the regulator was mounted on the right front wheelhousing.

Removal and Installation

To remove the regulator, disconnect the battery ground cable, disconnect the three-pronged plug, and unscrew the unit from the wheelhousing. Be careful to make a good ground connection on reinstallation. The manufacturer does not recommend any adjustments to the regulator.

STARTER

No maintenance is required on the starter between overhauls.

Removal and Installation

1. Disconnect the battery ground lead.
2. Remove the oil filter. Use a pan to catch the small amount of lost oil.

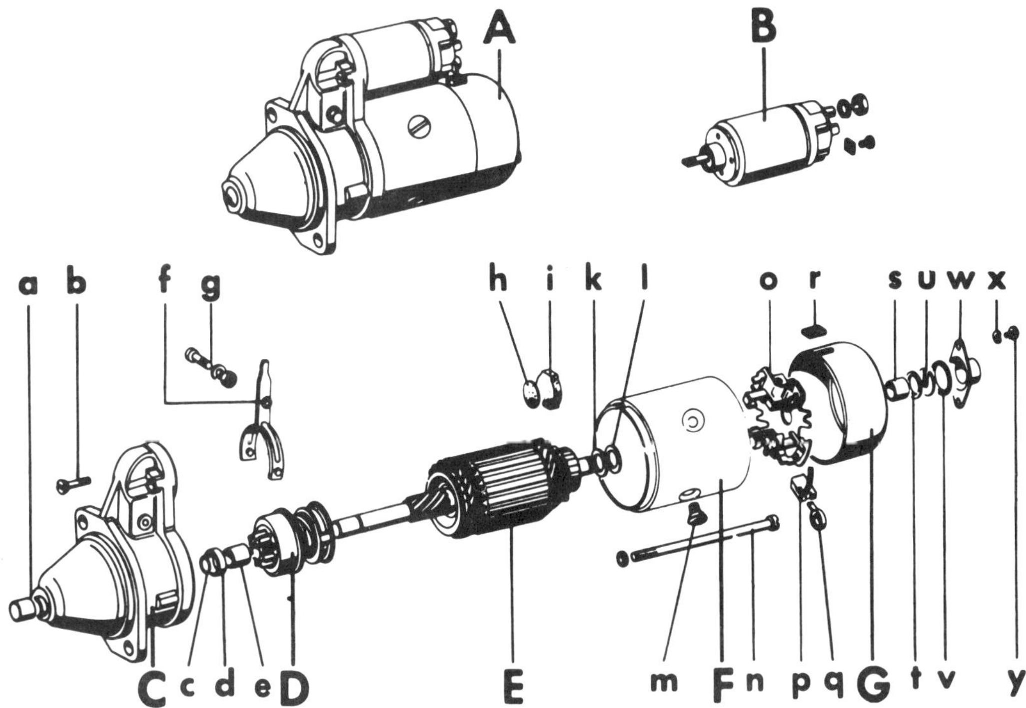

Exploded view of Super 90 starter

A Starter
B Solenoid switch
C Drive bearing
D Gear ring, complete
E Armature, complete
F Yoke
G Commutator bearing
a Bearing bushing and drive bearing
b Countersunk screw (for Solenoid switch)
c Snap-ring
d Stop-ring
e Bearing bushing (2 required for gear ring)
f Control lever
g Cylinder head screw with lock ring and hex nut (for control lever)
h Plate
i Rubber seal
k Washer (on armature shaft)
l Insulator (on armature shaft)
m Countersunk screw (4 req. for Pole shoes)
n Cylinder head screw (2 req. for washers)
o Brush holder plate
p Carbon brush (4 req.)
q Spring (4 req.)
r Rubber sleeve cable
s Bearing bushing (in commutator bearing)
t Shim (as required 0.1, 0.2, 0.3, 0.5, 0.8 mm)
u Fixing washer
v Rubber seal ring
w End cap
x Spring washer (domed)
y Cylinder head screw

3. Disconnect both leads from the upper terminal of the solenoid. Usually this is covered with a rubber boot.

4. Remove the lead from the lower solenoid terminal. The screw need only be loosened to remove this lead.

5. On the Super 90, unbolt and remove the crossbrace under the starter.

6. Unbolt the starter and pull it forward and out.

7. When replacing the starter, tighten the bolts to 43 ft lbs. If necessary, replace the lower mounting bolt with the head to the front of the car.

8. Thoroughly clean the seal and the sealing surface on the oil filter. Lightly lubricate both surfaces and tighten the oil filter about one turn by hand. This should be about 14–18 ft lbs.

9. Reconnect all the terminals.

10. Check and, if necessary, replenish the oil. Start the engine and check for oil leaks.

NOTE: *Some starters have an additional terminal (16), which is under full battery voltage, with a direct connection to the ignition coil.*

BATTERY

Refer to Chapter One for details on the battery.

Removal and Installation

1. Disconnect the negative (ground) cable and then the positive cable. Special pullers are available to remove battery terminals.

2. Remove the hold-down clamp.

3. Remove the battery, being careful not to spill the acid.

4. Clean the cable terminals of any corrosion, using a wire brush inside and out.

5. Install the battery. Replace the hold-down clamp.

6. Connect the positive and then the negative cable. Do not hammer them in place. The terminals should be coated lightly with petroleum jelly or grease to prevent corrosion.

Engine Mechanical

DESIGN

The Audi engine is a four-cylinder, four-stroke, carbureted, in-line engine. It is canted at an angle of 40 degrees to the left. The engine/transmission unit is mounted in the integral body and frame by engine carriers bolted to the engine block and by supports on the transmission.

Engine Removal and Installation

The transmission and engine must be lowered from the car as a unit. Thus the front of the car will have to be raised rather high or the car will have to be placed on a lift or a pit. The following procedure is for manual transmission cars; see "Automatic Transmission Removal and Installation" for details on the items that must be disconnected on the automatic transmission.

1. Remove the hood if a hoist is to be used to lower the engine. Mark the hinge location for reinstallation.

2. Unbolt and remove the apron just below the front bumper.

3. Disconnect the battery ground cable.

4. Remove the air cleaner and hose.

5. Drain the coolant. Disconnect all hoses between the radiator and the engine and the heater and the engine.

6. Disconnect the fuel hose at the fuel pump and plug the line.

7. Disconnect the power brake vacuum hose at the intake manifold.

8. Disconnect the speedometer cable at the transmission, the clutch cable at the mount, and the gearshift linkage at the transmission.

Battery and Starter Specifications

	BATTERY			*STARTER*			
				Lock Test			
Engine	*Ampere Hour Capacity*	*Volts*	*Terminal Grounded*	*Amps.*	*Volts*	*Torque (ft lbs)*	*Minimum Brush Length (in.)*
All	45/55	12	Neg	250–300	7	N.A.	0.47

General Engine Specifications

Year and Model	Engine Cu in. Displacement	Carburetor Type	SAE Horsepower @ rpm	SAE Torque @ rpm (ft lbs)	Bore × Stroke (in.)	Compression Ratio	Normal Oil Pressure (psi)
1970–1971 Super 90	107.5 (1,760 cc)	2 bbl	100 @ 5,200	116 @ 3,000	3.21 × 3.32	10.2 : 1	14–85
1972 Super 90	107.5 (1,760 cc)	2 bbl	N.A.	105 @ 3,000	3.21 × 3.32	8.2 : 1	14–85
1970–1971 100 LS	107.5 (1,760 cc)	2 bbl	115 @ 5,500	119 @ 3,200	3.21 × 3.32	10.2 : 1	14–85
1972–1973 100, 100 LS, 100 GL	114.2 (1,871 cc)	2 bbl	91 @ 5,500	110 @ 3,500	3.31 × 3.32	8.2 : 1	14–85

Valve Specifications

Engine	Seat Angle (deg)	Face Angle (deg)	Stem to Guide Clearance (in.)		Stem Diameter (in.)	
			Intake	Exhaust	Intake	Exhaust
Super 90	45	45°15′	0.001	0.002	0.3507	0.3890
100, 100 LS, 100 GL	45	45°15′	0.001	0.002	0.3507	0.3499

Note: Valve guides are removable.

Crankshaft and Connecting Rod Specifications

All measurements are given in inches.

Engine	Crankshaft				Connecting Rod		
	Main Bearing Journal Dia.	Main Bearing Oil Clearance	Shaft End-Play	Thrust on No.	Journal Diameter	Oil Clearance	Side Clearance
All	2.3322–2.3622	0.002–0.004	0.003–0.007	3	1.8598–1.8898	0.001–0.003	0.004–0.009

Piston and Ring Specifications

(All measurements in inches)

Engine	Piston Clearance	Ring Gap			Ring Side Clearance		
		Top Compression	Bottom Compression	Oil Control	Top Compression	Bottom Compression	Oil Control
Super 90	0.001	0.012–0.018	0.010–0.020	0.010–0.016	0.003–0.005	0.002–0.003	0.001–0.002
100, 100 LS, 100 GL	0.001	0.039	0.039	0.039	0.006	0.006	0.006

Note: Three piston sizes are available to accommodate overbores up to 0.040 in.

Torque Specifications

(All readings in ft lbs)

Engine	Cylinder Head Bolts	Rod Bearing Bolts	Main Bearing Bolts	Crankshaft Pulley Bolt	Flywheel to Crankshaft Bolts	Manifold	
						Intake	Exhaust
Super 90	65	25–31	29①	130–180	65	17	17
100, 100 LS, 100 GL	65	25–31	58②	130–180	65	18	18

① 23 on bearing cap no. 5
② 24 on bearing cap no. 5

9. Disconnect the accelerator linkage at the carburetor, mounting point, and connecting rod, and remove the throttle shaft.
10. Separate the brake line at the body mount and plug the line.
11. Remove the guard plate from the right engine mount.
12. Disconnect the following electrical wiring from the engine and transmission: ignition leads, idle cut-off valve, temperature switch, regulator, oil pressure switch, starter connections, back-up light switch, and ground lead.
13. Remove the oil filter on Super 90 models.
14. Remove the radiator and fan support together with the fan and stop pad, only if there isn't enough space to lower the engine with the fan attached. If there is space, unscrew the stop only.

(g) is the fan support, (h) is the stop pad, and (i) is the stop

15. Remove the front exhaust pipe.
16. Unbolt the driveshaft flange at the brake discs. Do not lose the thin insulator from between the brake disc and the flange. Turn the driveshaft flange slightly toward the wheel and wire it to the upper suspension control arm.
17. Detach the stabilizer bar from the lower control arms.
18. Position the jack or engine lifting apparatus on the engine and lift the weight from the engine mounts. Unbolt the rear crossmember from the body. Remove the retaining nut at the right engine/transmission mount. Note the positions of the washers and the sleeve on the mount.

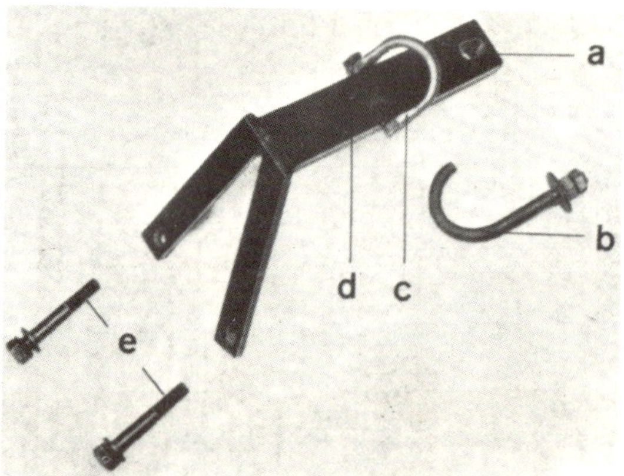

Engine lifting (or lowering) bracket. Bolt (b) goes through hole (a) and around the rear branch of the intake manifold. Bolts (e) go into the top of the transmission flange

c Lifting shackle
d Bracket

19. Remove the retaining nut from the left engine/transmission mount, but do not move the locknut. Lower the engine/transmission unit from the car.
20. Installation procedures are the reverse of removal. The engine and transmission unit must be aligned so that the same distance between the brake disc and wish-

When installing the engine, the same distance (x) must be maintained on both sides between the brake discs and the suspension wishbones. The maximum allowable deviation is 0.08 in.

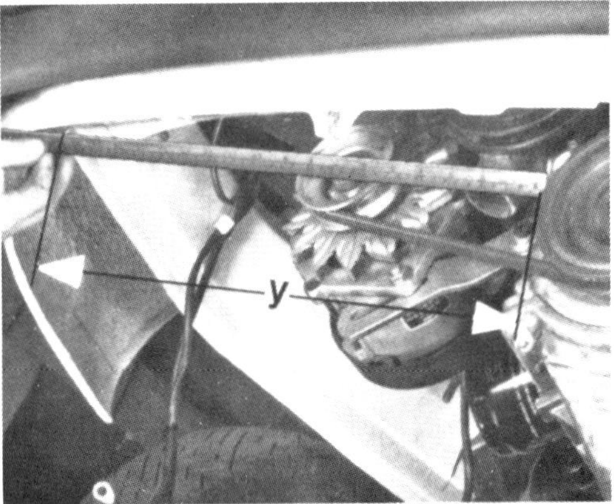

When installing the engine, the same distance (y) must be maintained between the pulley and the front of the side member on both sides

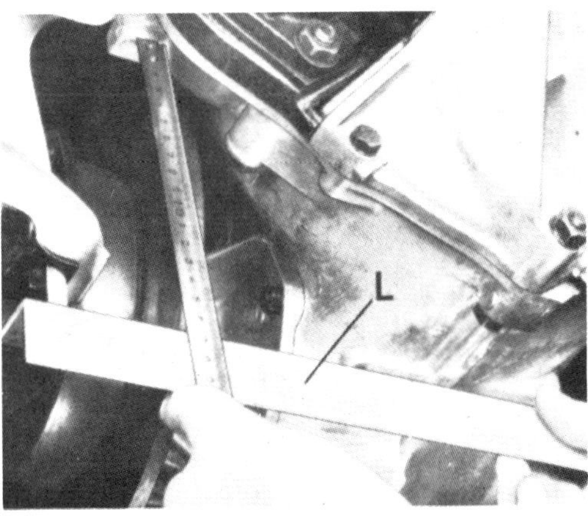

When installing the engine, the distance between the transmission casting at the point shown and a straightedge (L) must not vary more than 0.16 in. from side to side

bone appears on each side. The distance between the crankshaft pulley and the front of the side member must also be the same on each side. After the installation is complete, bleed the brakes.

CYLINDER HEAD

Removal and Installation

1. Drain the coolant from the radiator. Disconnect the spark plug wires.
2. Remove the sheet metal cover from the exhaust manifold. Remove the intake and exhaust manifolds.
3. Disconnect the hoses from the thermostat housing at the front of the head.
4. Remove the valve cover. Loosen the valve rocker arm adjusting nuts and remove the pushrods. Note their original locations; they must all go back in the same place.
5. Loosen the cylinder head bolts in the same order as shown for tightening. Remove the bolts. A metric allen wrench is required for the head bolts.

   NOTE: *Do not loosen the head bolts until the engine is thoroughly cool.*
6. Remove the head. If it sticks, operate the starter to loosen it by compression or rap it upward with a soft hammer. Do not force anything between the head and block. Check the head for warpage as detailed in the "Engine Rebuilding" section.
7. Reinstallation of the head is made easier by the use of guide studs installed in opposite corners of the block. These can be made by cutting the heads off two bolts of the same size as the head bolts.
8. Put the gasket in place on the block.
9. Guide the cylinder head into place.
10. Coat the head bolt threads with a graphite lubricant. Install them finger tight.
11. Tighten the bolts in the sequence shown in four stages until the proper torque is reached. The bolts should be torqued again after the first 500–1000 miles.
12. Install the pushrods in their original locations. Make a preliminary valve lash adjustment.
13. Replace the valve cover, using a new gasket. Replace the manifolds. Connect the coolant hoses and the spark plug wires.
14. Refill the cooling system.

15. Run the engine until it reaches normal operating temperature; watch for leaks. Make a final valve adjustment with the engine warm.

Cylinder Head Bolt Torque Sequence

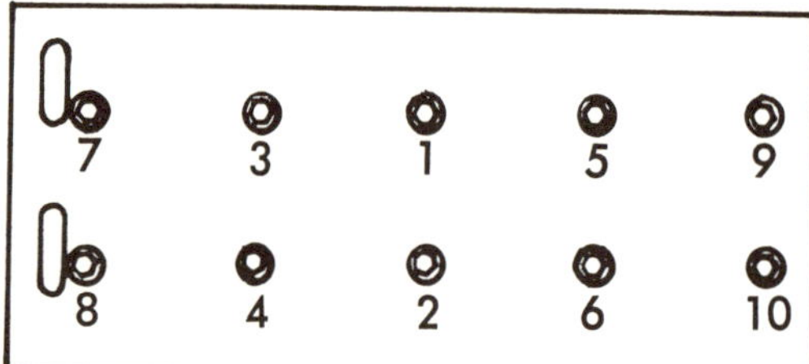

All models

Overhaul

See the "Engine Rebuilding" section at the end of this chapter for details on a valve job or cylinder head overhaul. This section should be consulted for checking head warpage, even if no other work is to be done on the head. If the rocker studs and pushrod guide plates have been removed, the guides must be aligned so that the pushrods will not contact them. The cylinder head must be heated to 248° F in an oven in order to install or remove the valve guides.

INTAKE MANIFOLD

Removal and Installation

1. Drain the coolant.
2. Remove the air cleaner.
3. Disconnect the coolant hoses from the manifold and the automatic choke. Disconnect the lead from the electric choke.
4. Disconnect the vacuum hose and the lead to the idle cutoff valve. Detach the fuel line and the accelerator linkage.
5. Remove the manifold nuts and the manifold support.
6. Pull the manifold off the studs. If it sticks, rap it with a soft hammer. Do not force anything between the manifold and the cylinder head. Discard the gaskets.
7. Installation is the reverse of the removal procedure. New gaskets must be used. Tighten the nuts to the specified torque. After refilling the cooling system, start the engine and check for leaks.

EXHAUST MANIFOLD

Removal and Installation

1. Disconnect the heated air intake hose from the manifold.
2. Unbolt the exhaust pipe from the manifold.
3. Remove the sheet metal cover.
4. Remove the manifold nuts. Pull the manifold off the studs. If it sticks, rap it with a soft hammer. Do not force anything between the manifold and the cylinder head. Discard the gaskets.
5. Installation is the reverse of removal. New gaskets must be used. Whether the gaskets have round or oval openings, they must be installed with the beaded side outward from the head and the notched edge down. Tighten the manifold nuts to the specified torque. Torque the front exhaust pipe flange nuts to 18–22 ft lbs, in steps. A new gasket should also be used between the exhaust pipe and the manifold.

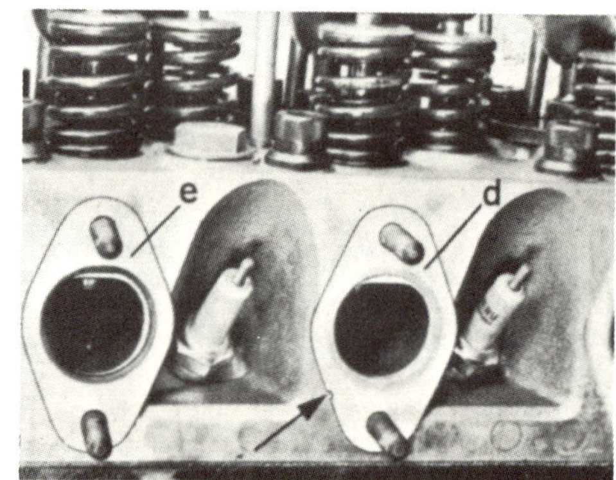

Exhaust manifold gaskets. (d) is the type with the oval opening which must be installed with the notched (arrow) side down, (e) is the type with the round opening. Both types must have the beaded edge around the opening outward.

EXHAUST SYSTEM

Removal

Front Exhaust Pipe

Loosen the clamp at the primary muffler and unbolt the flange at the exhaust manifold. Remove the front exhaust pipe.

Primary Muffler and Pipe

Loosen the clamps at the muffler inlet and at the end of the pipe. Disconnect the rubber loop at the muffler. Remove the muffler and pipe.

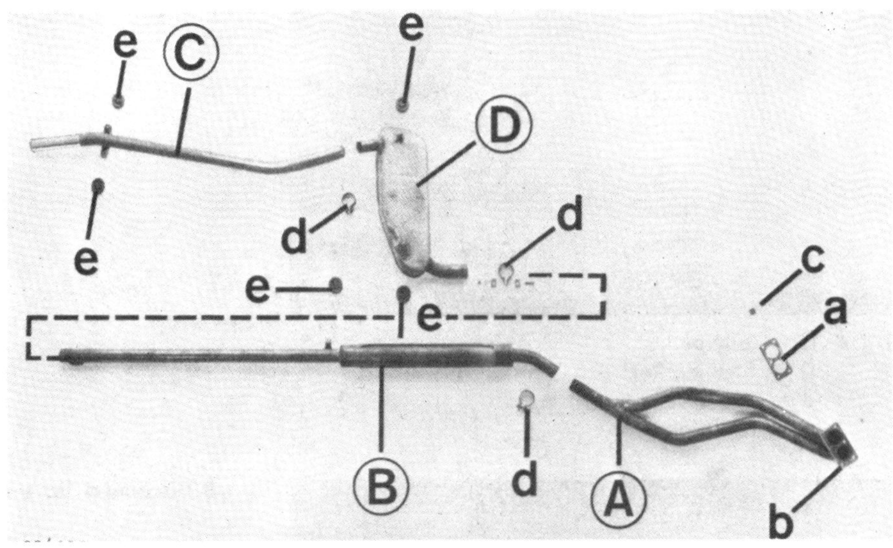

An exploded view of the complete exhaust system

A Exhaust pipe, front
B Primary muffler with pipe
C Tailpipe
D Final muffler
a Gasket
b Flange
c Nuts
d Clip with washers, screw, washer and nut
e Retaining strap

TAILPIPE

Loosen the clamp at the final muffler outlet, disconnect the straps from the tailpipe, and remove the tailpipe.

FINAL MUFFLER

Disconnect both the inlet and outlet clamps and remove the two retaining straps to remove the muffler.

Installation

To install the exhaust system components, reverse the removal procedure. When installing the front exhaust pipe flange use a new gasket and tighten the nuts evenly to 18–22 ft lbs. When installing the tailpipe, be sure that the rubber pad is in position to keep the pipe from hitting the body. Always use new clamps.

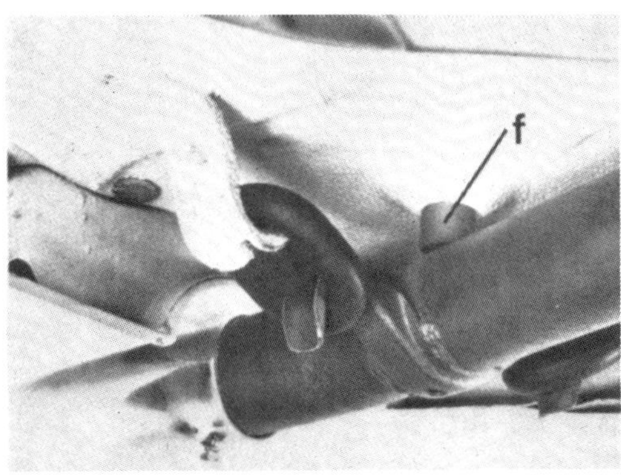

The rubber pad (f) prevents the exhaust pipe from hitting the body

TIMING CHAIN COVER

Removal and Installation

1. Place the car on a lift or over a pit.
2. Remove the apron from under the front bumper.
3. Have an assistant place the car in First gear and hold the brake on. Remove the crankshaft pulley nut. On cars with an automatic transmission, the nut can be removed by affixing a heavy wrench and rapping the wrench with a hammer. The nut must be unscrewed in the opposite direction of normal engine rotation.
4. Loosen the fan and alternator adjustments and remove the belts.
5. Remove the pulley, rapping it with a soft hammer if necessary. Be careful not to lose the shaft key.
6. Drain the oil.
7. Remove the oil pan, then the timing chain cover.
8. Reverse the procedure to install, using new gaskets. Timing chain cover bolt torque is 7 ft lbs.

Timing Chain Cover Oil Seal Replacement

When this seal fails, oil will be blown back along the bottom of the engine. It can be replaced without removing the engine. Current models have a lip in the cover which retains the oil seal to the inside. Thus the seal is pressed in from the front of the cover. A few older models have the retaining lip on the outside of the cover; the seal must be pressed in from the inside of the cover. Therefore, the oil seal may be replaced with the cover in place on the current models, while on older models the cover must be removed to replace the seal. The only way to determine which cover is installed is by inspection, after removing the crankshaft pulley. Virtually all US models use the current type.

To replace either type:

1. Remove the timing chain cover on older models. Follow Steps 1–6 of the "Timing Chain Cover Removal and Installation."
2. Carefully pry out the old seal with a screwdriver, being careful not to damage the housing.
3. Apply grease between the lips of the seal and apply a little oil to the outside edge.
4. On older models, press in the seal from the inside of the cover. Press or drive it in with a seal installer, or a suitable improvised tool, until it bottoms on the retaining lip. If there is no retaining lip, press the seal in until it is flush with the inside of the cover.
5. On current models, press or drive the seal in, with the metal side out, until it bottoms on the retaining lip. A good way to do this is to tighten a flat plate against the seal with the pulley retaining nut.
6. Reverse the procedure followed in Step 1 to reassemble the engine.

TIMING CHAIN AND TENSIONER

Removal and Installation

1. Remove the timing chain cover.
2. Some older Super 90 engines may have a leaf spring chain tensioner. If this is the case, simply unbolt and remove it. All other engines have a hydraulic chain tensioner. Bend open the lock plate, unscrew the chain tensioner plug, insert a phillips screwdriver and turn counterclockwise. If this is not done, the chain tensioner will fly apart as it is removed. On some models, the tensioner must be held together while it is removed. Unbolt and remove the tensioner.

Use a phillips screwdriver as shown to prevent the chain tensioner from coming apart when it is removed

3. Remove the camshaft sprocket retaining bolt.
4. Remove the camshaft sprocket, chain, and crankshaft sprocket together, using a puller on the crankshaft sprocket. Be careful not to lose the key for the crankshaft sprocket.
5. On reinstallation, heat the crankshaft sprocket to 140° F in an oven. Do not heat it with a flame, or it will warp. Install the shaft key and slide the sprocket into place until it rests against the stop.
6. Align the mark on the distributor body rim with the rotor. Set No. 1 cylinder precisely at Top Dead Center. Place the camshaft sprocket on the camshaft and align the sprocket punch mark with the notch in the chain guide rail.
7. Remove the camshaft sprocket, being careful not to turn the camshaft.
8. Place the timing chain over the crankshaft sprocket and place the camshaft sprocket in the chain, so that the camshaft

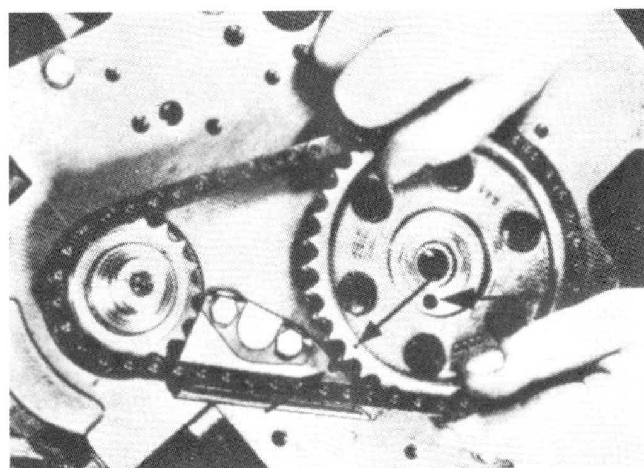

Timing chain alignment. The arrows show the camshaft sprocket punch mark, the notch in the chain guide rail, and the dowel which aligns the camshaft sprocket and camshaft

sprocket can be installed without moving either the camshaft or the crankshaft.

9. Torque the camshaft sprocket bolt to 58 ft lbs.

NOTE: *The factory specifies that timing chains with indented links should not be reused. They must be replaced with a straight-link chain.*

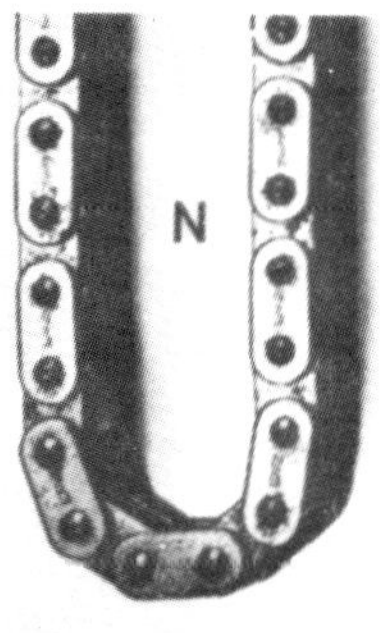

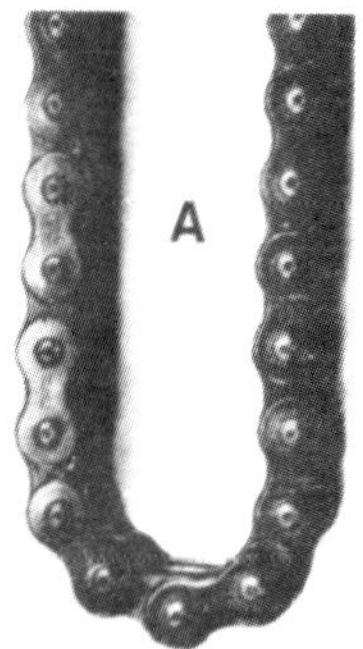

Only the timing chain with straight links (N) is to be used.

10. The manufacturer states that the leaf spring chain tensioner used on older Super 90 engines must be replaced with the hydraulic type. However, this entails drilling a hole into the engine block oil bore with the aid of special equipment. The engine also has to be lowered in the chassis to gain access. Assemble and install the chain tensioner, torquing the bolts to 9 ft lbs. Turn the chain plunger clockwise to release it. Current production models have a self releasing chain tensioner. Make absolutely sure that the hydraulic chain tensioner is free to move. Install the tensioner plunger and lock plate.

11. Replace the timing cover.

CAMSHAFT

Removal and Installation

This operation requires that the engine be removed from the car and rather extensively disassembled.

1. Remove the timing chain and tensioner.
2. Remove the cylinder head.
3. Remove the tappets (valve lifters). A special tool is used by dealers to lift them out. Keep them in order so they can be replaced in their original locations.
4. Remove the distributor.
5. Remove the oil pump.
6. Unbolt and remove the camshaft locating plate.
7. Carefully guide the camshaft out of the block, being careful not to bang the lobes into the bearings. This is a lot easier if a bolt is threaded into the front of the camshaft for use as a handle.
8. On reinstallation, oil the camshaft bearing surfaces. Insert the camshaft carefully.
9. Install the locating plate, torquing the bolts to 18 ft lbs.
10. Check the camshaft end-play in and out of the block, using a dial indicator. If it exceeds 0.004 in., install a new locating plate.
11. The rest of the reassembly procedure is the reverse of disassembly. Check the ignition timing when the job is complete.

PISTONS AND CONNECTING RODS

The connecting rods must be installed in the engine with the grooved side toward the camshaft. Both the pistons and the piston pins must be heated to 140° F in an oven in order to install the pins. Three piston sizes are available to accommodate overbores up to 0.040 in.

Engine Lubrication

OIL PAN

Removal and Installation

1. Place the car on a lift or over a pit.
2. Remove the apron from under the front bumper for better access.

3. Undo the radiator mounting bolts and press the radiator up out of the brackets.
4. Drain the oil.
5. Loosen and remove the allen head bolts which secure the pan. Tap it lightly with a soft hammer to break it loose. Remove the pan.
6. Clean the pan out thoroughly while it is off the engine.
7. Install new gaskets at either end of the oil pan. Apply a very thin coat of adhesive to them. Attach the pan rail gaskets to the block, using a slight amount of adhesive at both ends and in the middle. Put a tiny amount of adhesive at the extreme ends of the gaskets, adjacent to the rear main bearing cap and the timing cover. Stick on the small gasket segment below the starter.
8. Torque the larger pan bolts to 11 ft lbs and the rest to 6 ft lbs.
9. The rest of the installation is the reverse of removal. Fill the crankcase with oil and run the engine, checking for leaks.

Rear Main Bearing Oil Seal Replacement

When this seal fails, the usual result is oil leakage onto the clutch. This, of course, causes clutch slippage or failure to disengage. This repair requires that the engine be removed from the car and extensively disassembled.

1. Remove the engine.
2. Remove the transmission and clutch from the engine.
3. Remove the flywheel. Some method of preventing the flywheel from turning will have to be devised.

NOTE: *Mark the relationship between the flywheel and crankshaft to preserve balance.*

4. Remove the oil pan.
5. Unbolt and remove the rear main bearing cap.
6. The circular seal may now be removed.
7. Press the new seal evenly into place with the sealing lip toward the front of the engine. This is rather difficult without special seal installing tools.
8. Torque the bearing cap to specifications.
9. The remainder of the procedure is the reverse of disassembly. Make sure to align the flywheel marks made in Step 2.

OIL PUMP

Removal and Installation

1. Remove the distributor. Remove the oil pan.

(l) is the oil pan rail gaskets, stuck to the block at (x). (n) is a small gasket segment and the arrows show where adhesive is to be applied to the gaskets

2. Disconnect the oil line from the block and from the pump.

3. Unbolt the pump and pull it out of the block, being careful not to lose the bolt spacer.

4. Place No. 1 cylinder on Top Dead Center. This can be done by turning the engine with a finger held over the No. 1 spark plug hole. When compression is felt, turn the engine to align the 0° T mark on the crankshaft pulley with the timing pointer.

5. On replacement, turn the pump until the wide segment of the pump driveshaft faces forward. Turn the shaft 15 degrees counterclockwise and slide the oil pump shaft into the gear teeth of the camshaft.

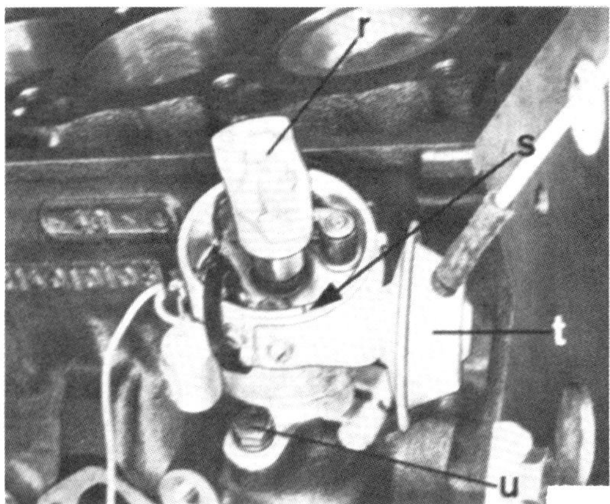

When installing the distributor, the rotor (r) must be aligned with the No. 1 cylinder notch (s). The vacuum unit (t) should parallel the engine block. (u) is the distributor mounting bolt.

The wide segment (c) on the oil pump driveshaft must face forward when installing the pump

The slots (a) in the oil pump driveshaft and the projections (b) on the distributor driveshaft are offset. (c) indicates the wide segment of each shaft. Because of this construction, the shafts can mate in only one way.

6. Install the spacer under the pump and mounting bolt and tighten the bolt finger tight.

7. Put the oil line in place. Turn the pump or add extra gaskets at either end of the oil line to prevent any strain on the line.

8. Torque the pump mounting bolt to 18 ft lbs and the oil line bolts to 7 ft lbs. Use the lock plates to hold the oil line bolts.

9. Align the distributor rotor with the No. 1 cylinder notch in the rim of the housing. Insert the distributor with the vacuum unit parallel to the engine block and pointing to the rear of the engine. When installing the distributor, wiggle the rotor back and forth to allow the shaft projections to engage the oil pump driveshaft slots. Tighten the distributor mounting bolt.

10. Replace and fill the oil pan.

11. Start the engine and watch for oil leaks. If it won't start, check the basic ignition timing as described in Chapter Two. If it does start, check the final ignition timing with a stroboscopic timing light.

Engine Cooling

Refer to Chapter One for coolant level checking and to the Appendix for Anti-Freeze Charts. At least every two years, the coolant should be drained and the system flushed with clean water. Service stations have reverse flushing equipment available. The coolant should always be maintained at a minimum of 0° F freezing protection, regardless of the prevailing temperature. This concentration assures rust protection and raises the boiling point well above that of pure water.

Coolant Draining and Refilling

1. Make sure that the engine is cool.
2. Set the heater water control lever at hot.
3. Remove the radiator cap and the drain plug from the bottom of the radiator. Open the system breather screw.

Radiator drain plug——100, 100 LS, and 100 GL shown

4. In order to drain the coolant completely, remove the drain plug from the front of the engine, adjacent to the alternator. The Super 90 also has a drain plug at the bottom of the heater, inside the car.

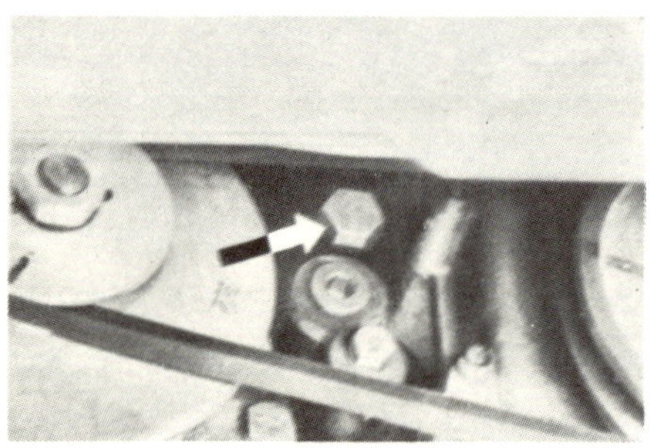

Engine block coolant drain plug

5. When the system has been flushed out thoroughly, replace the engine and radiator drain plugs.

NOTE: *Do not flush the system with cold water from a hose unless the engine is stone cold.*

6. Open the system breather screw if it was closed during the flushing process. Add the required amount of anti-freeze, then add water to fill the system.
7. Idle the engine to mix the water and anti-freeze. When coolant starts to flow out the breather, close it.

Cooling system breather plug——100, 100 LS, and 100 GL shown

8. Fill the radiator to the full mark. Check the level after the first hour's operation.

RADIATOR

The usual procedure for dealing with a damaged radiator is to remove it and have it repaired at a radiator specialty shop.

Removal and Installation

SUPER 90

1. Drain the coolant.
2. Remove the upper and lower hoses. Remove the small hose at the top.
3. Undo the mounting nuts and remove the radiator downward.
4. To install, reverse the removal procedures. Make sure that the gasket between the cowl and the radiator seals the crack completely. Be sure that the rubber fan ring is flat around the cowl.

100, 100 LS, 100 GL

1. Drain the coolant.
2. Remove the upper radiator hose.
3. Detach the mounting strut at the top of the radiator and swing it forward.
4. Detach the lower radiator hose.
5. Unbolt the radiator mountings.
6. Lift the radiator out.
7. To install, reverse the removal procedures. Make sure that the rubber sealing strips between the radiator and radiator cowl are in place.

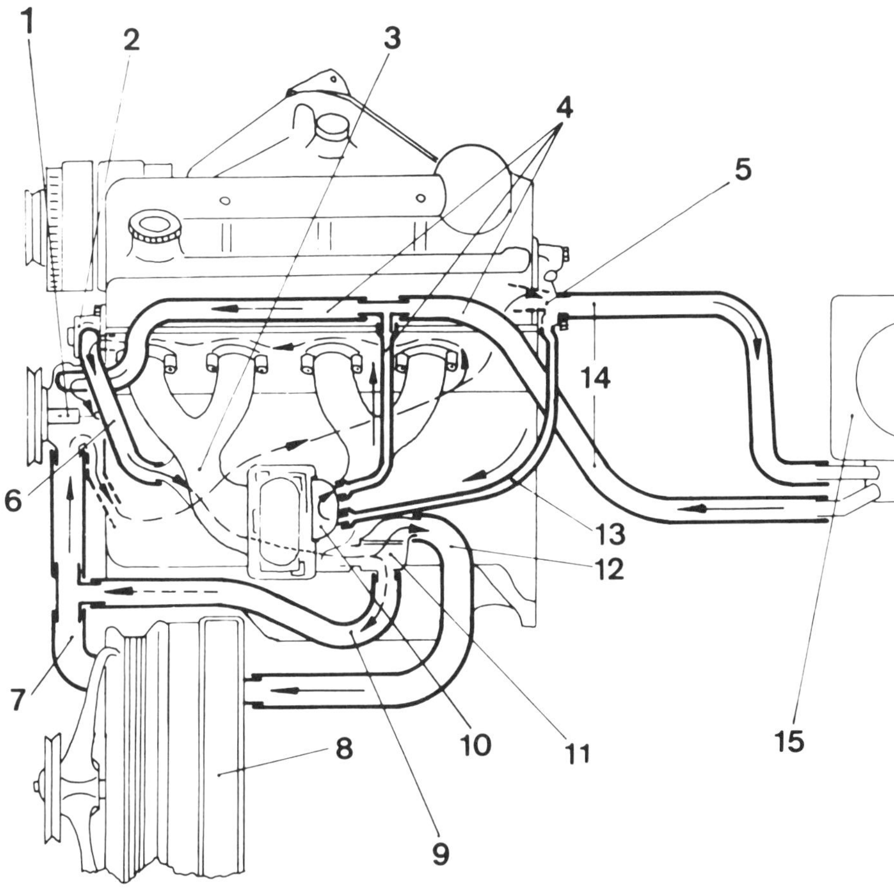

Coolant flow—1970–1971 100 LS shown

1. Water pump
2. Flange, front of cylinder head
3. Intake manifold
4. Return line, heater and automatic choke
5. Flange, rear of cylinder head
6. Connecting line to intake manifold
7. Radiator circuit from radiator to water pump
8. Radiator and fan (or electric fan)
9. Bypass line from intake manifold to water pump
10. Preheating, automatic choke
11. Thermostat, intake manifold
12. Radiator circuit
13. Automatic choke circuit
14. Heater circuit
15. Heat exchanger, heater

WATER PUMP

Removal and Installation

SUPER 90

1. Loosen the adjustment and remove the water pump drive belt.
2. Drain the coolant.
3. Remove the bolt that holds the small diameter hose to the front of the pump.
4. Detach the inlet and outlet hoses from the pump.
5. Remove the three allen head bolts and remove the pump.
6. Reverse the procedure for installation, using new gaskets and adjusting the water pump drive belt tension. Tighten the pump mounting bolts to 18 ft lbs.

100, 100 LS, 100 GL

1. Loosen the adjustment and remove the water pump drive belt.
2. Drain the coolant.
3. Remove the alternator pivot bolt at the front.
4. Loosen the clamp and pull the lower hose off the pump.
5. Remove the thermostat housing.
6. Unbolt the fan pulley. The pulley may be prevented from turning by wedging a screwdriver between the pulley hub and one of the bolts.
7. The pulley may be carefully pried off the hub with two large screwdrivers.
8. Loosen the clamp and pull the upper hose off the pump.

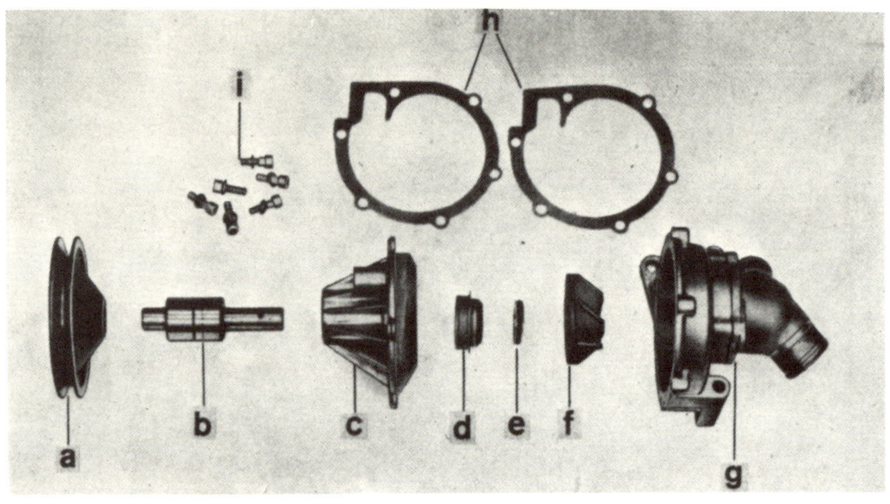

Exploded view of Super 90 water pump

a Pulley
b Water pump bearing with shaft
c Bearing housing
d Sliding seal ring
e Counter ring with rubber ring
f Impeller
g Housing
h Gaskets
i Bolts

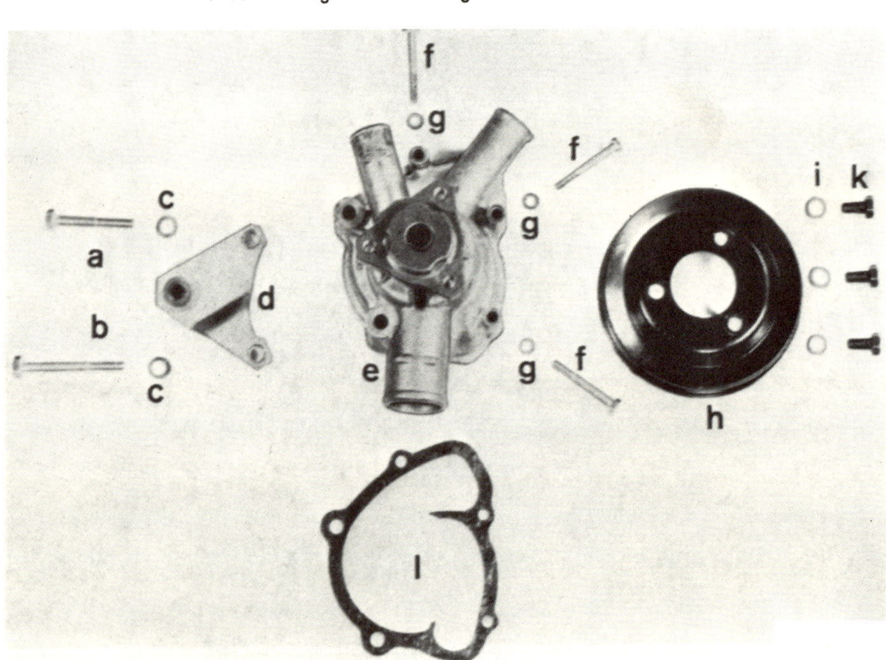

Exploded view of 100, 100 LS, and 100 GL water pump

a Bolt
b Bolt
c Lockwasher
d Mounting plate, alternator
e Water pump
f Bolt
g Lockwasher
h Pulley
i Lockwasher
k Bolt
l Water pump gasket

9. Remove the five bolts and remove the pump.

10. Reverse the procedure for installation, using new gaskets and adjusting the alternator drive belt tension. Pump mounting bolt torque is 15 ft lbs for the large bolts, and 9 ft lbs for the small ones. Thermostat housing bolt torque is 15 ft lbs. Pulley bolt torque is 7 ft lbs.

THERMOSTAT

The thermostat normally installed is rated at 181° F (83° C). A winter thermostat, which is rated at 189° F (87° C), is also available. Poor heater performance is often caused by a thermostat stuck in the open position.

Removal and Installation

1. Drain the coolant from the radiator.
2. Remove the air cleaner on the Super 90.
3. The thermostat is inside a cast housing on the engine, connected to the upper radiator hose. Unbolt the cover and remove the gasket and the thermostat.
4. When replacing the thermostat on the 100, 100 LS, and 100 GL, the bar on the thermostat should be facing up and running from front to rear. On the Super 90, the bar should be facing up and pointing at the projection on the housing. Some thermostats have an arrow on the bar which should also point at the projection. The housing bolts should be torqued to 7 ft lbs. Always use a new gasket.
5. Replace the Super 90 air cleaner and refill the radiator.

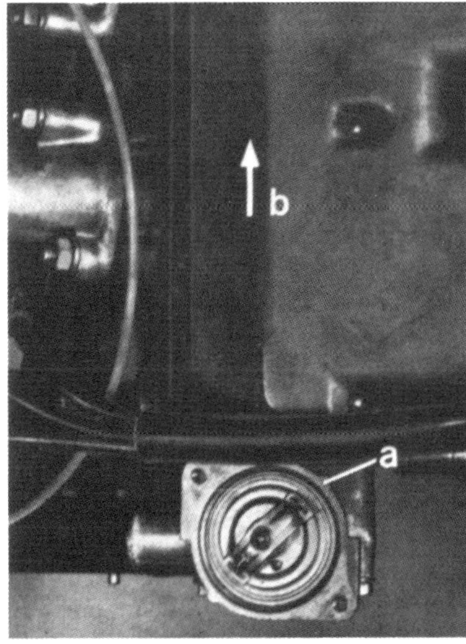

When installing the Super 90 thermostat, the bar (or arrow) should point at the projection (a). (b) points to the front

RADIATOR FAN

On the Super 90, the radiator fan is driven by the same belt that drives the water pump. On the 100, 100 LS, and 100 GL, the radiator fan is driven by a separate belt, the water pump being driven by the same belt that drives the alternator. Current models have an electric fan which requires no belt or adjustment.

Correct installation of the 100, 100 LS, and 100 GL thermostat

Belt Tension Adjustment

1. Loosen the two bolts which hold the fan housing to the fan support arm.
2. Move the fan and housing out to tighten the belt. The belt is correctly tensioned when the longest span of belt between pulleys can be depressed about ½ in. by moderate thumb pressure.
3. Tighten the bolts.

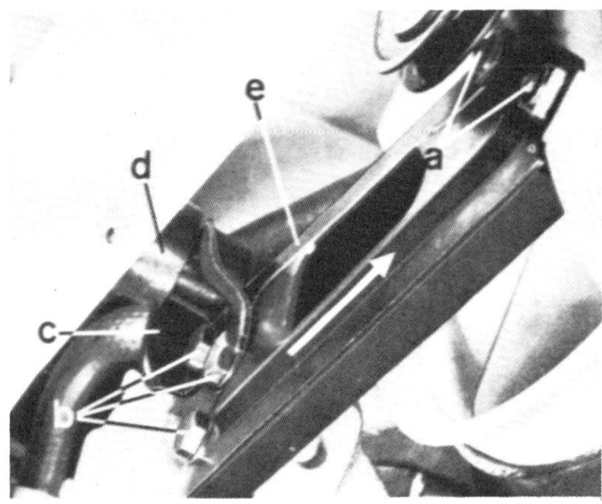

Radiator fan belt tension is adjusted with the bolts (a)

b Mounting bolts
c Pad
d Stop
e Fan support

This section describes, in detail, the procedures involved in rebuilding a typical engine. The procedures specifically refer to an inline engine, however, they are basically identical to those used in rebuilding engines of nearly all design and configurations. Procedures for servicing atypical engines (i.e., horizontally opposed) are described in the appropriate section, although in most cases, cylinder head reconditioning procedures described in this chapter will apply.

The section is divided into two sections. The first, Cylinder Head Reconditioning, assumes that the cylinder head is removed from the engine, all manifolds are removed, and the cylinder head is on a workbench. The camshaft should be removed from overhead cam cylinder heads. The second section, Cylinder Block Reconditioning, covers the block, pistons, connecting rods and crankshaft. It is assumed that the engine is mounted on a work stand, and the cylinder head and all accessories are removed.

Procedures are identified as follows:

Unmarked—Basic procedures that must be performed in order to successfully complete the rebuilding process.

Starred (*)—Procedures that should be performed to ensure maximum performance and engine life.

Double starred (**)—Procedures that may be performed to increase engine performance and reliability. These procedures are usually reserved for extremely heavy-duty or competition usage.

In many cases, a choice of methods is also provided. Methods are identified in the same manner as procedures. The choice of method for a procedure is at the discretion of the user.

The tools required for the basic rebuilding procedure should, with minor exceptions, be those

TORQUE (ft. lbs.)*

U.S.

Bolt Diameter (inches)	Bolt Grade (SAE) 1 and 2	5	6	8	Wrench Size (inches) Bolt	Nut
1/4	5	7	10	10.5	3/8	7/16
5/16	9	14	19	22	1/2	9/16
3/8	15	25	34	37	9/16	5/8
7/16	24	40	55	60	5/8	3/4
1/2	37	60	85	92	3/4	13/16
9/16	53	88	120	132	7/8	7/8
5/8	74	120	167	180	15/16	1
3/4	120	200	280	296	1-1/8	1-1/8
7/8	190	302	440	473	1-5/16	1-5/16
1	282	466	660	714	1-1/2	1-1/2

Metric

Bolt Diameter (mm)	Bolt Grade 5D	8G	10K	12K	Wrench Size (mm) Bolt and Nut
6	5	6	8	10	10
8	10	16	22	27	14
10	19	31	40	49	17
12	34	54	70	86	19
14	55	89	117	137	22
16	83	132	175	208	24
18	111	182	236	283	27
22	182	284	394	464	32
24	261	419	570	689	36

*—Torque values are for lightly oiled bolts. CAUTION: Bolts threaded into aluminum require much less torque.

General Torque Specifications

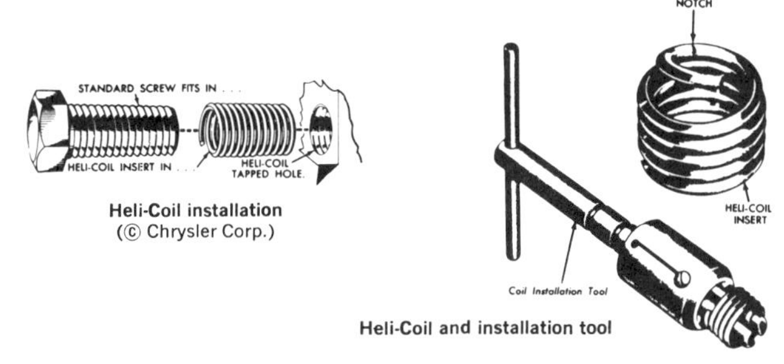

Heli-Coil installation
(© Chrysler Corp.)

Heli-Coil and installation tool

Heli-Coil Insert			*Drill*	*Tap*	*Insert. Tool*	*Extracting Tool*
Thread Size	*Part No.*	*Insert Length (In.)*	*Size*	*Part No.*	*Part No.*	*Part No.*
1/2 -20	1185-4	3/8	17/64(.266)	4 CPB	528-4N	1227-6
5/16-18	1185-5	15/32	Q(.332)	5 CPB	528-5N	1227-6
3/8 -16	1185-6	9/16	X(.397)	6 CPB	528-6N	1227-6
7/16-14	1185-7	21/32	29/64(.453)	7 CPB	528-7N	1227-16
1/2 -13	1185-8	3/4	33/64(.516)	8 CPB	528-8N	1227-16

Heli-Coil Specifications

included in a mechanic's tool kit. An accurate torque wrench, and a dial indicator (reading in thousandths) mounted on a universal base should be available. Bolts and nuts with no torque specification should be tightened according to size (see chart). Special tools, where required, all are readily available from the major tool suppliers (i.e., Craftsman, Snap-On, K-D). The services of a competent automotive machine shop must also be readily available.

When assembling the engine, any parts that will be in frictional contact must be pre-lubricated, to provide protection on initial start-up. Vortex Pre-Lube, STP, or any product specifically formulated for this purpose may be used. NOTE: *Do not use engine oil.* Where semi-permanent (locked but removable) installation of bolts or nuts is desired, threads should be cleaned and coated with Loctite. Studs may be permanently installed using Loctite Stud and Bearing Mount.

Aluminum has become increasingly popular for use in engines, due to its low weight and excellent heat transfer characteristics. The following precautions must be observed when handling aluminum engine parts:

—Never hot-tank aluminum parts.

—Remove all aluminum parts (identification tags, etc.) from engine parts before hot-tanking (otherwise they will be removed during the process).

—Always coat threads lightly with engine oil or anti-seize compounds before installation, to prevent seizure.

—Never over-torque bolts or spark plugs in aluminum threads. Should stripping occur, threads can be restored according to the following procedure, using Heli-Coil thread inserts:

Tap drill the hole with the stripped threads to the specified size (see chart). Using the specified tap (NOTE: *Heli-Coil tap sizes refer to the size thread being replaced, rather than the actual tap size*), tap the hole for the Heli-Coil. Place the insert on the proper installation tool (see chart). Apply pressure on the insert while winding it clockwise into the hole, until the top of the insert is one turn below the surface. Remove the installation tool, and break the installation tang from the bottom of the insert by moving it up and down. If the Heli-Coil must be removed, tap the removal tool firmly into the hole, so that it engages the top thread, and turn the tool counter-clockwise to extract the insert.

Snapped bolts or studs may be removed, using a stud extractor (unthreaded) or Vise-Grip pliers (threaded). Penetrating oil (e.g., Liquid Wrench) will often aid in breaking frozen threads. In cases where the stud or bolt is flush with, or below the surface, proceed as follows:

Drill a hole in the broken stud or bolt, approximately ½ its diameter. Select a screw extractor (e.g., Easy-Out) of the proper size, and tap it into the stud or bolt. Turn the extractor counter-clockwise to remove the stud or bolt.

Magnaflux and Zyglo are inspection techniques used to locate material flaws, such as stress cracks. Magnafluxing coats the part with fine magnetic particles, and subjects the part to a magnetic field. Cracks cause breaks

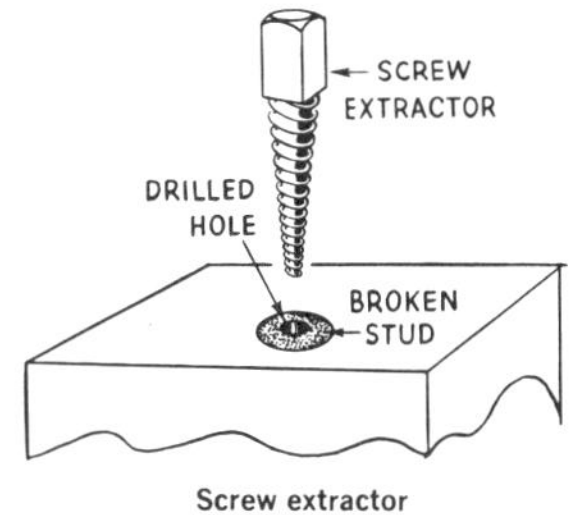

Screw extractor

in the magnetic field, which are outlined by the particles. Since Magnaflux is a magnetic process, it is applicable only to ferrous materials. The Zyglo process coats the material with a fluorescent dye penetrant, and then subjects it to blacklight inspection, under which cracks glow bright-

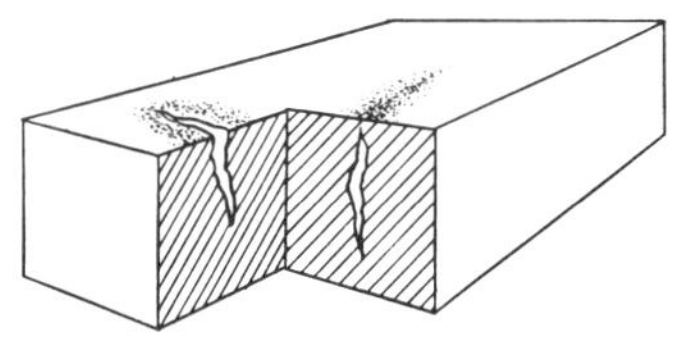

Magnaflux indication of cracks

ly. Parts made of any material may be tested using Zyglo. While Magnaflux and Zyglo are excellent for general inspection, and locating hidden defects, specific checks of suspected cracks may be made at lower cost and more readily using spot check dye. The dye is sprayed onto the suspected area, wiped off, and the area is then sprayed with a developer. Cracks then will show up brightly. Spot check dyes will only indicate surface cracks; therefore, structural cracks below the surface may escape detection. When questionable, the part should be tested using Magnaflux or Zyglo.

CYLINDER HEAD RECONDITIONING

Procedure	*Method*
Identify the valves: Valve identification (© SAAB)	Invert the cylinder head, and number the valve faces front to rear, using a permanent felt-tip marker.
Remove the rocker arms:	Remove the rocker arms with shaft(s) or balls and nuts. Wire the sets of rockers, balls and nuts together, and identify according to the corresponding valve.
Remove the valves and springs:	Using an appropriate valve spring compressor (depending on the configuration of the cylinder head), compress the valve springs. Lift out the keepers with needlenose pliers, release the compressor, and remove the valve, spring, and spring retainer.
Check the valve stem-to-guide clearance:  **Checking the valve stem-to-guide clearance** (© American Motors Corp.)	Clean the valve stem with lacquer thinner or a similar solvent to remove all gum and varnish. Clean the valve guides using solvent and an expanding wire-type valve guide cleaner. Mount a dial indicator so that the stem is at 90° to the valve stem, as close to the valve guide as possible. Move the valve off its seat, and measure the valve guide-to-stem clearance by moving the stem back and forth to actuate the dial indicator. Measure the valve stems using a micrometer, and compare to specifications, to determine whether stem or guide wear is responsible for excessive clearance.
De-carbon the cylinder head and valves: 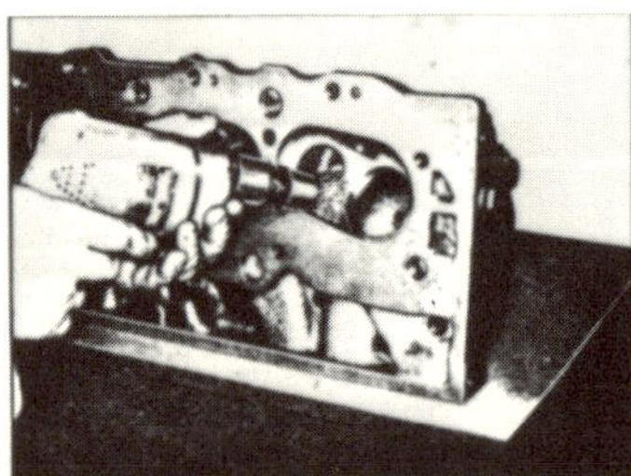 **Removing carbon from the cylinder head** (© Chevrolet Div. G.M. Corp.)	Chip carbon away from the valve heads, combustion chambers, and ports, using a chisel made of hardwood. Remove the remaining deposits with a stiff wire brush. NOTE: *Ensure that the deposits are actually removed, rather than burnished.*

Procedure	*Method*
Hot-tank the cylinder head:	Have the cylinder head hot-tanked to remove grease, corrosion, and scale from the water passages. NOTE: *In the case of overhead cam cylinder heads, consult the operator to determine whether the camshaft bearings will be damaged by the caustic solution.*
Degrease the remaining cylinder head parts:	Using solvent (i.e., Gunk), clean the rockers, rocker shaft(s) (where applicable), rocker balls and nuts, springs, spring retainers, and keepers. Do not remove the protective coating from the springs.
Check the cylinder head for warpage: 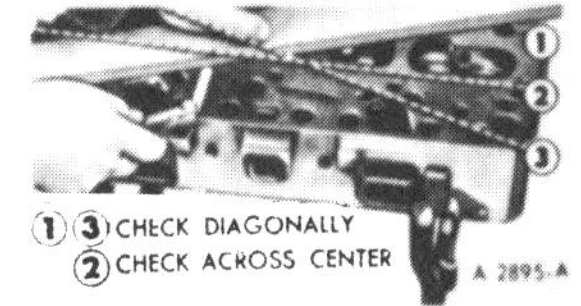 **Checking the cylinder head for warpage** (© Ford Motor Co.)	Place a straight-edge across the gasket surface of the cylinder head. Using feeler gauges, determine the clearance at the center of the straight-edge. Measure across both diagonals, along the longitudinal centerline, and across the cylinder head at several points. If warpage exceeds .003″ in a 6″ span, or .006″ over the total length, the cylinder head must be resurfaced. NOTE: *If warpage exceeds the manufacturers maximum tolerance for material removal, the cylinder head must be replaced.* When milling the cylinder heads of V-type engines, the intake manifold mounting position is altered, and must be corrected by milling the manifold flange a proportionate amount.
** Porting and gasket matching: 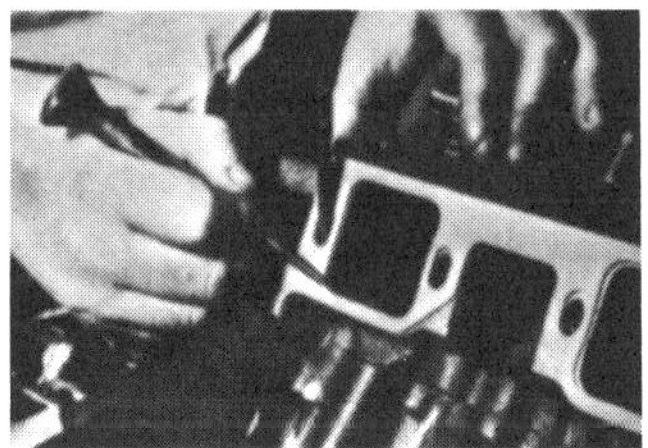 **Marking the cylinder head for gasket matching** (© Petersen Publishing Co.)  **Port configuration before and after gasket matching** (© Petersen Publishing Co.)	** Coat the manifold flanges of the cylinder head with Prussian blue dye. Glue intake and exhaust gaskets to the cylinder head in their installed position using rubber cement and scribe the outline of the ports on the manifold flanges. Remove the gaskets. Using a small cutter in a hand-held power tool (i.e., Dremel Moto-Tool), gradually taper the walls of the port out to the scribed outline of the gasket. Further enlargement of the ports should include the removal of sharp edges and radiusing of sharp corners. Do not alter the valve guides. NOTE: *The most efficient port configuration is determined only by extensive testing. Therefore, it is best to consult someone experienced with the head in question to determine the optimum alterations.*

Procedure	*Method*
** Polish the ports: 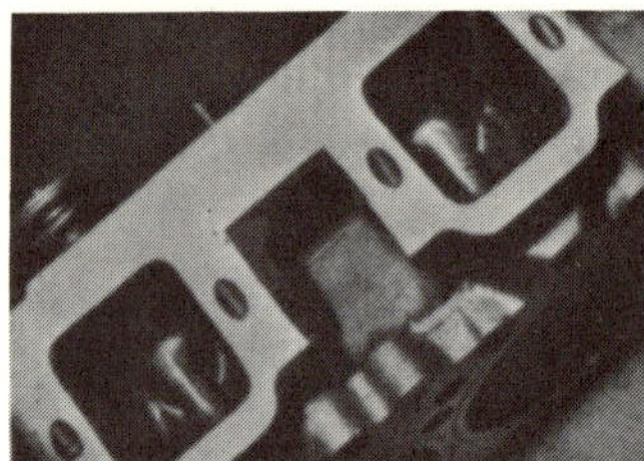 Relieved and polished ports (© Petersen Publishing Co.) 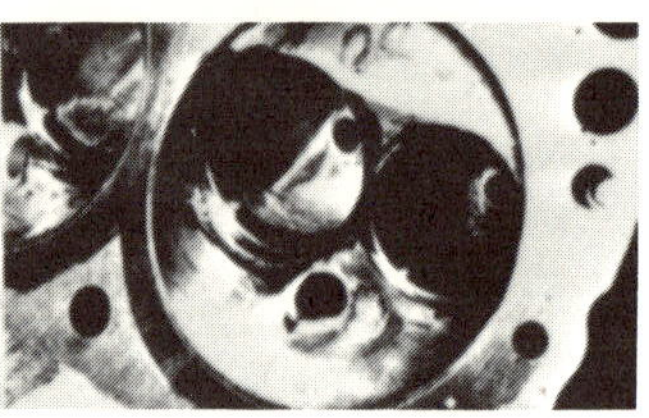 Polished combustion chamber (© Petersen Publishing Co.)	** Using a grinding stone with the above mentioned tool, polish the walls of the intake and exhaust ports, and combustion chamber. Use progressively finer stones until all surface imperfections are removed. NOTE: *Through testing, it has been determined that a smooth surface is more effective than a mirror polished surface in intake ports, and vice-versa in exhaust ports.*
* Knurling the valve guides: 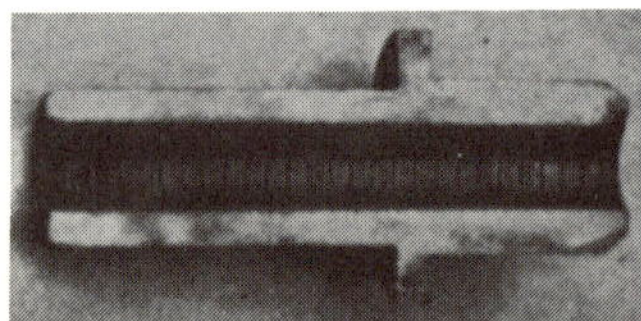 Cut-away view of a knurled valve guide (© Petersen Publishing Co.)	* Valve guides which are not excessively worn or distorted may, in some cases, be knurled rather than replaced. Knurling is a process in which metal is displaced and raised, thereby reducing clearance. Knurling also provides excellent oil control. The possibility of knurling rather than replacing valve guides should be discussed with a machinist.
Replacing the valve guides: NOTE: *Valve guides should only be replaced if damaged or if an oversize valve stem is not available.* 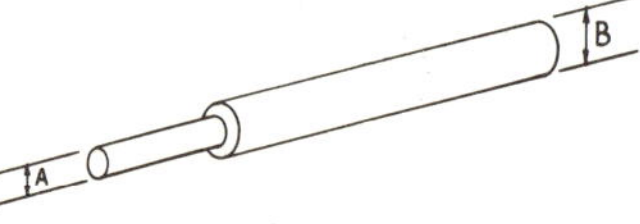 Valve guide removal tool 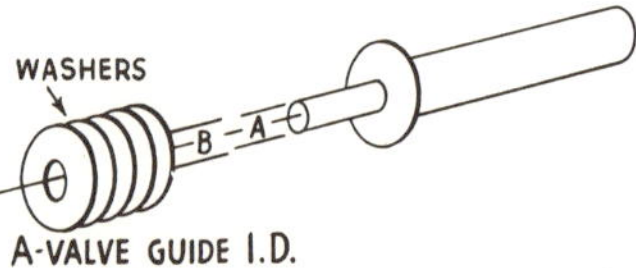 Valve guide installation tool (with washers used during installation)	Depending on the type of cylinder head, valve guides may be pressed, hammered, or shrunk in. In cases where the guides are shrunk into the head, replacement should be left to an equipped machine shop. In other cases, the guides are replaced as follows: Press or tap the valve guides out of the head using a stepped drift (see illustration). Determine the height above the boss that the guide must extend, and obtain a stack of washers, their I.D. similar to the guide's O.D., of that height. Place the stack of washers on the guide, and insert the guide into the boss. NOTE: *Valve guides are often tapered or beveled for installation.* Using the stepped installation tool (see illustration), press or tap the guides into position. Ream the guides according to the size of the valve stem.

Procedure	*Method*
Replacing valve seat inserts:	Replacement of valve seat inserts which are worn beyond resurfacing or broken, if feasible, must be done by a machine shop.
Resurfacing (grinding) the valve face:	Using a valve grinder, resurface the valves according to specifications. CAUTION: *Valve face angle is not always identical to valve seat angle.* A minimum margin of 1/32″ should remain after grinding the valve. The valve stem tip should also be squared and resurfaced, by placing the stem in the V-block of the grinder, and turning it while pressing lightly against the grinding wheel.

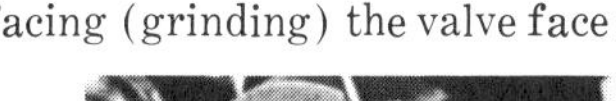
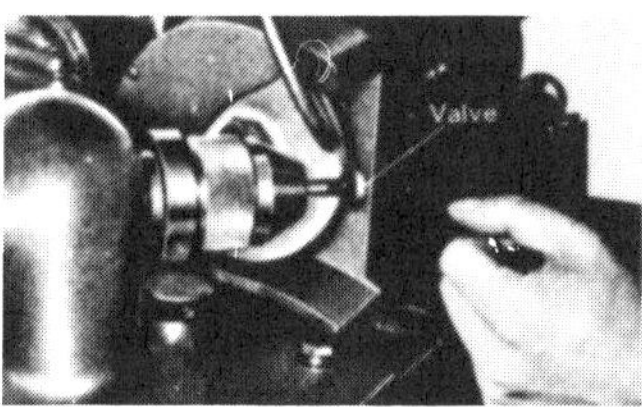

Grinding a valve (© Subaru)

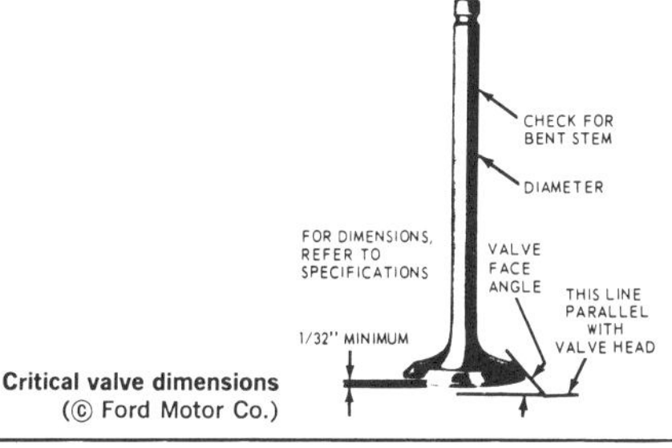

Critical valve dimensions (© Ford Motor Co.)

Resurfacing the valve seats using reamers:	Select a reamer of the correct seat angle, slightly larger than the diameter of the valve seat, and assemble it with a pilot of the correct size. Install the pilot into the valve guide, and using steady pressure, turn the reamer clockwise. CAUTION: *Do not turn the reamer counter-clockwise.* Remove only as much material as necessary to clean the seat. Check the concentricity of the seat (see below). If the dye method is not used, coat the valve face with Prussian blue dye, install and rotate it on the valve seat. Using the dye marked area as a centering guide, center and narrow the valve seat to specifications with correction cutters. NOTE: *When no specifications are available, minimum seat width for exhaust valves should be 5/64″, intake valves 1/16″.* After making correction cuts, check the position of the valve seat on the valve face using Prussian blue dye.

Reaming the valve seat (© S.p.A. Fiat)

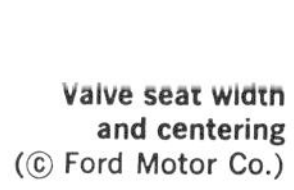

Valve seat width and centering (© Ford Motor Co.)

* Resurfacing the valve seats using a grinder:	Select a pilot of the correct size, and a coarse stone of the correct seat angle. Lubricate the pilot if necessary, and install the tool in the valve guide. Move the stone on and off the seat at approximately two cycles per second, until all flaws are removed from the seat. Install a fine stone, and finish the seat. Center and narrow the seat using correction stones, as described above.

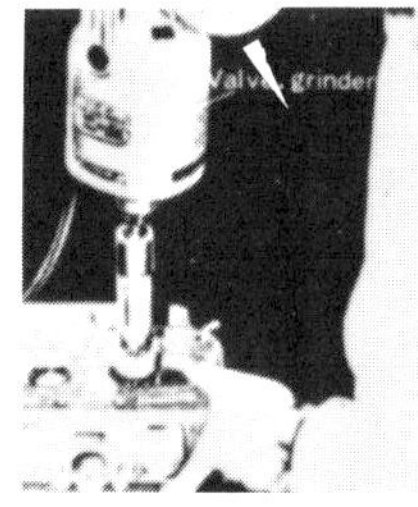
Grinding a valve seat (© Subaru)

Procedure	*Method*
Checking the valve seat concentricity: 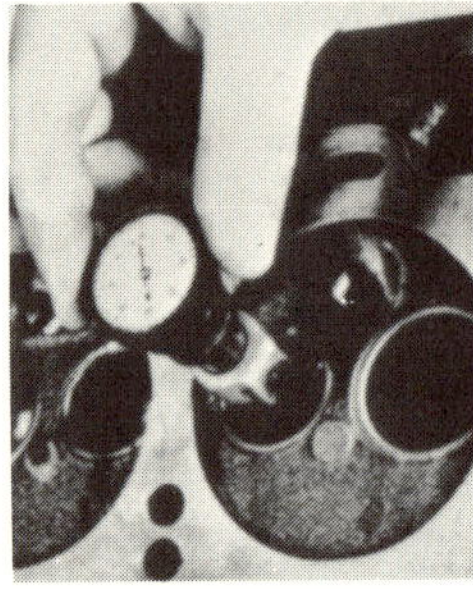 **Checking the valve seat concentricity using a dial gauge** (© American Motors Corp.)	Coat the valve face with Prussian blue dye, install the valve, and rotate it on the valve seat. If the entire seat becomes coated, and the valve is known to be concentric, the seat is concentric. * Install the dial gauge pilot into the guide, and rest the arm on the valve seat. Zero the gauge, and rotate the arm around the seat. Run-out should not exceed .002″.
* Lapping the valves: NOTE: *Valve lapping is done to ensure efficient sealing of resurfaced valves and seats. Valve lapping alone is not recommended for use as a resurfacing procedure.*  **Hand lapping the valves** 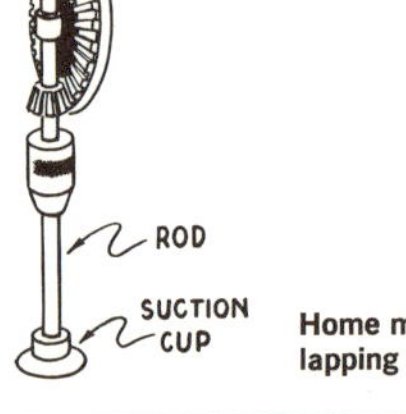 **Home made mechanical valve lapping tool**	* Invert the cylinder head, lightly lubricate the valve stems, and install the valves in the head as numbered. Coat valve seats with fine grinding compound, and attach the lapping tool suction cup to a valve head (NOTE: *Moisten the suction cup*). Rotate the tool between the palms, changing position and lifting the tool often to prevent grooving. Lap the valve until a smooth, polished seat is evident. Remove the valve and tool, and rinse away all traces of grinding compound. ** Fasten a suction cup to a piece of drill rod, and mount the rod in a hand drill. Proceed as above, using the hand drill as a lapping tool. CAUTION: *Due to the higher speeds involved when using the hand drill, care must be exercised to avoid grooving the seat.* Lift the tool and change direction of rotation often.
Check the valve springs: 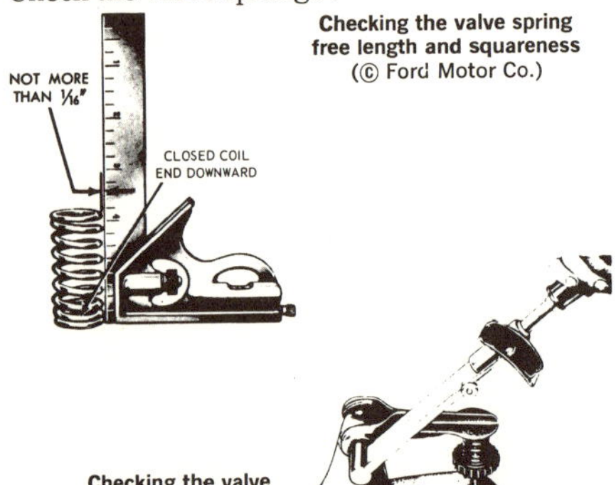 **Checking the valve spring free length and squareness** (© Ford Motor Co.) **Checking the valve spring tension** (© Chrysler Corp.)	Place the spring on a flat surface next to a square. Measure the height of the spring, and rotate it against the edge of the square to measure distortion. If spring height varies (by comparison) by more than 1/16″ or if distortion exceeds 1/16″, replace the spring. ** In addition to evaluating the spring as above, test the spring pressure at the installed and compressed (installed height minus valve lift) height using a valve spring tester. Springs used on small displacement engines (up to 3 liters) should be ± 1 lb. of all other springs in either position. A tolerance of ± 5 lbs. is permissible on larger engines.

Procedure	Method
 * Install valve stem seals:  **Valve stem seal installation** (© Ford Motor Co.)	* Due to the pressure differential that exists at the ends of the intake valve guides (atmospheric pressure above, manifold vacuum below), oil is drawn through the valve guides into the intake port. This has been alleviated somewhat since the addition of positive crankcase ventilation, which lowers the pressure above the guides. Several types of valve stem seals are available to reduce blow-by. Certain seals simply slip over the stem and guide boss, while others require that the boss be machined. Recently, Teflon guide seals have become popular. Consult a parts supplier or machinist concerning availability and suggested usages. NOTE: *When installing seals, ensure that a small amount of oil is able to pass the seal to lubricate the valve guides; otherwise, excessive wear may result.*
Install the valves:	Lubricate the valve stems, and install the valves in the cylinder head as numbered. Lubricate and position the seals (if used, see above) and the valve springs. Install the spring retainers, compress the springs, and insert the keys using needlenose pliers or a tool designed for this purpose. NOTE: *Retain the keys with wheel bearing grease during installation.*
Checking valve spring installed height: 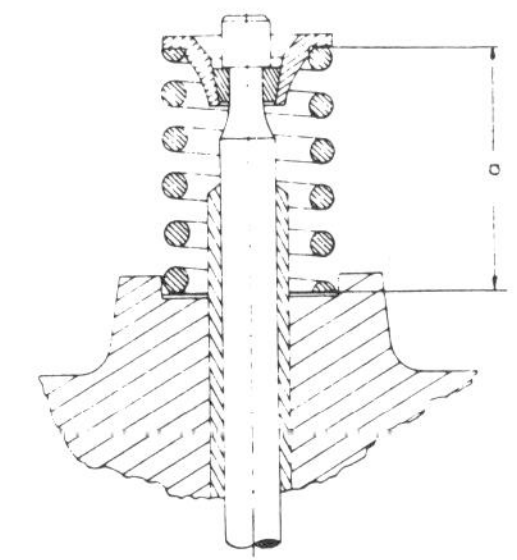 **Valve spring installed height dimension** (© Porsche) 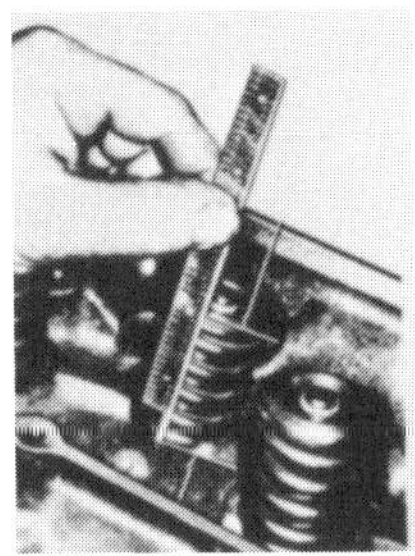 **Measuring valve spring installed height** (© Petersen Publishing Co.)	Measure the distance between the spring pad and the lower edge of the spring retainer, and compare to specifications. If the installed height is incorrect, add shim washers between the spring pad and the spring. CAUTION: *Use only washers designed for this purpose.*
** CC'ing the combustion chambers:	** Invert the cylinder head and place a bead of sealer around a combustion chamber. Install an apparatus designed for this purpose (burette mounted on a clear plate; see illustration) over the combustion chamber, and fill with the specified fluid to an even mark on the burette. Record the burette reading, and fill the combustion chamber with fluid. (NOTE: *A hole drilled in the plate will permit air to escape*). Subtract the burette reading, with the combustion chamber filled, from the previous reading, to determine combustion chamber volume in cc's. Duplicate this procedure in all combustion

Procedure	*Method*
 CC'ing the combustion chamber (© Petersen Publishing Co.)	chambers on the cylinder head, and compare the readings. The volume of all combustion chambers should be made equal to that of the largest. Combustion chamber volume may be increased in two ways. When only a small change is required (usually), a small cutter or coarse stone may be used to remove material from the combustion chamber. NOTE: *Check volume frequently.* Remove material over a wide area, so as not to change the configuration of the combustion chamber. When a larger change is required, the valve seat may be sunk (lowered into the head). NOTE: *When altering valve seat, remember to compensate for the change in spring installed height.*
Inspect the rocker arms, balls, studs, and nuts (where applicable): 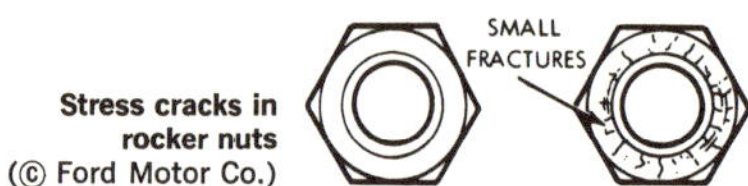 Stress cracks in rocker nuts (© Ford Motor Co.)	Visually inspect the rocker arms, balls, studs, and nuts for cracks, galling, burning, scoring, or wear. If all parts are intact, liberally lubricate the rocker arms and balls, and install them on the cylinder head. If wear is noted on a rocker arm at the point of valve contact, grind it smooth and square, removing as little material as possible. Replace the rocker arm if excessively worn. If a rocker stud shows signs of wear, it must be replaced (see below). If a rocker nut shows stress cracks, replace it. If an exhaust ball is galled or burned, substitute the intake ball from the same cylinder (if it is intact), and install a new intake ball. NOTE: *Avoid using new rocker balls on exhaust valves.*
Replacing rocker studs: 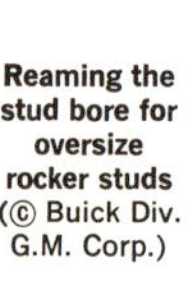  Reaming the stud bore for oversize rocker studs (© Buick Div. G.M. Corp.) 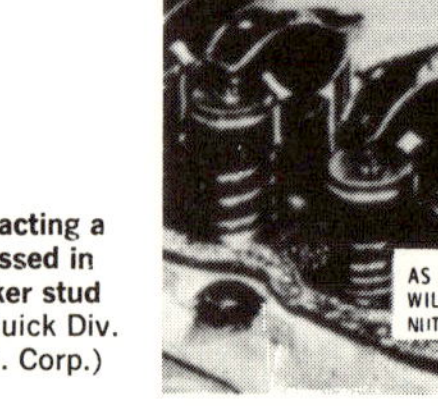 Extracting a pressed in rocker stud (© Buick Div. G.M. Corp.)	In order to remove a threaded stud, lock two nuts on the stud, and unscrew the stud using the lower nut. Coat the lower threads of the new stud with Loctite, and install. Two alternative methods are available for replacing pressed in studs. Remove the damaged stud using a stack of washers and a nut (see illustration). In the first, the boss is reamed .005-.006″ oversize, and an oversize stud pressed in. Control the stud extension over the boss using washers, in the same manner as valve guides. Before installing the stud, coat it with white lead and grease. To retain the stud more positively, drill a hole through the stud and boss, and install a roll pin. In the second method, the boss is tapped, and a threaded stud installed. Retain the stud using Loctite Stud and Bearing Mount.

Procedure	*Method*
Inspect the rocker shaft(s) and rocker arms (where applicable):  Disassembled rocker shaft parts arranged for inspection (© American Motors Corp.) 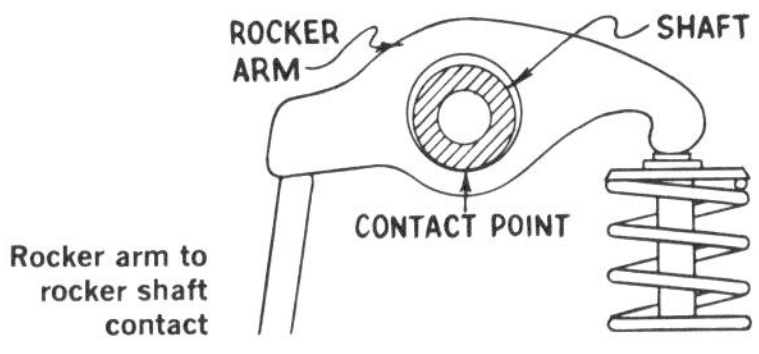 Rocker arm to rocker shaft contact	Remove rocker arms, springs and washers from rocker shaft. NOTE: *Lay out parts in the order they are removed.* Inspect rocker arms for pitting or wear on the valve contact point, or excessive bushing wear. Bushings need only be replaced if wear is excessive, because the rocker arm normally contacts the shaft at one point only. Grind the valve contact point of rocker arm smooth if necessary, removing as little material as possible. If excessive material must be removed to smooth and square the arm, it should be replaced. Clean out all oil holes and passages in rocker shaft. If shaft is grooved or worn, replace it. Lubricate and assemble the rocker shaft.
Inspect the camshaft bushings and the camshaft (overhead cam engines):	See next section.
Inspect the pushrods:	Remove the pushrods, and, if hollow, clean out the oil passages using fine wire. Roll each pushrod over a piece of clean glass. If a distinct clicking sound is heard as the pushrod rolls, the rod is bent, and must be replaced.
	* The length of all pushrods must be equal. Measure the length of the pushrods, compare to specifications, and replace as necessary.
Inspect the valve lifters: 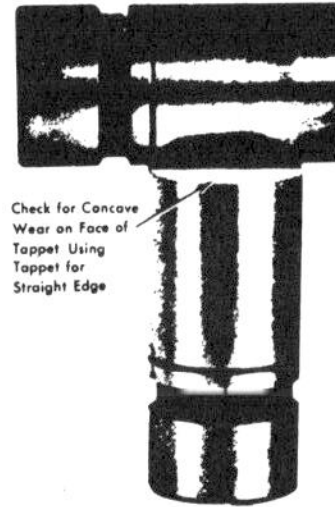 Checking the lifter face (© American Motors Corp.)	Remove lifters from their bores, and remove gum and varnish, using solvent. Clean walls of lifter bores. Check lifters for concave wear as illustrated. If face is worn concave, replace lifter, and carefully inspect the camshaft. Lightly lubricate lifter and insert it into its bore. If play is excessive, an oversize lifter must be installed (where possible). Consult a machinist concerning feasibility. If play is satisfactory, remove, lubricate, and reinstall the lifter.
* Testing hydraulic lifter leak down: 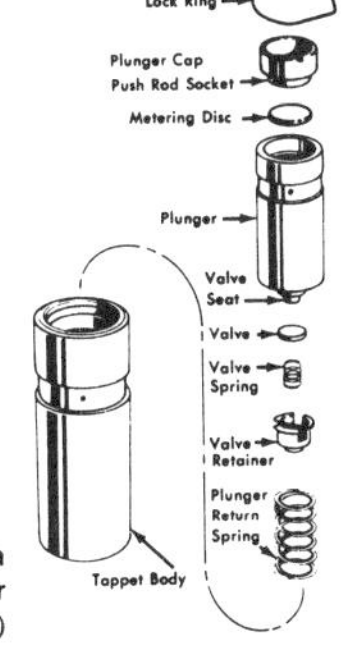 Exploded view of a typical hydraulic lifter (© American Motors Corp.)	Submerge lifter in a container of kerosene. Chuck a used pushrod or its equivalent into a drill press. Position container of kerosene so pushrod acts on the lifter plunger. Pump lifter with the drill press, until resistance increases. Pump several more times to bleed any air out of lifter. Apply very firm, constant pressure to the lifter, and observe rate at which fluid bleeds out of lifter. If the fluid bleeds very quickly (less than 15 seconds), lifter is defective. If the time exceeds 60 seconds, lifter is sticking. In either case, recondition or replace lifter. If lifter is operating properly (leak down time 15-60 seconds), lubricate and install it.

CYLINDER BLOCK RECONDITIONING

Procedure	*Method*

Checking the main bearing clearance:

Plastigage installed on main bearing journal
(© Chevrolet Div. G.M. Corp.)

Measuring Plastigage to determine main bearing clearance
(© Chevrolet Div. G.M. Corp.)

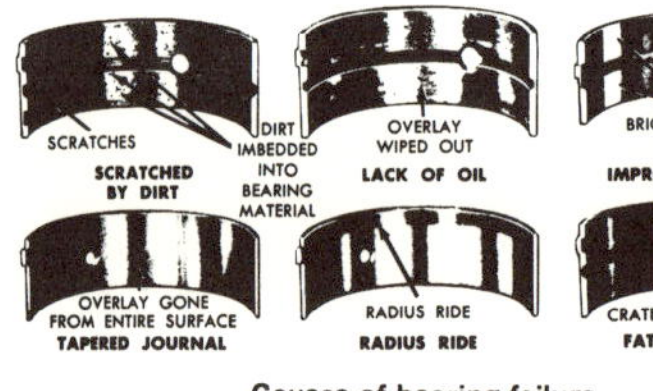

Causes of bearing failure
(© Ford Motor Co.)

Invert engine, and remove cap from the bearing to be checked. Using a clean, dry rag, thoroughly clean all oil from crankshaft journal and bearing insert. NOTE: *Plastigage is soluble in oil; therefore, oil on the journal or bearing could result in erroneous readings.* Place a piece of Plastigage along the full length of journal, reinstall cap, and torque to specifications. Remove bearing cap, and determine bearing clearance by comparing width of Plastigage to the scale on Plastigage envelope. Journal taper is determined by comparing width of the Plastigage strip near its ends. Rotate crankshaft 90° and retest, to determine journal eccentricity. NOTE: *Do not rotate crankshaft with Plastigage installed.* If bearing insert and journal appear intact, and are within tolerances, no further main bearing service is required. If bearing or journal appear defective, cause of failure should be determined before replacement.

* Remove crankshaft from block (see below). Measure the main bearing journals at each end twice (90° apart) using a micrometer, to determine diameter, journal taper and eccentricity. If journals are within tolerances, reinstall bearing caps at their specified torque. Using a telescope gauge and micrometer, measure bearing I.D. parallel to piston axis and at 30° on each side of piston axis. Subtract journal O.D. from bearing I.D. to determine oil clearance. If crankshaft journals appear defective, or do not meet tolerances, there is no need to measure bearings; for the crankshaft will require grinding and/or undersize bearings will be required. If bearing appears defective, cause for failure should be determined prior to replacement.

Checking the connecting rod bearing clearance:

Plastigage installed on connecting rod bearing journal
(© Chevrolet Div. G.M. Corp.)

Connecting rod bearing clearance is checked in the same manner as main bearing clearance, using Plastigage. Before removing the crankshaft, connecting rod side clearance also should be measured and recorded.

* Checking connecting rod bearing clearance, using a micrometer, is identical to checking main bearing clearance. If no other service

Procedure	 *Method*
 **Measuring Plastigage to determine connecting rod bearing clearance** (© Chevrolet Div. G.M. Corp.)	is required, the piston and rod assemblies need not be removed.
Removing the crankshaft:  **Connecting rod matching marks** (© Ford Motor Co.)	Using a punch, mark the corresponding main bearing caps and saddles according to position (i.e., one punch on the front main cap and saddle, two on the second, three on the third, etc.). Using number stamps, identify the corresponding connecting rods and caps, according to cylinder (if no numbers are present). Remove the main and connecting rod caps, and place sleeves of plastic tubing over the connecting rod bolts, to protect the journals as the crankshaft is removed. Lift the crankshaft out of the block.
Remove the ridge from the top of the cylinder: 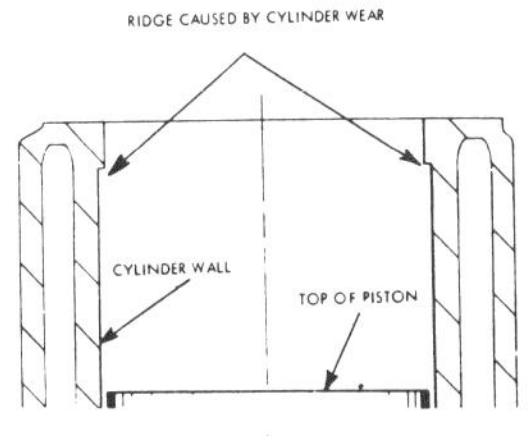 **Cylinder bore ridge** (© Pontiac Div. G.M. Corp.)	In order to facilitate removal of the piston and connecting rod, the ridge at the top of the cylinder (unworn area; see illustration) must be removed. Place the piston at the bottom of the bore, and cover it with a rag. Cut the ridge away using a ridge reamer, exercising extreme care to avoid cutting too deeply. Remove the rag, and remove cuttings that remain on the piston. CAUTION: *If the ridge is not removed, and new rings are installed, damage to rings will result.*
Removing the piston and connecting rod:  **Removing the piston** (© SAAB)	Invert the engine, and push the pistons and connecting rods out of the cylinders. If necessary, tap the connecting rod boss with a wooden hammer handle, to force the piston out. CAUTION: *Do not attempt to force the piston past the cylinder ridge* (see above).

Procedure	*Method*
Service the crankshaft:	Ensure that all oil holes and passages in the crankshaft are open and free of sludge. If necessary, have the crankshaft ground to the largest possible undersize.
	** Have the crankshaft Magnafluxed, to locate stress cracks. Consult a machinist concerning additional service procedures, such as surface hardening (e.g., nitriding, Tuftriding) to improve wear characteristics, cross drilling and chamfering the oil holes to improve lubrication, and balancing.
Removing freeze plugs:	Drill a hole in the center of the freeze plugs, and pry them out using a screwdriver or drift.
Remove the oil gallery plugs:	Threaded plugs should be removed using an appropriate (usually square) wrench. To remove soft, pressed in plugs, drill a hole in the plug, and thread in a sheet metal screw. Pull the plug out by the screw using pliers.
Hot-tank the block:	Have the block hot-tanked to remove grease, corrosion, and scale from the water jackets. NOTE: *Consult the operator to determine whether the camshaft bearings will be damaged during the hot-tank process.*
Check the block for cracks:	Visually inspect the block for cracks or chips. The most common locations are as follows: Adjacent to freeze plugs. Between the cylinders and water jackets. Adjacent to the main bearing saddles. At the extreme bottom of the cylinders. Check only suspected cracks using spot check dye (see introduction). If a crack is located, consult a machinist concerning possible repairs.
	** Magnaflux the block to locate hidden cracks. If cracks are located, consult a machinist about feasibility of repair.
Install the oil gallery plugs and freeze plugs:	Coat freeze plugs with sealer and tap into position using a piece of pipe, slightly smaller than the plug, as a driver. To ensure retention, stake the edges of the plugs. Coat threaded oil gallery plugs with sealer and install. Drive replacement soft plugs into block using a large drift as a driver.
	* Rather than reinstalling lead plugs, drill and tap the holes, and install threaded plugs.

Procedure	*Method*
Check the bore diameter and surface:	Visually inspect the cylinder bores for roughness, scoring, or scuffing. If evident, the cylinder bore must be bored or honed oversize to eliminate imperfections, and the smallest possible oversize piston used. The new pistons should be given to the machinist with the block, so that the cylinders can be bored or honed exactly to the piston size (plus clearance). If no flaws are evident, measure the bore diameter using a telescope gauge and micrometer, or dial gauge, parallel and perpendicular to the engine centerline, at the top (below the ridge) and bottom of the bore. Subtract the bottom measurements from the top to determine taper, and the parallel to the centerline measurements from the perpendicular measurements to determine eccentricity. If the measurements are not within specifications, the cylinder must be bored or honed, and an oversize piston installed. If the measurements are within specifications the cylinder may be used as is, with only finish honing (see below). NOTE: *Prior to submitting the block for boring, perform the following operation(s).*

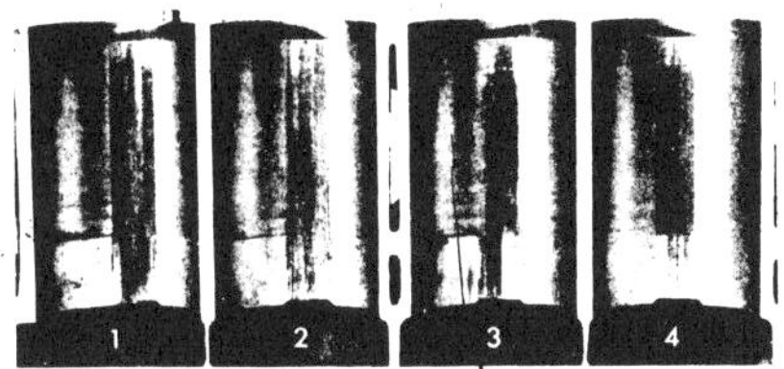

1, 2, 3 Piston skirt seizure resulted in this pattern. Engine must be rebored

4. Piston skirt and oil ring seizure caused this damage. Engine must be rebored

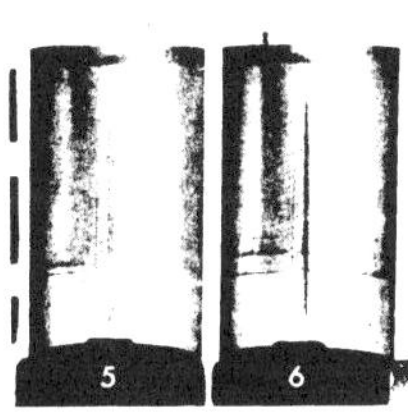

5, 6 Score marks caused by a split piston skirt. Damage is not serious enough to warrant reboring

7. Ring seized longitudinally, causing a score mark 1 3/16" wide, on the land side of the piston groove. The honing pattern is destroyed and the cylinder must be rebored

8. Result of oil ring seizure. Engine must be rebored

9. Oil ring seizure here was not serious enough to warrant reboring. The honing marks are still visible

Cylinder wall damage
(© Daimler-Benz A.G.)

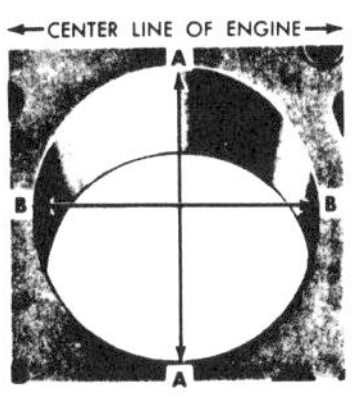

Cylinder bore measuring positions
(© Ford Motor Co.)

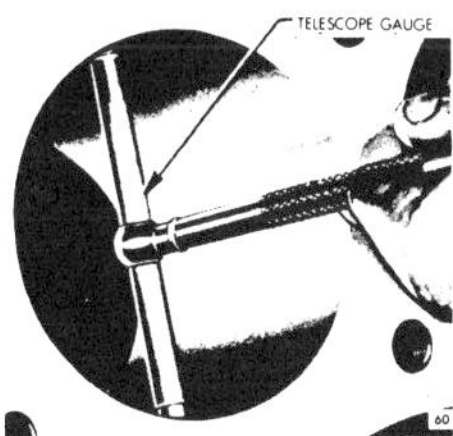

Measuring the cylinder bore with a telescope gauge
(© Buick Div. G.M. Corp.)

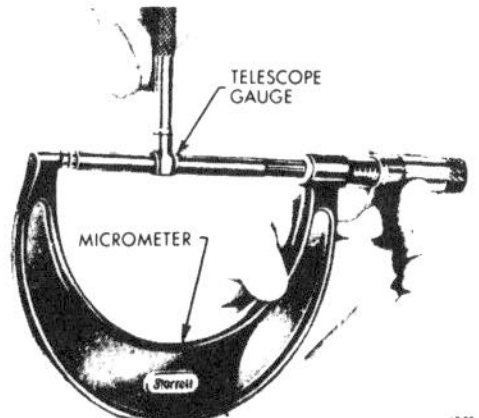

Determining the cylinder bore by measuring the telescope gauge with a micrometer
(© Buick Div. G.M. Corp.)

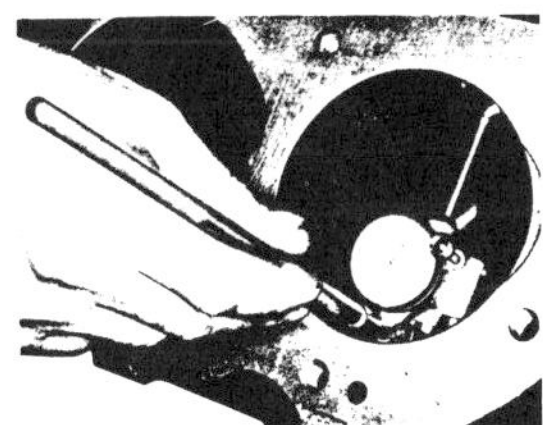

Measuring the cylinder bore with a dial gauge
(© Chevrolet Div. G.M. Corp.)

Procedure	Method
Check the block deck for warpage:	Using a straightedge and feeler gauges, check the block deck for warpage in the same manner that the cylinder head is checked (see Cylinder Head Reconditioning). If warpage exceeds specifications, have the deck resurfaced. NOTE: *In certain cases a specification for total material removal (Cylinder head and block deck) is provided. This specification must not be exceeded.*
* Check the deck height:	The deck height is the distance from the crankshaft centerline to the block deck. To measure, invert the engine, and install the crankshaft, retaining it with the center main cap. Measure the distance from the crankshaft journal to the block deck, parallel to the cylinder centerline. Measure the diameter of the end (front and rear) main journals, parallel to the centerline of the cylinders, divide the diameter in half, and subtract it from the previous measurement. The results of the front and rear measurements should be identical. If the difference exceeds .005″, the deck height should be corrected. NOTE: *Block deck height and warpage should be corrected concurrently.*
Check the cylinder block bearing alignment: 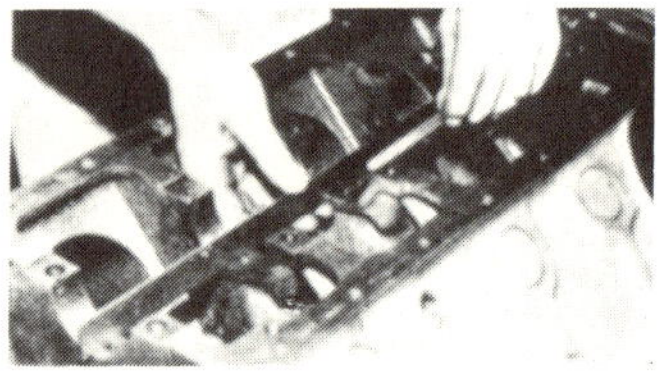 **Checking main bearing saddle alignment** (© Petersen Publishing Co.)	Remove the upper bearing inserts. Place a straightedge in the bearing saddles along the centerline of the crankshaft. If clearance exists between the straightedge and the center saddle, the block must be alignbored.
Clean and inspect the pistons and connecting rods: 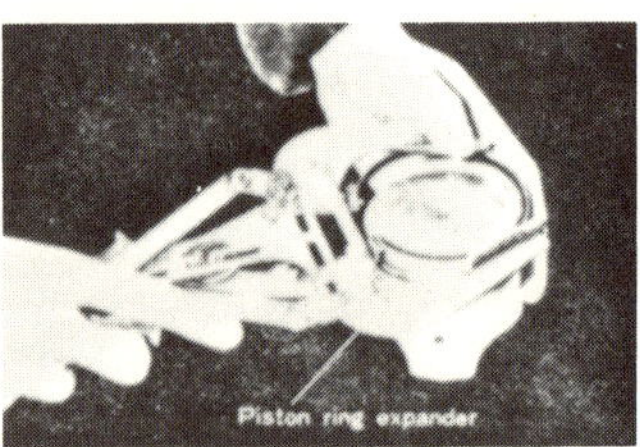 **Removing the piston rings** (© Subaru)	Using a ring expander, remove the rings from the piston. Remove the retaining rings (if so equipped) and remove piston pin. NOTE: *If the piston pin must be pressed out, determine the proper method and use the proper tools; otherwise the piston will distort.* Clean the ring grooves using an appropriate tool, exercising care to avoid cutting too deeply. Thoroughly clean all carbon and varnish from the piston with solvent. CAUTION: *Do not use a wire brush or caustic solvent on pistons.* Inspect the pistons for scuffing, scoring, cracks, pitting, or excessive ring groove wear. If wear is evident, the piston must be replaced. Check the connecting rod length by measuring the rod from the inside of the large end to the inside of the small end using calipers (see

Procedure	*Method*
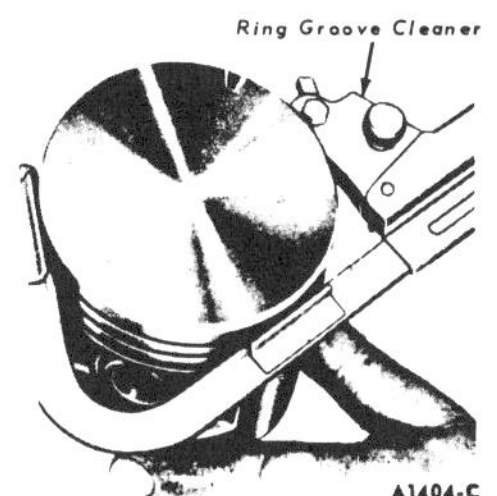 Cleaning the piston ring grooves (© Ford Motor Co.) 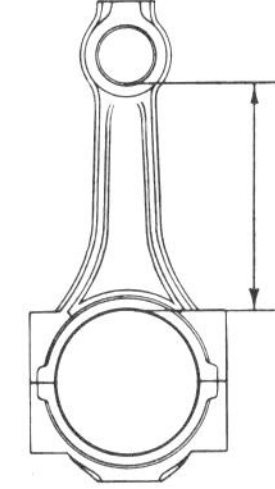 Connecting rod length checking dimension	illustration). All connecting rods should be equal length. Replace any rod that differs from the others in the engine.
	* Have the connecting rod alignment checked in an alignment fixture by a machinist. Replace any twisted or bent rods.
	* Magnaflux the connecting rods to locate stress cracks. If cracks are found, replace the connecting rod.
Fit the pistons to the cylinders: 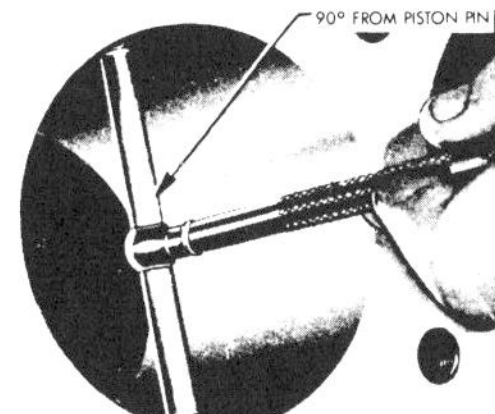 Measuring the cylinder with a telescope gauge for piston fitting (© Buick Div. G.M. Corp.) 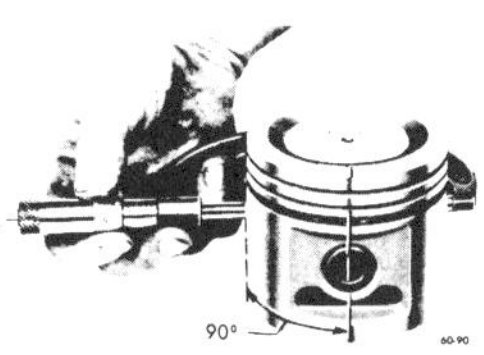 Measuring the piston for fitting (© Buick Div. G.M. Corp.)	Using a telescope gauge and micrometer, or a dial gauge, measure the cylinder bore diameter perpendicular to the piston pin, 2½" below the deck. Measure the piston perpendicular to its pin on the skirt. The difference between the two measurements is the piston clearance. If the clearance is within specifications or slightly below (after boring or honing), finish honing is all that is required. If the clearance is excessive, try to obtain a slightly larger piston to bring clearance within specifications. Where this is not possible, obtain the first oversize piston, and hone (or if necessary, bore) the cylinder to size.
Assemble the pistons and connecting rods: 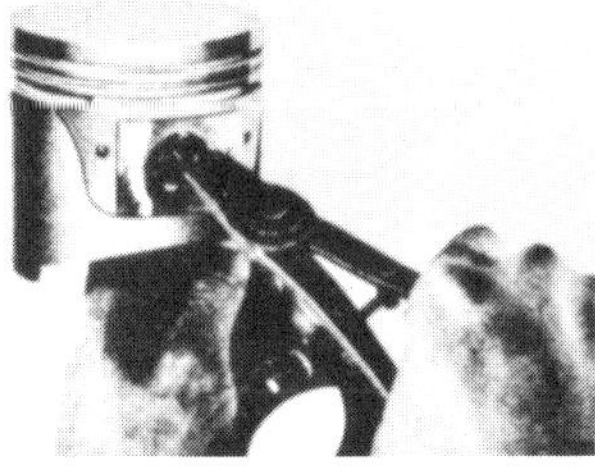 Installing piston pin lock rings (© Nissan Motor Co., Ltd.)	Inspect piston pin, connecting rod small end bushing, and piston bore for galling, scoring, or excessive wear. If evident, replace defective part(s). Measure the I.D. of the piston boss and connecting rod small end, and the O.D. of the piston pin. If within specifications, assemble piston pin and rod. CAUTION: *If piston pin must be pressed in, determine the proper method and use the proper tools; otherwise the piston will distort.* Install the lock rings; ensure that they seat properly. If the parts are not within specifications, determine the service method for the type of engine. In some cases, piston and pin are serviced as an assembly when either is defective. Others specify reaming the piston and connecting rods for an oversize pin. If the connecting rod bushing is worn, it may in many cases be replaced. Reaming the piston and replacing the rod bushing are machine shop operations.

Procedure	*Method*
Clean and inspect the camshaft:	Degrease the camshaft, using solvent, and clean out all oil holes. Visually inspect cam lobes and bearing journals for excessive wear. If a lobe is questionable, check all lobes as indicated below. If a journal or lobe is worn, the camshaft must be reground or replaced. NOTE: *If a journal is worn, there is a good chance that the bushings are worn.* If lobes and journals appear intact, place the front and rear journals in V-blocks, and rest a dial indicator on the center journal. Rotate the camshaft to check straightness. If deviation exceeds .001″, replace the camshaft.

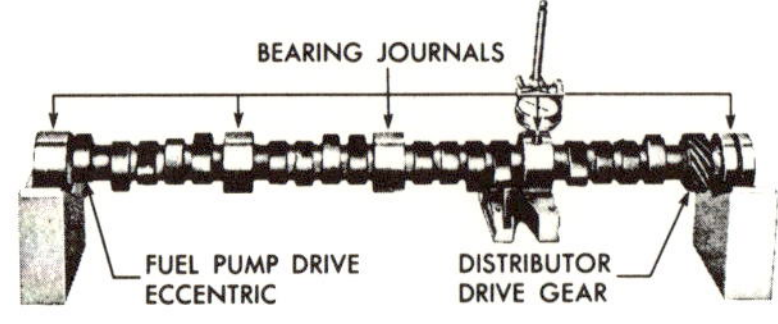

Checking the camshaft for straightness
(© Chevrolet Motor Div. G.M. Corp.)

* Check the camshaft lobes with a micrometer, by measuring the lobes from the nose to base and again at 90° (see illustration). The lift is determined by subtracting the second measurement from the first. If all exhaust lobes and all intake lobes are not identical, the camshaft must be reground or replaced.

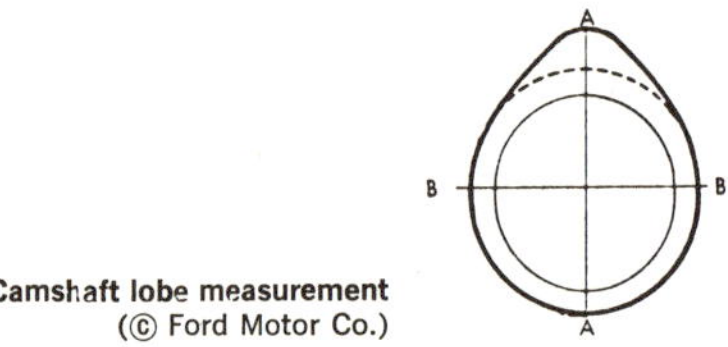

Camshaft lobe measurement
(© Ford Motor Co.)

Procedure	*Method*
Replace the camshaft bearings:	If excessive wear is indicated, or if the engine is being completely rebuilt, camshaft bearings should be replaced as follows: Drive the camshaft rear plug from the block. Assemble the removal puller with its shoulder on the bearing to be removed. Gradually tighten the puller nut until bearing is removed. Remove remaining bearings, leaving the front and rear for last. To remove front and rear bearings, reverse position of the tool, so as to pull the bearings in toward the center of the block. Leave the tool in this position, pilot the new front and rear bearings on the installer, and pull them into position. Return the tool to its original position and pull remaining bearings into position. NOTE: *Ensure that oil holes align when installing bearings.* Replace camshaft rear plug, and stake it into position to aid retention.

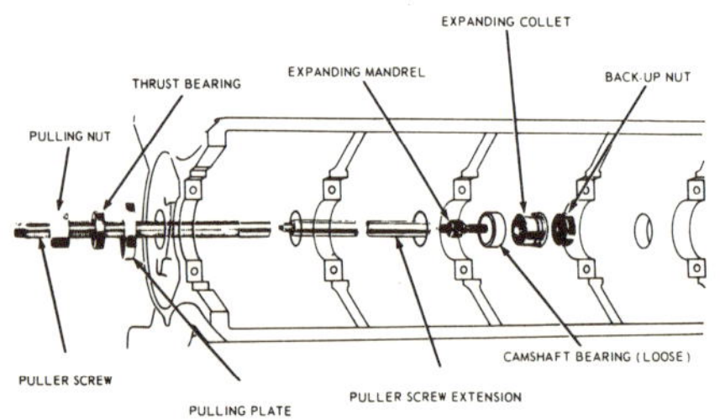

Camshaft removal and installation tool (typical)
(© Ford Motor Co.)

Procedure	*Method*
Finish hone the cylinders:	Chuck a flexible drive hone into a power drill, and insert it into the cylinder. Start the hone, and move it up and down in the cylinder at a rate which will produce approximately a 60° cross-hatch pattern (see illustration). NOTE: *Do not extend the hone below the cylinder bore.* After developing the pattern, remove the hone and recheck piston fit. Wash the cylinders with a detergent and water solution to remove abrasive dust, dry, and wipe several times with a rag soaked in engine oil.

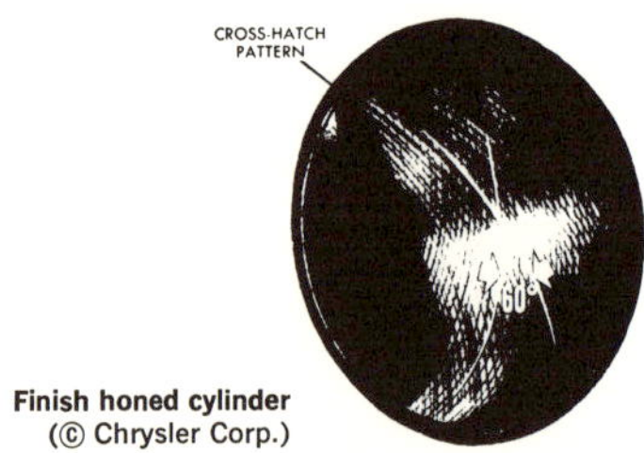

Finish honed cylinder
(© Chrysler Corp.)

Procedure	*Method*
Check piston ring end-gap: 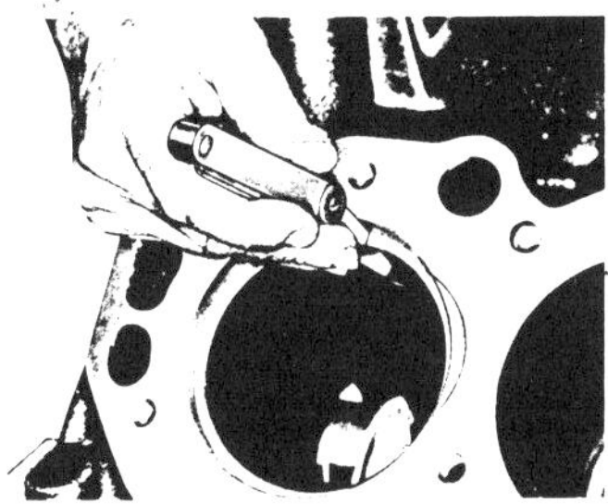 Checking ring end-gap (© Chevrolet Motor Div. G.M. Corp.)	Compress the piston rings to be used in a cylinder, one at a time, into that cylinder, and press them approximately 1″ below the deck with an inverted piston. Using feeler gauges, measure the ring end-gap, and compare to specifications. Pull the ring out of the cylinder and file the ends with a fine file to obtain proper clearance. CAUTION: *If inadequate ring end-gap is utilized, ring breakage will result.*
Install the piston rings: 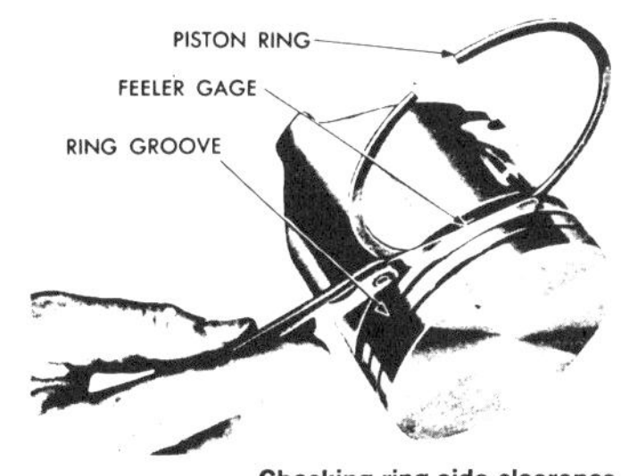 Checking ring side clearance (© Chrysler Corp.) 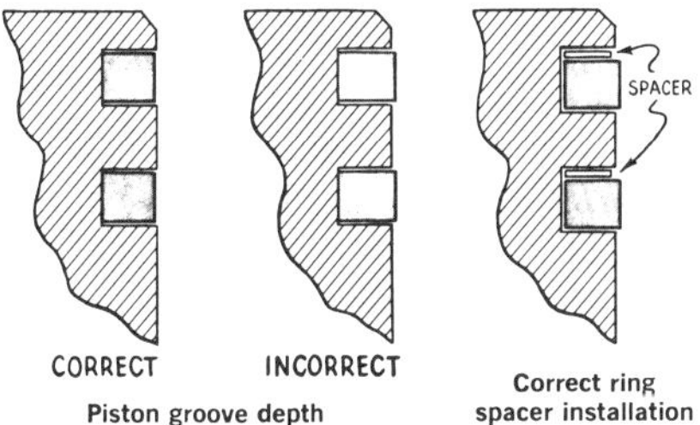 Piston groove depth; Correct ring spacer installation	Inspect the ring grooves in the piston for excessive wear or taper. If necessary, recut the groove(s) for use with an overwidth ring or a standard ring and spacer. If the groove is worn uniformly, overwidth rings, or standard rings and spacers may be installed without recutting. Roll the outside of the ring around the groove to check for burrs or deposits. If any are found, remove with a fine file. Hold the ring in the groove, and measure side clearance. If necessary, correct as indicated above. NOTE: *Always install any additional spacers above the piston ring.* The ring groove must be deep enough to allow the ring to seat below the lands (see illustration). In many cases, a "go-no-go" depth gauge will be provided with the piston rings. Shallow grooves may be corrected by recutting, while deep grooves require some type of filler or expander behind the piston. Consult the piston ring supplier concerning the suggested method. Install the rings on the piston, lowest ring first, using a ring expander. NOTE: *Position the ring markings as specified by the manufacturer (see car section).*
Install the camshaft:	Liberally lubricate the camshaft lobes and journals, and slide the camshaft into the block. CAUTION: *Exercise extreme care to avoid damaging the bearings when inserting the camshaft.* Install and tighten the camshaft thrust plate retaining bolts.
Check camshaft end-play: 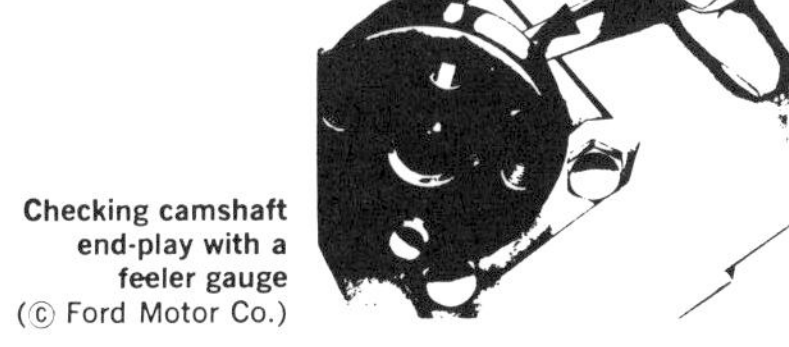 Checking camshaft end-play with a feeler gauge (© Ford Motor Co.)	Using feeler gauges, determine whether the clearance between the camshaft boss (or gear) and backing plate is within specifications. Install shims behind the thrust plate, or reposition the camshaft gear and retest end-play.

Procedure	*Method*
 Checking camshaft end-play with a dial indicator	* Mount a dial indicator stand so that the stem of the dial indicator rests on the nose of the camshaft, parallel to the camshaft axis. Push the camshaft as far in as possible and zero the gauge. Move the camshaft outward to determine the amount of camshaft end-play. If the end-play is not within tolerance, install shims behind the thrust plate, or reposition the camshaft gear and retest.
Install the rear main seal (where applicable): 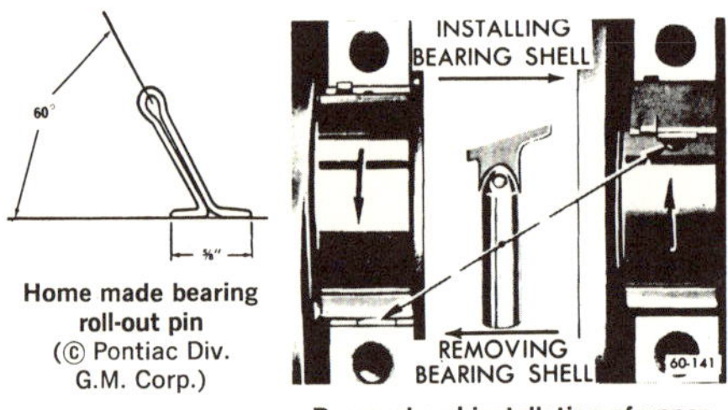 Seating the rear main seal (© Buick Div. G.M. Corp.)	Position the block with the bearing saddles facing upward. Lay the rear main seal in its groove and press it lightly into its seat. Place a piece of pipe the same diameter as the crankshaft journal into the saddle, and firmly seat the seal. Hold the pipe in position, and trim the ends of the seal flush if required.
Install the crankshaft: Home made bearing roll-out pin (© Pontiac Div. G.M. Corp.) Removal and installation of upper bearing insert using a roll-out pin (© Buick Div. G.M. Corp.)	Thoroughly clean the main bearing saddles and caps. Place the upper halves of the bearing inserts on the saddles and press into position. NOTE: *Ensure that the oil holes align.* Press the corresponding bearing inserts into the main bearing caps. Lubricate the upper main bearings, and lay the crankshaft in position. Place a strip of Plastigage on each of the crankshaft journals, install the main caps, and torque to specifications. Remove the main caps, and compare the Plastigage to the scale on the Plastigage envelope. If clearances are within tolerances, remove the Plastigage, turn the crankshaft 90°, wipe off all oil and retest. If all clearances are correct, remove all Plastigage, thoroughly

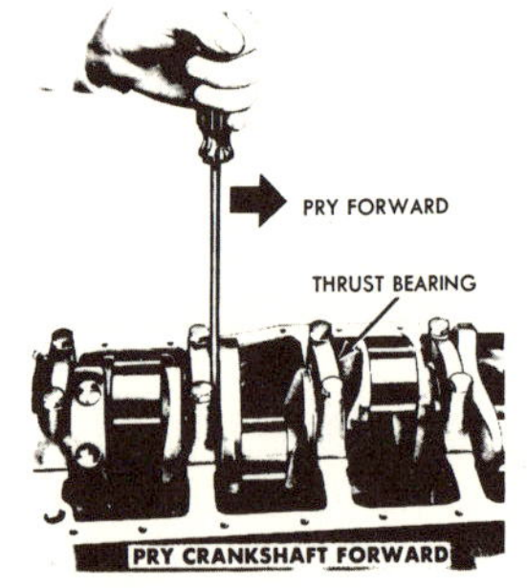

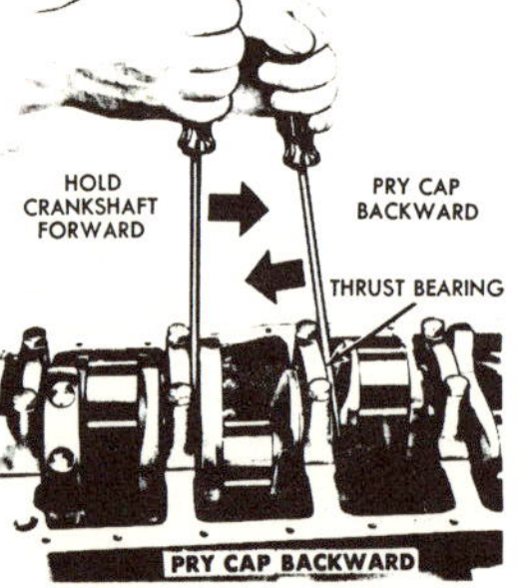

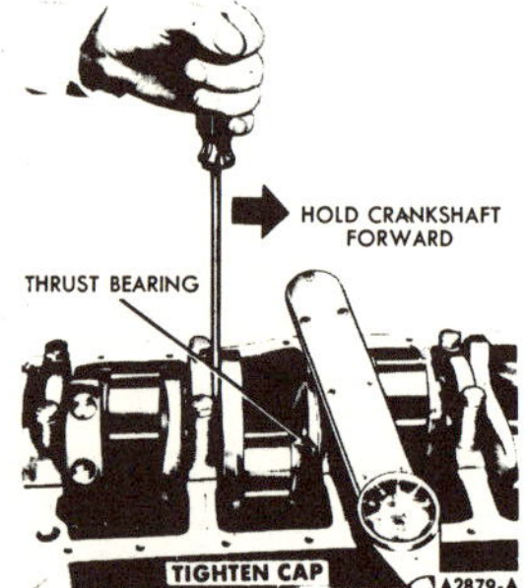

Aligning the thrust bearing
(© Ford Motor Co.)

<table>
<tr><th>Procedure</th><th>Method</th></tr>
<tr><td></td><td>lubricate the main caps and bearing journals, and install the main caps. If clearances are not within tolerance, the upper bearing inserts may be removed, without removing the crankshaft, using a bearing roll out pin (see illustration). Roll in a bearing that will provide proper clearance, and retest. Torque all main caps, excluding the thrust bearing cap, to specifications. Tighten the thrust bearing cap finger tight. To properly align the thrust bearing, pry the crankshaft the extent of its axial travel several times, the last movement held toward the front of the engine, and torque the thrust bearing cap to specifications. Determine the crankshaft end-play (see below), and bring within tolerance with thrust washers.</td></tr>
<tr><td>Measure crankshaft end-play:

Checking crankshaft end-play with a dial indicator (© Ford Motor Co.)

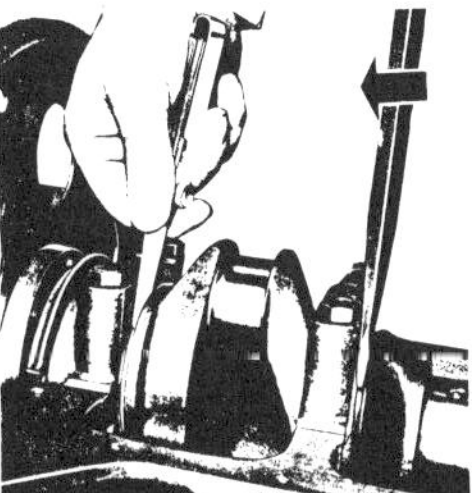
Checking crankshaft end-play with a feeler gauge (© Chevrolet Div. (G.M. Corp.)</td><td>Mount a dial indicator stand on the front of the block, with the dial indicator stem resting on the nose of the crankshaft, parallel to the crankshaft axis. Pry the crankshaft the extent of its travel rearward, and zero the indicator. Pry the crankshaft forward and record crankshaft end-play. NOTE: Crankshaft end-play also may be measured at the thrust bearing, using feeler gauges (see illustration).</td></tr>
<tr><td>Install the pistons:</td><td>Press the upper connecting rod bearing halves into the connecting rods, and the lower halves into the connecting rod caps. Position the piston ring gaps according to specifications (see car section), and lubricate the pistons. Install a ring compresser on a piston, and press two long (8") pieces of plastic tubing over the rod bolts. Using the plastic tubes as a guide, press the pistons into the bores and onto the crankshaft with a wooden hammer handle. After seating the rod on the crankshaft journal, remove the tubes and install the cap finger tight. Install the remaining pistons in the same man-</td></tr>
</table>

Procedure	Method
 **Tubing used as guide when installing a piston** (© Oldsmobile Div. G.M. Corp.) 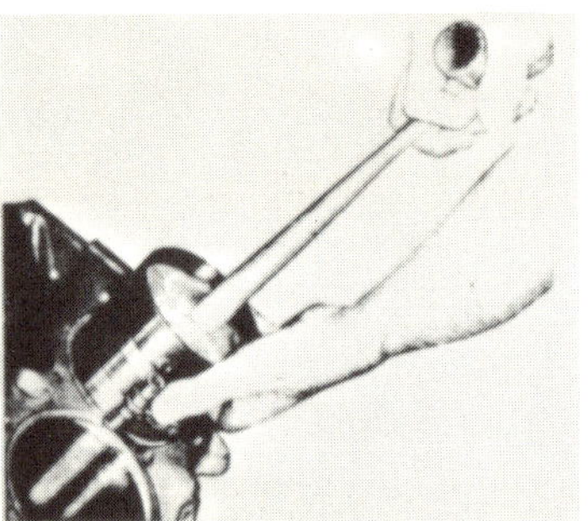 **Installing a piston** (© Chevrolet Div. G.M. Corp.)	ner. Invert the engine and check the bearing clearance at two points (90° apart) on each journal with Plastigage. NOTE: *Do not turn the crankshaft with Plastigage installed.* If clearance is within tolerances, remove *all* Plastigage, thoroughly lubricate the journals, and torque the rod caps to specifications. If clearance is not within specifications, install different thickness bearing inserts and recheck. CAUTION: *Never shim or file the connecting rods or caps.* Always install plastic tube sleeves over the rod bolts when the caps are not installed, to protect the crankshaft journals.
Check connecting rod side clearance:  **Checking connecting rod side clearance** (© Chevrolet Div. G.M. Corp.)	Determine the clearance between the sides of the connecting rods and the crankshaft, using feeler gauges. If clearance is below the minimum tolerance, the rod may be machined to provide adequate clearance. If clearance is excessive, substitute an unworn rod, and recheck. If clearance is still outside specifications, the crankshaft must be welded and reground, or replaced.
Inspect the timing chain:	Visually inspect the timing chain for broken or loose links, and replace the chain if any are found. If the chain will flex sideways, it must be replaced. Install the timing chain as specified. NOTE: *If the original timing chain is to be reused, install it in its original position.*

Procedure	*Method*
Check timing gear backlash and runout:  Checking camshaft gear backlash (© Chevrolet Div. G.M. Corp.)  Checking camshaft gear runout (© Chevrolet Div. G.M. Corp.)	Mount a dial indicator with its stem resting on a tooth of the camshaft gear (as illustrated). Rotate the gear until all slack is removed, and zero the indicator. Rotate the gear in the opposite direction until slack is removed, and record gear backlash. Mount the indicator with its stem resting on the edge of the camshaft gear, parallel to the axis of the camshaft. Zero the indicator, and turn the camshaft gear one full turn, recording the runout. If either backlash or runout exceed specifications, replace the worn gear(s).

Completing the Rebuilding Process

Following the above procedures, complete the rebuilding process as follows:

Fill the oil pump with oil, to prevent cavitating (sucking air) on initial engine start up. Install the oil pump and the pickup tube on the engine. Coat the oil pan gasket as necessary, and install the gasket and the oil pan. Mount the flywheel and the crankshaft vibrational damper or pulley on the crankshaft. NOTE: *Always use new bolts when installing the flywheel.* Inspect the clutch shaft pilot bushing in the crankshaft. If the bushing is excessively worn, remove it with an expanding puller and a slide hammer, and tap a new bushing into place.

Position the engine, cylinder head side up. Lubricate the lifters, and install them into their bores. Install the cylinder head, and torque it as specified in the car section. Insert the pushrods (where applicable), and install the rocker shaft(s) (if so equipped) or position the rocker arms on the pushrods. If solid lifters are utilized, adjust the valves to the "cold" specifications.

Mount the intake and exhaust manifolds, the carburetor(s), the distributor and spark plugs. Adjust the point gap and the static ignition timing. Mount all accessories and install the engine in the car. Fill the radiator with coolant, and the crankcase with high quality engine oil.

Break-in Procedure

Start the engine, and allow it to run at low speed for a few minutes, while checking for leaks. Stop the engine, check the oil level, and fill as necessary. Restart the engine, and fill the cooling system to capacity. Check the point dwell angle and adjust the ignition timing and the valves. Run the engine at low to medium speed (800-2500 rpm) for approximately ½ hour, and retorque the cylinder head bolts. Road test the car, and check again for leaks.

Follow the manufacturer's recommended engine break-in procedure and maintenance schedule for new engines.

Chapter Four
Emission Controls and Fuel System

Emission Controls

Several emission control devices are used to control different sources of emissions. Engine crankcase emissions are controlled by routing them directly into the carburetor air cleaner or into the fuel vapor control system, which is connected to the air cleaner.

Fuel vapor emissions from the carburetor float bowl and the fuel tank are handled by the fuel vapor control system. This system has an activated carbon container in the engine compartment to store vapors until they can be drawn in through the air cleaner and burned.

The 100, 100 LS, and 100 GL use certain basic equipment to control exhaust emissions. The Super 90 uses some of this equipment. The common parts of the system are: a triple port intake manifold and an air cleaner with a temperature controlled inlet beginning in 1972; a double vacuum unit distributor on 1970–1971 models and a heating circuit to preheat the intake manifold. A single vacuum unit distributor was introduced in 1972.

The triple port intake manifold has a separate intake for water, used to preheat the manifold. The preheating and the separate conduction of the fuel-air mixture from each carburetor stage leads to more complete combustion and a lower level of exhaust emissions.

The distributor uses both centrifugal and vacuum advance mechanisms. When

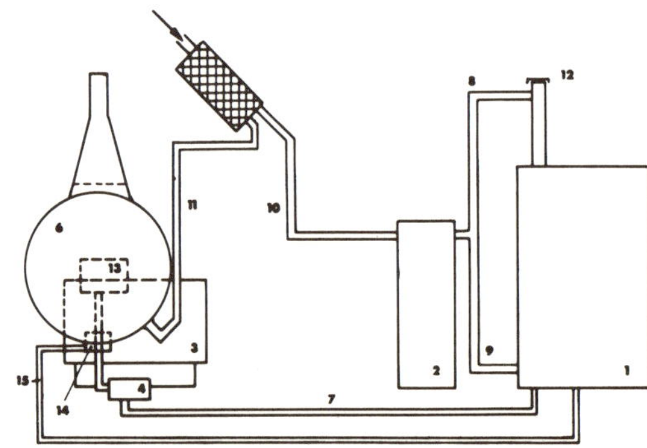

Fuel vapor emission control system, 1972–1973. Earlier versions do not have items 14 and 15

1. Fuel tank
2. Vapor expansion container
3. Engine
4. Fuel pump
5. Activated carbon container
6. Air cleaner
7. Fuel line from tank to pump
8. Breather line from filler neck to expansion container
9. Breather line from tank to expansion container
10. Breather line to carbon container
11. Line from carbon container to air cleaner
12. Non-vented tank filler cap
13. Carburetor
14. Fuel return valve
15. Line from return valve to tank

adjusting the ignition timing at idle speed on 1970–1971 models, both vacuum hoses must be disconnected. When reconnecting them, make sure that the hose from the carburetor connects to the plastic tube and the hose from the intake manifold connects to the metal tube.

1970–1971 distributor vacuum hoses. (a) is the vacuum unit (EC) is the hose to the carburetor, and (RI) is the hose to the intake manifold

All 1973 models are equipped with a capacitive discharge ignition system. This system eliminates the normal decline in ignition system performance between tune-ups, keeping exhaust emissions at a minimum.

NOTE: *Some tachometers, dwell-meters, and oscilloscopes will not work with this system.*

1973 automatic transmission models have an exhaust gas recirculation system, while manual transmission models have a system which permits full distributor vacuum advance only in Fourth gear. The exhaust gas recirculation system is controlled by carburetor vacuum. When the throttle opens a specified amount (18°), carburetor vacuum causes the recirculation valve to open. This allows the intake manifold to draw in a small amount of exhaust gas from the exhaust system. The system does not function at idle or at full throttle. The filter in the system should be replaced every 20,000 miles or two years. The manual transmission system has a solenoid-actuated vacuum control for the distributor

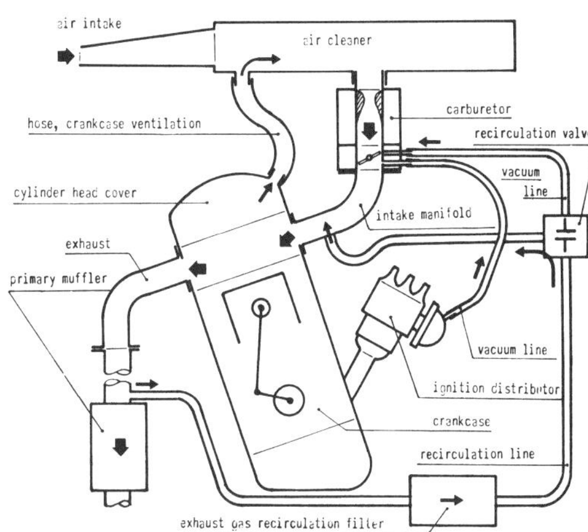

1973 exhaust gas recirculation system used with automatic transmission

vacuum advance system. This vacuum control is actuated by a Fourth gear switch on the transmission. Thus vacuum advance is allowed for better performance in Fourth gear.

For adjustments of emission levels, see "Tune-Up Procedures."

Fuel System

FUEL PUMP

Removal and Installation

SUPER 90

The Super 90 fuel pump is on the side of the block, beneath the intake manifold.

1. Detach the hose at the carburetor, since the other end is hard to reach.
2. Remove and plug the pump intake hose.
3. Remove the mounting bolts.

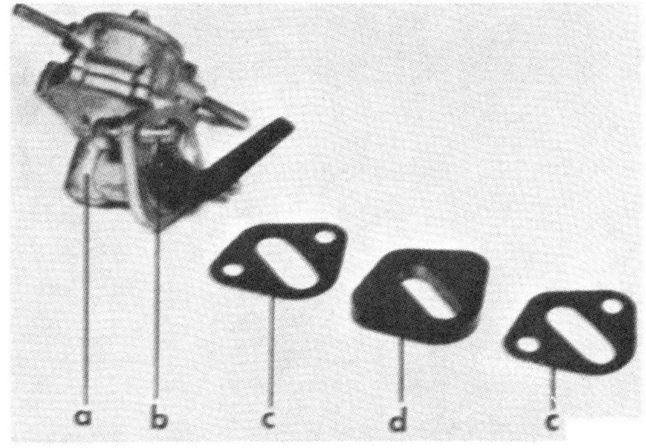

(a) is the Super 90 fuel pump (b) is the mounting bolts (c) is the gaskets, and (d) is the insulator

4. Remove the crankcase dipstick and reach around the radiator to pull the pump out to the rear. Be careful not to spill any fuel into the crankcase.

5. When replacing the pump, use new gaskets and rock the pump back and forth to make sure that the lever rests on the camshaft.

100, 100 LS, 100 GL

The fuel pump is on the left side of the engine block.

1. Disconnect the hoses from the pump. Plug the inlet hose.
2. Remove the mounting bolts and pull out the pump.
3. When replacing the pump, use a new insulator.

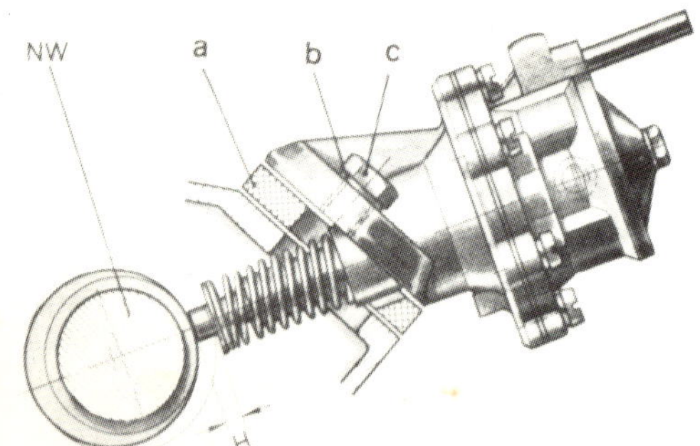

100, 100 LS, 100 GL fuel pump. (NW) is the camshaft (a) is the insulator, (b) is the lockwasher, and (c) is the mounting bolt

Measuring Output Pressure

A fuel pump pressure testing gauge can be connected between the fuel pump and the carburetor. With the engine running at about 2,000 rpm, the pressure should be approximately as specified in the Tune-Up Specifications Chart.

CARBURETORS

The carburetors used are:

Model	*Year*	*Carburetor*
Super 90	1970–1971	Solex 32/32 DIDTA
Super 90	1972	Solex 32/32 TDID
100 LS	1970–1971	Solex 32/32 TDID
100, 100 LS, 100 GL	1972–1973	Solex 32/35 TDID

NOTE: *Solex carburetors are marked with the model number on the float bowl and on the outside of the upper cover.*

These are all progressive two barrel units; that is, the secondary throttle opens only on wide throttle opening. This results in good high rpm performance, as well as smooth and economical low-speed operation. See Chapter One for fuel filter maintenance.

Removal and Installation

1. Remove the air cleaner.
2. Disconnect the fuel hose, being careful not to spill any fuel on hot engine parts.
3. If a choke with coolant connections is used, remove the radiator cap. Disconnect the coolant lines and fasten them up in some way to avoid losing any coolant. Disconnect the lead from the electric choke.
4. Disconnect the vacuum line and the electrical lead to the idle cutoff valve.
5. Remove the clip which secures the throttle linkage, at the carburetor. Detach the linkage, being careful not to lose any plastic washers or bushings.
6. Unbolt the carburetor from the manifold and remove it.
7. When replacing, use a new gasket between the carburetor and manifold. The gasket does not quite match the shape of the manifold port by design; do not cut it to match. Tighten the mounting bolts evenly, to 14 ft lbs.

Overhaul

Whenever dirt or wear causes a carburetor to perform poorly, it should be rebuilt. Carburetor overhaul kits are available for this purpose. They are discussed in more detail later in this section. Some of the better overhaul kits contain complete step by step instructions along with exploded views and gauges. Other kits, probably intended for the professional, have only a few general overhaul hints. The second type can be confusing to the novice, especially since a kit may have extra parts so that one kit can cover several variations of the same basic carburetor. In any event, it is inadvisable to dismantle any carburetor without at least replacing all the gaskets. The carburetor adjustments should all be checked after overhaul.

Efficient carburetion depends greatly on

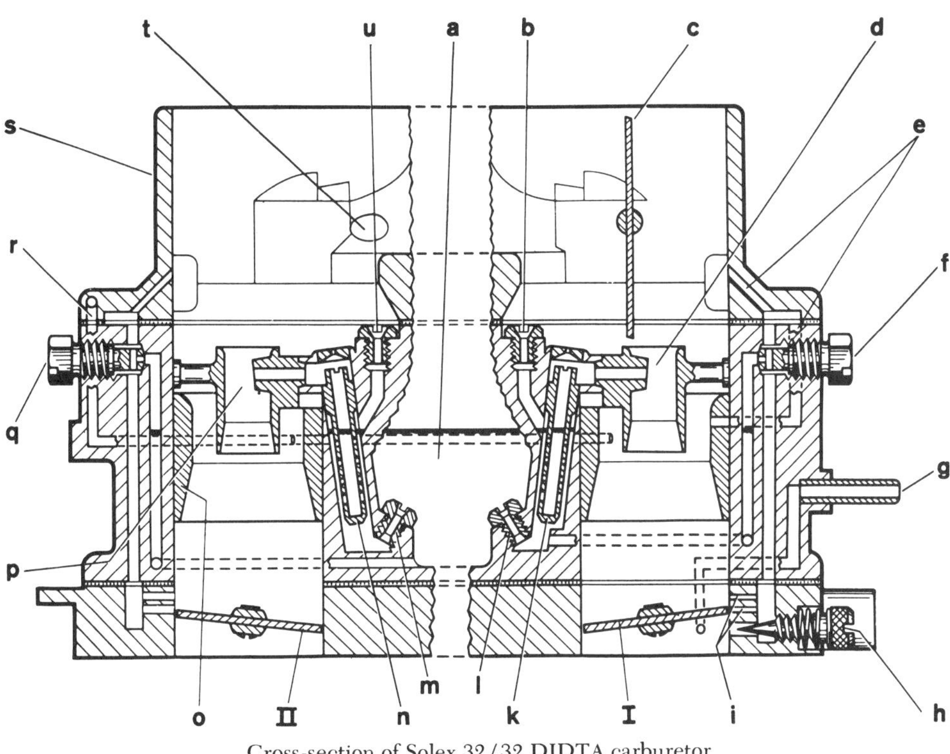

Cross-section of Solex 32/32 DIDTA carburetor

I Primary throttle
II Secondary throttle
a Float chamber
b Air correction jet (primary)
c Choke
d Outlet arm with atomizer
e Idle air bore
f Idle jet (Primary)
g Connection tube, ignition timing
h Idle mixture regulating screw
i Bypass bores
k Mixture tube (primary)
l Main jet (primary)
m Main jet (secondary)
n Mixture tube (secondary)
o Venturi (secondary)
p Outlet arm with atomizer (secondary)
q Idle jet (secondary)
r Bore, vacuum unit
s Carburetor cover
t Breathing bore
u Air correction jet (secondary)

careful cleaning and inspection during overhaul since dirt, gum, water, or varnish in or on the carburetor parts are often responsible for poor performance.

Overhaul your carburetor in a clean, dust-free area. Carefully disassemble the carburetor, referring often to the diagrams. Keep all similar and look-alike parts segregated during disassembly and cleaning to avoid accidental interchange during assembly. Make a note of all jet sizes.

When the carburetor is disassembled, wash all parts (except diaphragms, electric choke units, pump plunger, and any other plastic, leather, fiber, or rubber parts) in clean carburetor solvent. Do not leave parts in the solvent any longer than is necessary to sufficiently loosen the deposits. Excessive cleaning may remove the special finish from the float bowl and choke valve bodies, leaving these parts unfit for service. Rinse all parts in clean solvent and blow them dry with compressed air or allow them to air dry. Wipe clean all cork, plastic, leather, and fiber parts with a clean, lint-free cloth.

Blow out all passages and jets with compressed air and be sure that there are no restrictions or blockages. Never use wire or similar tools to clean jets, fuel passages, or air bleeds. Clean all jets and valves separately to avoid accidental interchange.

Check all parts for wear or damage. If wear or damage is found, replace the defective parts. Especially check the following:

1. Check the float needle and seat for wear. If wear is found, replace the complete assembly.

2. Check the float hinge pin for wear and the float(s) for dents or distortion. Replace the float if fuel has leaked into it.

3. Check the throttle and choke shaft bores for wear or an out-of-round condition. Damage or wear to the throttle arm, shaft, or shaft bore will often require re-

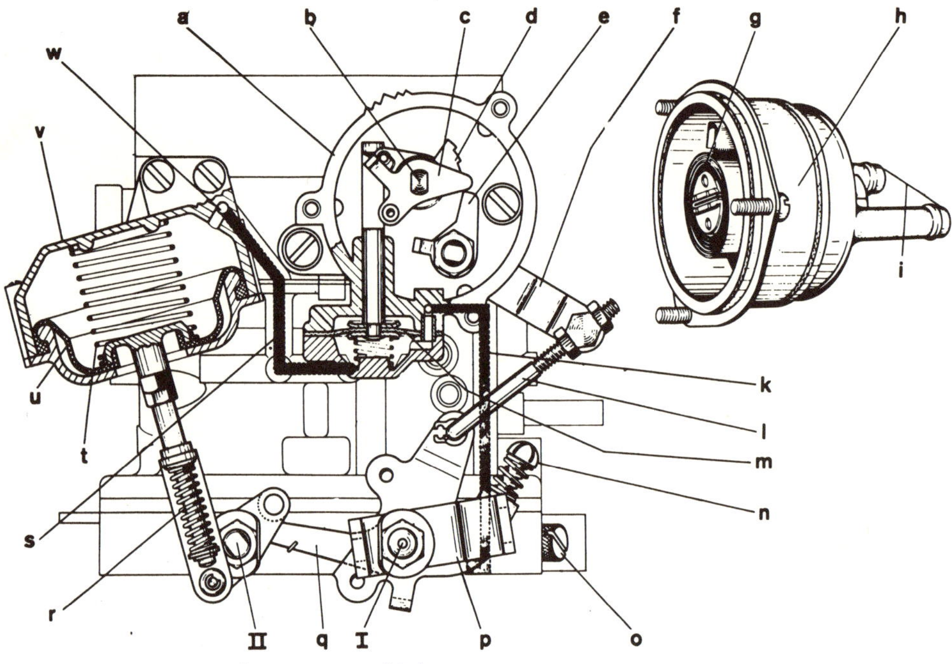

Cross-section of Solex 32/32 DIDTA carburetor

I Throttle shaft (primary)
II Throttle shaft (secondary)
a Automatic choke housing
b Choke shaft
c Catch lever
d Stepped washer
e Stop lever
f Starter lever
g Bimetallic spring
h Bimetallic spring housing
i Warm water connection
k Vacuum channel
l Starter rod
m Reduction diaphragm
n Idle adjustment screw
o Idle mixture regulating screw
p Throttle lever
q Return lever
r Diaphragm rod (secondary)
s Vacuum spring
t Diaphragm spring
u Vacuum diaphragm
v Vacuum unit
w Vacuum bore

placement of the throttle body. These parts require a close tolerance of fit; wear may allow air leakage, which could affect starting and idling.

NOTE: *Throttle shafts and bushings are not included in overhaul kits. They must be purchased separately.*

4. Inspect the idle mixture adjusting needle for burrs or grooves. Any such condition requires replacement of the needle, since you will not be able to obtain a satisfactory idle.

5. Test the accelerator pump check valves. They should pass air one way but not the other. Test for proper seating by blowing and sucking on the valve. Replace the valve if necessary. If the valve is satisfactory, wash the valve again to remove breath moisture.

6. Check the bowl cover for warped surfaces with a straightedge.

7. Closely inspect the valves and seats for wear and damage, replacing as necessary.

8. After the carburetor is assembled, check the choke valve for freedom of operation.

Carburetor overhaul kits are recommended for each overhaul. These kits contain all gaskets and new parts to replace those that deteriorate most rapidly. Failure to replace all parts supplied with the kit (especially gaskets) can result in poor performance later.

Solex supplies overhaul kits of three basic types: minor repair; major repair; and gasket kits. Basically, they contain the following:

Minor Repair Kits:

- All gaskets
- Float needle valve
- Volume control screw
- All diaphragms
- Spring for the pump diaphragm

Major Repair Kits:

- All jets and gaskets
- All diaphragms
- Float needle valve
- Volume control screw
- Pump ball valve

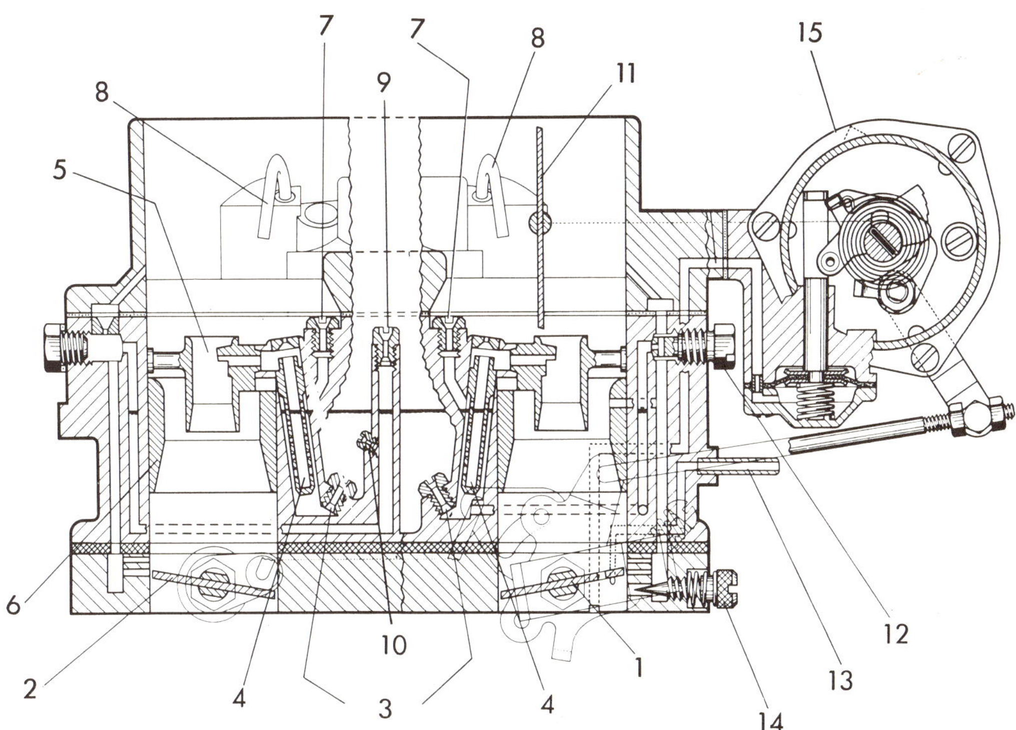

Cross-section of Solex 32/32 TDID carburetor. The 32/35 TDID is very similar but has an electric choke

1. Primary throttle
2. Secondary throttle
3. Main jet
4. Mixture tube
5. Outlet arm with atomizer
6. Venturi
7. Air correction jet
8. Enrichment tube
9. Breather jet
10. Transfer jet
11. Choke
12. Idle jet
13. Connection tube, ignition timing
14. Idle mixture regulating screw
15. Automatic choke

Main jet carrier
Float
Complete intermediate rod
Intermediate pump lever
Complete injector tube
Some cover hold-down screws and washers

Gasket Kits:

All gaskets

After cleaning and checking all components, reassemble the carburetor, using new parts and referring to the diagrams. When reassembling, make sure that all screws and jets are tight in their seats, but do not overtighten. Tighten all screws gradually, in rotation. Do not tighten needle valves into their seats; uneven jetting will result. Always use new gaskets. Be sure to adjust the float level (if applicable) when reassembling.

Throttle Linkage Adjustment

Throttle linkage adjustments are not normally required. However, it is a good idea to make sure that the throttle valve(s)

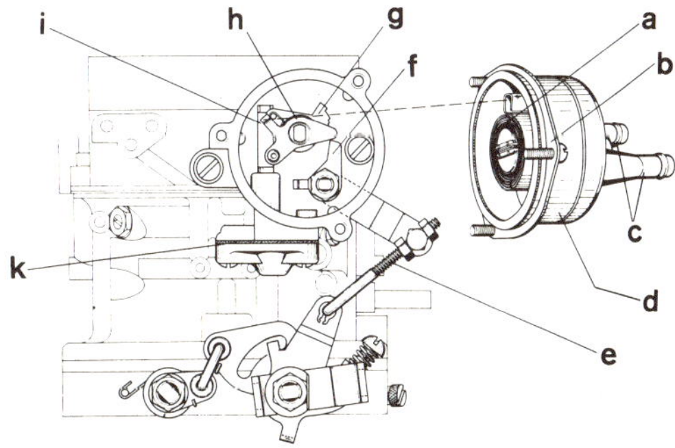

Cross-section of Solex 32/32 TDID carburetor. The 32/35 TDID is very similar but has an electric choke

a Bimetallic spring
b Retaining ring
c Water connection
d Choke cover
e Connecting rod
f Stop lever
g Stepped washer
h Follower
i Diaphragm rod
k Diaphragm

in the carburetor open all the way when the accelerator pedal is held in the wide-open throttle position. Only the primary throttle valve will open on the 32/32 DIDTA carburetor; the secondary throttle is vacuum operated. There is an adjust-

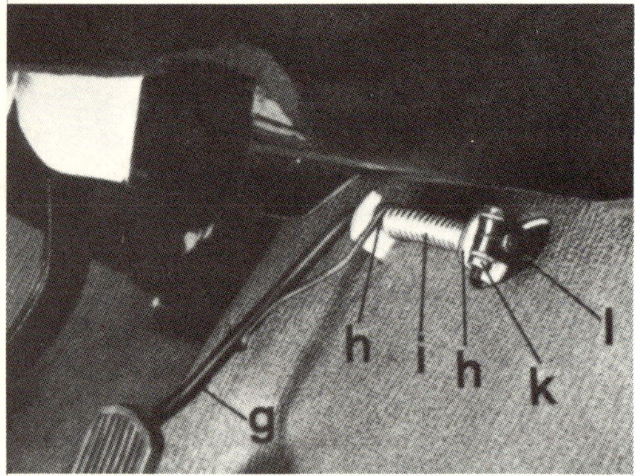

Super 90 throttle linkage—(k) is the clamp bolt

g Lever with slider-behind accelerator pedal
h Bushing
i Spring
h Bushing
l Lever

ment point on the linkage inside the car. To adjust, simply loosen the clamp bolt and vary the position of the two levers. There is also an adjustable accelerator pedal stop on the floor of the Super 90 to prevent overtravel of the linkage.

Fuel Level Adjustment—32/32 DIDTA

This adjustment is made with the carburetor installed on the engine. Incorrect fuel level can cause stalling or a high-speed miss.

1. Idle the engine for one minute.
2. Stop the engine. Remove the air cleaner.
3. Detach the fuel line.
4. Remove the five carburetor cover mounting screws.
5. Plug the fuel inlet with a finger and lift off the carburetor cover and gasket. Set them to the side, leaving the linkages attached.
6. Using a sliding T-scale, measure the distance from the top of the fuel surface to the edge of the housing. It should be 0.67–0.74 in. on carburetors with finned floats (after No. 7279), and 0.63–0.71 in. on earlier models.
7. The measurement may be corrected by varying the thickness of the fiber sealing ring under the float needle valve.

Float Level Adjustment—32/32 and 32/35 TDID

This adjustment can be made with the carburetor either installed or removed. Incorrect float level can cause stalling or a high-speed miss.

1. If the carburetor is on the car, perform Steps 1–5 of "Fuel Level Adjustment — 32/32 DIDTA."
2. Disconnect the linkage between the upper and lower parts of the carburetor.
3. Turn the carburetor cover upside down.
4. Measure the distance between the upper edge of the bead around the float and the carburetor cover flange surface. It should be as follows:

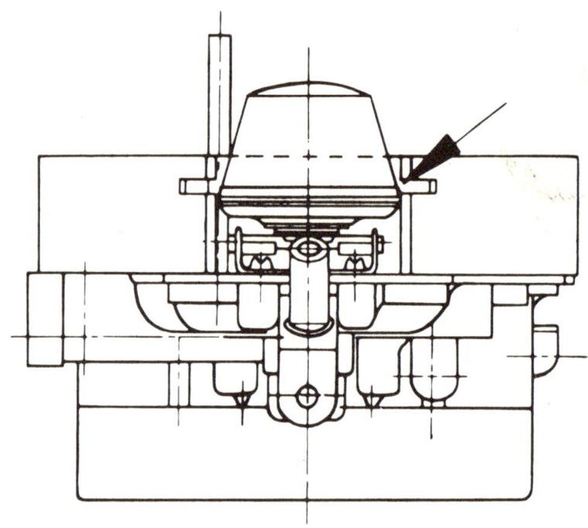

32/32 and 32/35 TDID float level measurement —the arrow points to the upper edge of the float bead

Carburetor	*Float Level (in.)*
32/32 TDID	0.51–0.59
32/35 TDID	0.61–0.69

5. The metal tab of the float lever can be bent to correct the height.
6. If necessary, the fuel level can also be checked as described for the 32/32 DIDTA. It should be 0.53–0.55 in. for both models.

Accelerator Pump Injection Rate Adjustment

This adjustment applies to all carburetors. It must be done with the carburetor removed from the car. Improper adjustment can cause a hesitation when opening the throttle.

1. Place the carburetor over a clean container. Make sure that the float bowl is full.
2. Pump the throttle linkage full stroke

10–20 times. Injection should start as soon as the linkage is moved.

3. Measure the amount of fuel pumped, with a chemist's graduated cylinder. Divide the amount in cc (ml) by the number of strokes to get the average volume per stroke. The figure should be:

Carburetor	*Injection Rate (cc)*
32/32 DIDTA up to No. 7279	1.3
32/32 DIDTA after No. 7279	0.9–1.1
32/32 TDID, 100 LS	1.4–1.5
32/32 TDID, Super 90	1.1–1.4
32/35 TDID	1.4–1.9

4. To increase the injection rate, place more washers between the cotter pin and the pump lever. To decrease the rate, remove washers or move the cotter pin further out.

Accelerator pump output is adjusted with washers between the cotter pin and the pump lever (b)

Accelerator pump diaphragm assembly—(c) is the cover screws (d) is the cover (e) is the diaphragm, and (f) is the spring

5. If the specified rate cannot be obtained, check the diaphragm and the injection tube.

Automatic Choke Adjustment

The standard adjustment on all versions of the automatic choke is with the movable notch aligned with the large central tooth on the housing. To adjust, loosen the three clamping screws and move the outer part of the choke unit.

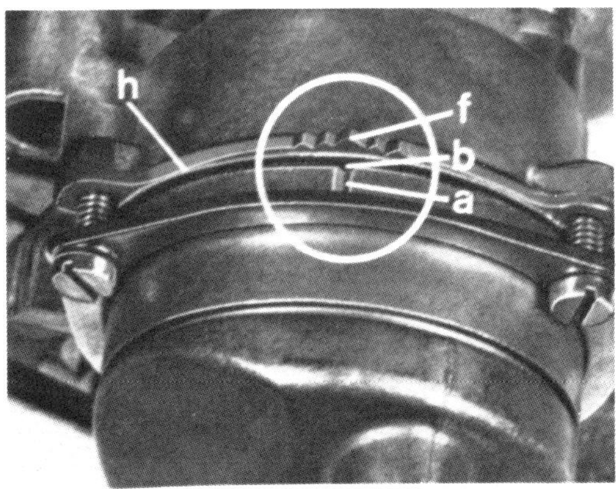

The automatic choke is correctly adjusted when (a), (b), and (f) are aligned (h) is an insulator

Choke Gap Adjustment

This adjustment can be made with the carburetor in place, but it is much easier with it removed. The procedure applies to all carburetors.

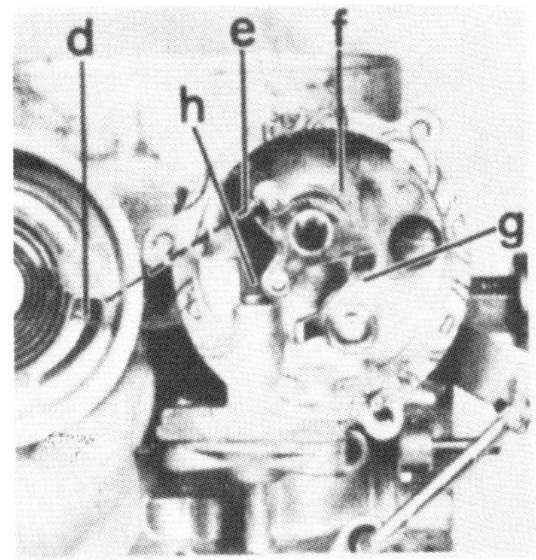

When checking the choke gap, press the diaphragm rod (h) down against the stop and hold the follower (e) against the stop

d Bimetallic spring eyelet
f Stepped washer
g Stop lever

1. Close the choke tightly.
2. Press the diaphragm rod down against the stop.
3. Hold the follower against the stop.
4. Check the gap between the upper edge of the choke valve and the housing wall with a drill. The gap should be:

Carburetor	*Choke Gap (in.)*
32/32 DIDTA	0.087–0.095
32/32 TDID, 100 LS	0.118–0.134
32/32 TDID, Super 90	0.094–0.106
32/35 TDID	0.132–0.144

5. To correct the gap, bend the pin up or down slightly.

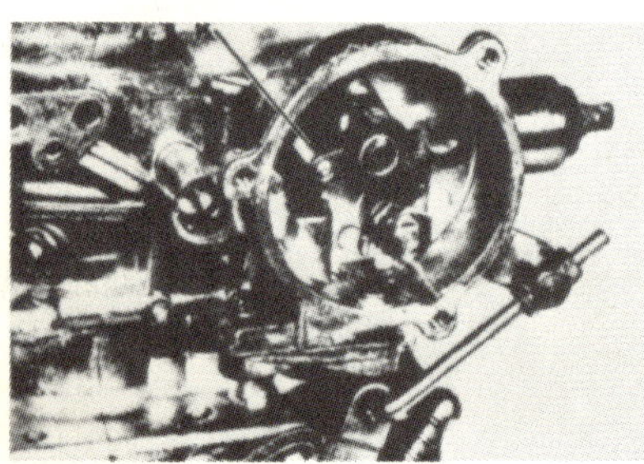

Bend pin (k) to adjust the choke gap

Throttle Gap Adjustment

This adjustment could possibly be made with the carburetor in place, but it is much easier with it removed.

1. Close the choke tightly. The stop lever should rest on the highest step of the stepped washer, holding the throttle open slightly.
2. Check the gap between the lower edge of the throttle valve and the housing wall with a drill. The measurement should be:

Carburetor	*Throttle Gap (in.)*
32/32 DIDTA	0.056–0.064
32/32 TDID	0.051–0.059
32/35 TDID	0.055–0.059

3. Adjust the gap by means of the two nuts on the connecting rod.

When checking the throttle gap, the stop lever (l) should rest on the highest step of the stepped washer (m) and hold the throttle open by means of the connecting rod (n). (p) indicates the adjusting nuts.

Idle Speed and Mixture Adjustments

See "Tune-Up Procedures" for these adjustments. The procedure to be used depends on the type of carburetor. There are two types: standard and idle air bypass. The standard has only one adjusting screw, the idle mixture screw, on the body of the carburetor. These units are found mainly on early and non-US models. The idle air bypass carburetor is the current

Solex carburetor jets and other components, cover removed

1. Idle fuel jet with electric cutoff
2. Diaphragm pump check valve
3. Primary main jet
4. Secondary main jet
5. Secondary idle reserve jet
6. Secondary breathing jet
7. Primary venturi
8. Primary air correction jet
9. Injection tube
10. Primary breathing bore
11. Secondary breathing bore
12. Secondary air correction jet
13. Secondary venturi

emission control type. It can be identified by the two adjusting screws on the body of the carburetor. These are the idle mixture and idle air control screws.

Jet Sizes

Carburetor	Main Jet		Air Correction Jet	
	Primary	*Secondary*	*Primary*	*Secondary*
32/32 DIDTA	120*	140	150	100
32/32 TDID, 100 LS	102.5	140	120	100
32/32 TDID, Super 90	102.5	145	120	100
32/35 TDID	127.5	135	150	100
32/35 TDID, automatic	125	135	150	100

* 115 for economy and city driving

Solex 32/32 TDID carburetor

21. Primary throttle valve shaft
22. Operating lever
23. Secondary connecting rod
24. Secondary throttle valve shaft
25. Thermal starting valve
26. Electric connection for thermal starting valve
27. Secondary atomizer retaining screw
28. Plug
29. Float chamber
30. Choke
31. Primary enrichment tube
32. Secondary enrichment tube
33. Interior breathing bore

Solex 32/32 TDID carburetor

1. Automatic choke water connection
2. Retaining ring
3. Automatic choke
4. Choke lever
5. Choke connecting rod
6. Throttle lever
7. Idle adjusting screw
8. Carburetor cover
9. Carburetor body
10. Throttle valve
11. Primary atomizer retaining screw
12. Idle mixture control screw
13. Vacuum connection
14. Idle air control screw
15. Connecting rod and spring
16. Pump lever
17. Diaphragm pump
18. Idle fuel jet with electric cutoff
19. Cover cap screws
20. Fuel tube

Solex 32/32 TDID carburetor

15. Connecting rod and spring
16. Pump lever
20. Fuel tube
34. Secondary throttle valve stop lever
35. Primary throttle valve shaft pump lever
36. Accelerator pump diaphragm cover

Carburetor Adjustment Specifications

Carburetor	*Fuel Level (in.)*	*Float Level (in.)*	*Accelerator Pump Injection Rate (cc/stroke)*	*Choke Gap (in.)*	*Throttle Gap (in.)*	*Automatic Choke Setting*
32/32 DIDTA up to No. 7279	0.63–0.71	——	1.3	0.087–0.095	0.056–0.064	Index
32/32 DIDTA after No. 7279	0.67–0.74	——	0.9–1.1	0.087–0.095	0.056–0.064	Index
32/32 TDID, Super 90	0.53–0.55	0.51–0.59	1.1–1.4	0.094–0.106	0.051–0.059	Index
32/32 TDID, 100 LS	0.53–0.55	0.51–0.59	1.4–1.5	0.118–0.134	0.051–0.059	Index
32/35 TDID	0.53–0.55	0.61–0.69	1.4–1.9	0.132–0.144	0.055–0.059	Index

Heater

The heater blower may have to be removed in case of excessive motor noise or electrical failure. The heater core may have to be removed for repair in case of clogging or coolant leakage. Core repair service can usually be obtained at radiator repair shops. To remove either the heater blower or the core, it is necessary to remove the heater unit from the car and disassemble it.

Removal and Installation

SUPER 90

1. Drain the radiator coolant, disconnect the battery, and remove the instrument panel lower trim for access.
2. Drain the remaining coolant from the plug in the bottom of the heater.
3. If necessary, unscrew the blower duct at the bottom of the heater and remove it.
4. Unbolt and remove the hood latch cable inside the car.
5. Disconnect the brown and red wires.
6. Detach the defroster hoses and push them toward the engine compartment.
7. Disconnect the heater control cable from the lever to the right of the steering column. Disconnect the cables from the lower and center heater control levers.

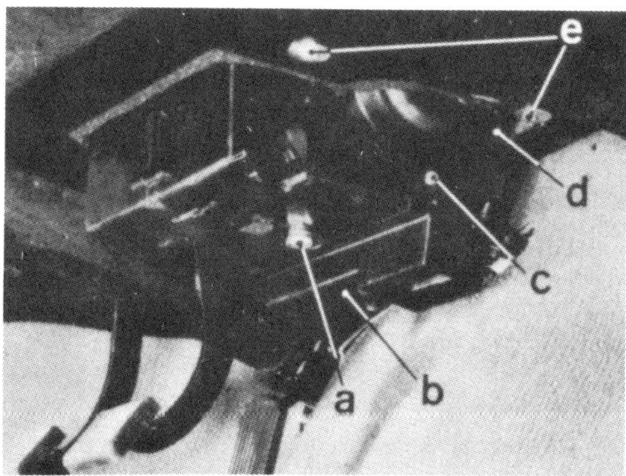

The Super 90 heater has a drain plug (a) at the bottom

a Drain plug
b Blower duct
c Retaining screw for b
d Retaining screw for b
e Self-tapping screw with washer

8. Remove the left and right water drain hoses. Disconnect the heater hoses from under the hood. The hoses will often stick to the heater inlet and outlet tubes. If this is the case, cut the hoses off. Do not twist or pull on the tubes; core damage will result.
9. Unbolt and remove the heater.
10. Installation is the reverse of removal. Adjust the control cables so that they allow the full control lever movement. Refill the cooling system, run the en-

gine with the heater in the hot position for ten minutes, and recheck the coolant level. See "Coolant Draining and Refilling" in Chapter Three.

100, 100 LS, 100 GL

1. Set the heater controls on the hot position. Drain the coolant, disconnect the battery, and remove the lower instrument panel trim and center shelf.
2. Remove the breather screw from the hose inside the engine compartment, being careful not to damage the firewall seal.
3. Detach both heater hoses. The hoses will often stick to the heater inlet and outlet tubes. If this is the case, cut the hoses off. Do not twist or pull on the tubes; core damage will result.
4. Disconnect the cables that control the foot area flaps, the windshield flap, and the heater valve.
5. Remove the plug connector from the controls and the lead from terminal 15 of the emergency warning light switch.
6. From the passenger compartment, unbolt the heater and pull it down.
7. Installation is the reverse of removal. When installing the cables, place the heater levers in the off position. Place the leg of the spring clip in the mount and install the spring clip. The cable sleeve must protrude at least 0.2 in. beyond the spring clip. Refill the cooling system, run the engine with the heater in the hot position for ten minutes, and recheck the coolant level. See "Coolant Draining and Refilling" in Chapter Three.

Radio

The radio is usually a dealer installed or aftermarket unit. Thus no specific removal and installation procedures can be given. The following information applies generally to all car radios.

Care should be taken during installation to avoid reversing the ground and power leads. Reversal of these leads will cause serious damage to the radio. The power lead usually has an in-line fuse.

If the speaker needs replacement, it should be replaced with one of the same impedance, measured in ohms. Mismatched impedance can cause rapid transistor failure as well as poor radio performance. This should also be taken into consideration when adding a second speaker.

The radio should never be operated without a speaker connected or with the speaker leads shorted. This will result in transistor failure.

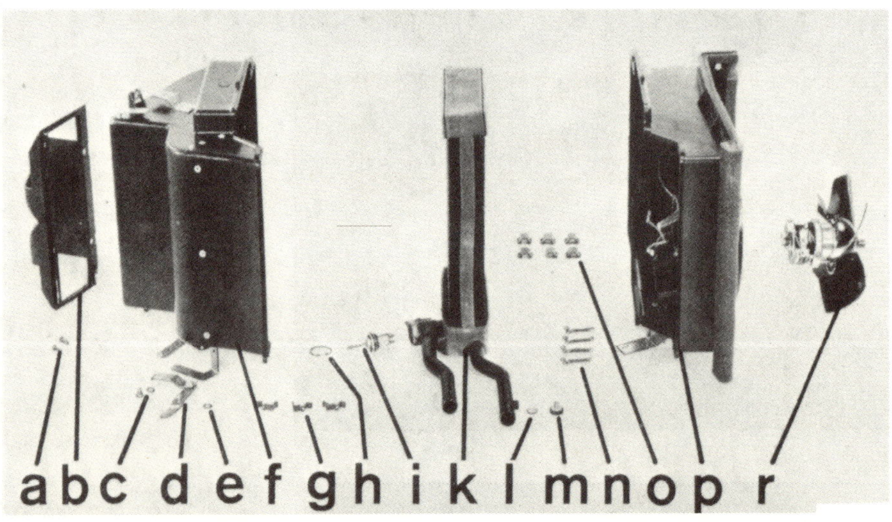

Exploded view of 100, 100 LS, and 100 GL heater

a Self-tapping screw
b Foot area nozzle
c Hex head screw
d Adjusting lever
e Nut
f Housing lower section
g Spring clip, cable
h Snap-ring
i Plunger
k Heater core
l Seal
m Breather screw
n Spring, blower motor
o Clip, housing halves
p Housing upper section
r Motor and fan

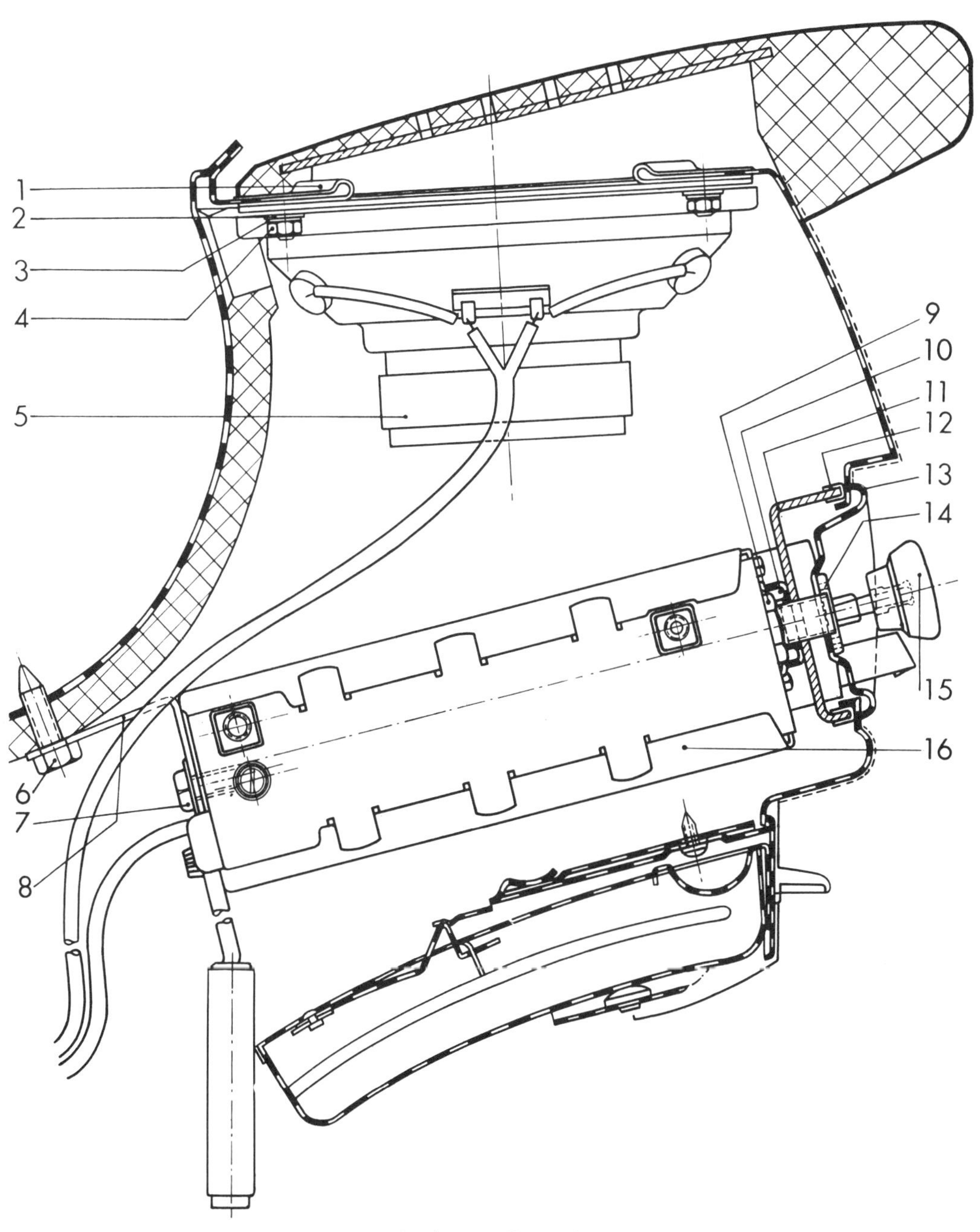

Typical radio installation details

1. Clip
2. Washer
3. Lockwasher
4. Nut
5. Speaker
6. Screw
7. Screw
8. Mounting bracket
9. Nut
10. Spacer
11. Bracket
12. Rubber insulator
13. Face plate
14. Nut
15. Knob
16. Receiver

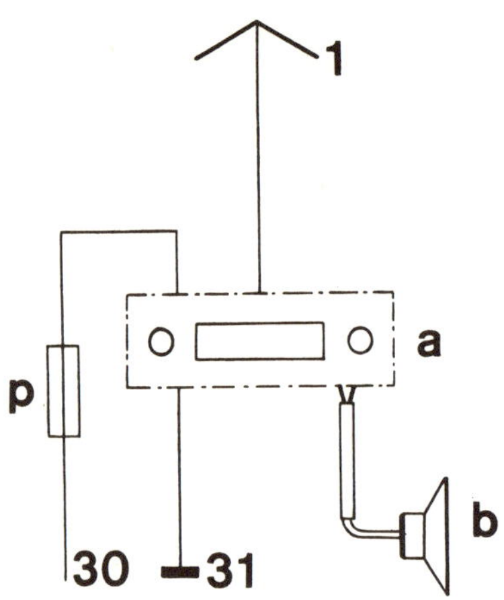

Radio wiring diagram

1. Antenna
30. Terminal 30 of the light switch
31. Ground connection

a Receiver
b Speaker
p In-line fuse

Antenna Trimmer Adjustment

The antenna trimmer should be adjusted whenever the radio, antenna cable, or antenna is replaced, or when reception is poor.

1. Tune the radio to a weak station at about 14 on the AM band.
2. Adjust the antenna to the normal height, or to 31 in. for FM receivers.
3. Turn the trimmer screw to get the maximum volume. The screw is usually on the back or side of the radio case, in the dial, or sometimes hidden behind one of the dial knobs.

Windshield Wiper System

Wiper Motor and Linkage Removal and Installation—Super 90

The wiper motor and the linkage can be removed from inside the engine compartment after removing the heater.

1. Disconnect the battery ground cable. Remove the wiper arms. They are mounted either with a cap nut and domed washer, or by a spring which engages a groove.
2. Pull the windshield washer pump from the instrument panel and disconnect the hoses.
3. Remove the ring nut from the instrument panel, remove the switch, and disconnect the wires.
4. Remove the brown wire from the instruments.
5. Drain the coolant and remove the heater.
6. Remove the nuts from the wiper arm mounts.
7. Disconnect the hoses from the washer jets.
8. Tilt the wiper motor and linkage assembly to remove it.
9. Installation is the reverse of removal. Seal the cable hole in the firewall to prevent leaks. Operate the wiper motor to be sure that the wipers park properly. Remove the motor crank arm and remount it if the wipers don't park correctly.

Wiper Motor Removal and Installation—100, 100 LS, 100 GL

The motor can be removed from inside the engine compartment.

1. Disconnect the battery ground cable.
2. Remove the right and left knee padding.
3. Working in the engine compartment, pull out the rubber grommet to give the wiring harness more play. Pull out the wiper switch and remove the leads.
4. Bend open the metal tabs which hold the wiring harness and remove the harness which runs below the spray jets together with the spray jet line.
5. Loosen the nut and pry off the lever for the linkage.
6. Remove the motor and harness.
7. Reverse the procedure for installation.

Wiper Linkage Removal and Installation—100, 100 LS, 100 GL

The linkage can be removed from inside the engine compartment.

1. Remove the wiper arms from the studs by prying off the cap and removing the retaining nut.
2. Remove the lower nut, washer, and seal from the recess in the body.
3. Remove the mounting bolts in the engine compartment and tilt the linkage to remove.
4. Installation of the wiper linkage and the motor is done by reversing the removal procedure. The lever connected to the

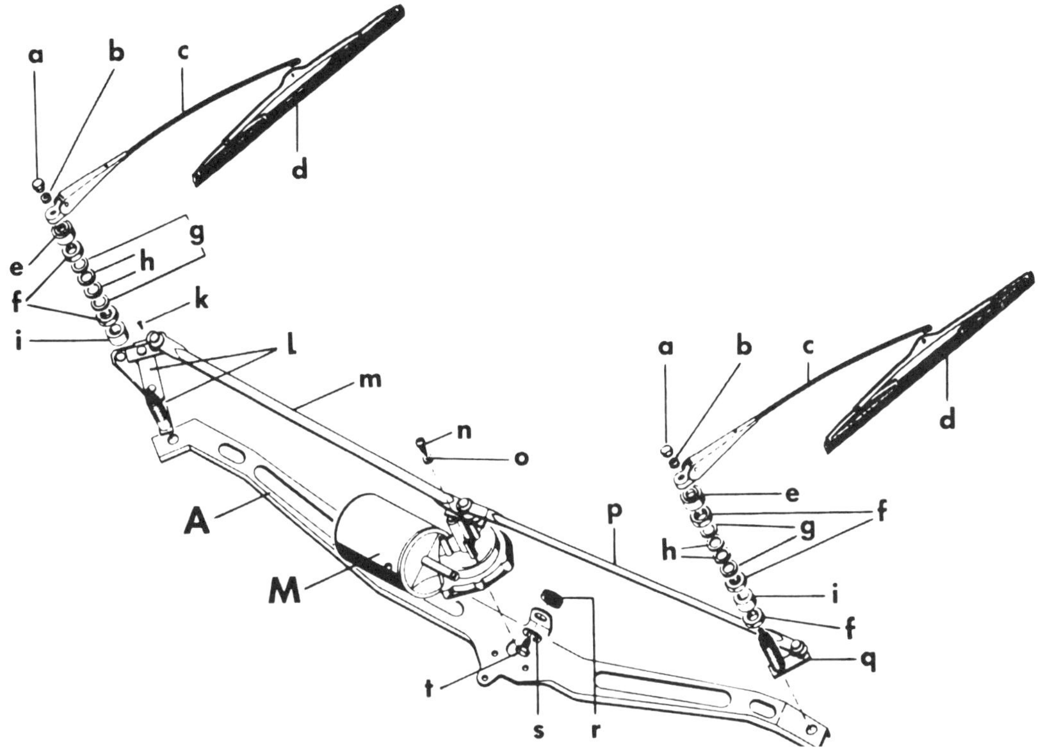

Exploded view of Super 90 wiper linkage and motor

A Windshield wiper base
M Wiper motor
a Cap nut
b Washer
c Wiper arm
d Wiper blade
e Seal cap
f Hex nut
g Washer
h Leather washer
i Spacer
k Round head rivet
l Square joint
m Rod (thick)
n Self-tapping screw
o Lockwasher
p Rod (thin)
q Wiper bearing
r Rubber grommet
s Washer
t Hex head self-tapping screw

wiper motor should be installed at approximately 90° to the front-to-rear centerline of the vehicle. The wiper arm blades have different angles. The arm with the blade at the greater angle is installed on the driver's side.

On the 100, 100 LS, and 100 GL, the wiper motor lever (m) should be at an angle of 90° to the front-to-rear centerline

m Lever o Connecting rod

BLADES

Whenever wiper smearing becomes evident, the condition of the rubber blades should be checked. Smearing is often caused by a buildup of road dirt on the blades. This can be prevented by cleaning the blade rubbing surfaces carefully each time the car is washed.

Removal and Installation

1. Pull the wiper arms away from the windshield.
2. Turn the blade at right angles to the arm.
3. Press in on the flat spring. This releases the blade.

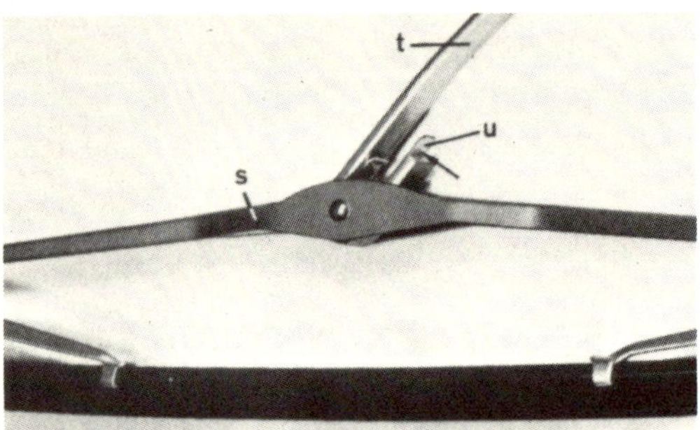

Wiper blade installation details
s Wiper blade t Wiper arm u Flat spring

4. On installation, simply put the hook on the wiper arm through the blade and pull back to seat the cross pin under the spring.

Instruments

The instruments can be removed separately in the Super 90, but the entire instrument cluster must be removed in the 100, 100 LS, and 100 GL.

Fuel and Water Temperature Gauge Removal and Installation—Super 90

1. Disconnect the battery ground cable.
2. Unscrew and remove the blower duct from the bottom of the heater.
3. Remove the instrument panel bottom trim. If it is held in place by round plastic clips, use a punch to drive the plastic pins through. The pins will be needed for installation.
4. Pull the three bulbs from the back of the housing.
5. Unscrew the knurled nuts and remove the retaining bracket.

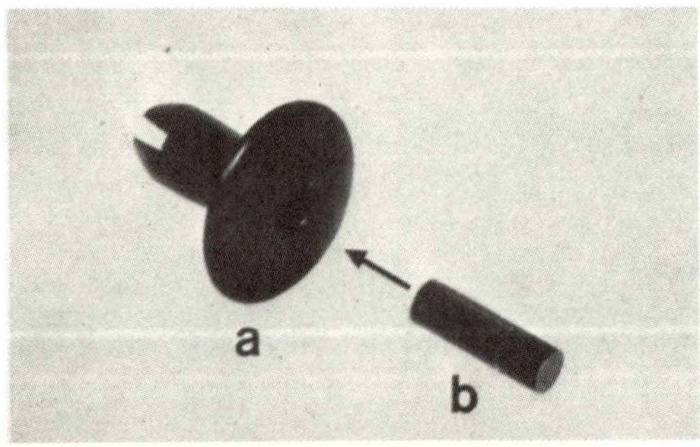

To disengage the plastic clips (a) drive the pins (b) in the direction indicated. The pins should be driven in the same direction on replacement

6. Pull the instrument through the panel and detach all the connections.
7. Reverse the procedure for installation.

Clock Removal and Installation—Super 90

The clock is easier to remove if one of the large instruments is removed first.

1. Follow Steps 1–3 of "Fuel and Water Temperature Gauge Removal and Installation—Super 90."
2. Unscrew the retaining nuts and remove the retaining bracket.
3. Pull the light bulb from the side of the case.
4. Remove the clock. Detach the wire.
5. Reverse the procedure for installation.

Speedometer Removal and Installation—Super 90

1. Follow Steps 1–3 of "Fuel and Water Temperature Gauge Removal and Installation—Super 90."
2. Unscrew the cable from the back of the case.
3. Remove the nut and the retaining bracket.
4. Remove the speedometer and detach the wires.
5. Reverse the procedure for installation.

Instrument Cluster Removal and Installation—100, 100 LS, 100 GL

1. Disconnect the battery ground cable.
2. Remove the screws which hold the padding on top of the instrument panel. Remove the padding.
3. Remove the nuts at the rear of instrument cluster and remove the cover.
4. Pull the cluster out toward the driver's seat.
5. Pull off the electrical connections and unscrew the speedometer cable.
6. Remove the instrument cluster. It may be further disassembled as necessary.

Headlights

Audis imported to the US use standard American replacement sealed beam units, available at auto supply and discount houses. See the Light Bulb Specifications Chart for the unit numbers.

Removal and Installation

1. Remove the radiator grille.
2. On the 100, 100 LS, and 100 GL, pull the three prong connector from the back of the sealed beam unit.
3. The sealed beam units are each held in place by a ring fastened by one screw at the top and two at the bottom. Remove these screws and remove the ring. On the Super 90, be careful not to disturb the headlight adjusting screws. These are positioned at 12 and 3 o'clock on the left headlight and at 12 and 9 o'clock on the right.
4. Remove the sealed beam unit. On the Super 90, detach the three prong connector from the back of the unit now.
5. Reverse the procedure for installation. The headlight units have lugs so that they can be installed only one way. Headlight alignment should be checked if possible.

Light Bulb Specifications

Unit	US Replacement Number Super 90	US Replacement Number 100, 100 LS, 100 GL
Single headlight	6012, 6014	—
Outer headlight	—	4002
Inner headlight	—	4001
Front parking light/ turn signal	1034	1034
Front side marker	57	1816
Rear turn signal	1073	1073
Tail light	67	—
Rear side marker	57	—
Tail/stop light	1034	1034
Backup light	1073	1073
License plate light	57	—
Interior light	—	211

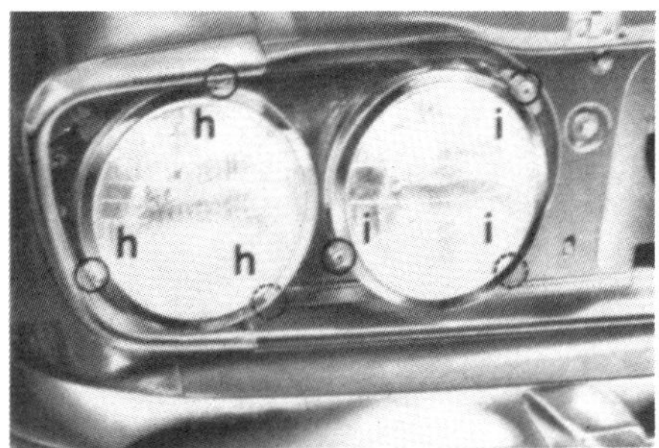

The screws holding the headlight retaining rings are shown by (h) and (i)

Alignment

The grille need not be removed for headlight adjustment. On the Super 90, the adjusting screws are at the front, as described under "Headlight Removal and Installation." On the 100, 100 LS, and 100 GL, two large adjusting knobs are provided inside the engine compartment on the back of the headlight units. The top adjustment regulates beam height, and the one to the side regulates beam horizontal adjustment.

FUSE BOX LOCATION

On the Super 90, the fuse box is on the left, under the hood. It has a transparent cover. The turn signal flasher, emergenc flasher, and the headlight relays are directly behind it.

On the 100, 100 LS, and 100 GL, the fuse box is near the clutch pedal on the left side of the car. The turn signal flasher, windshield washer, and headlight relays are mounted on the fuse box.

The fuse box on the 100, 100 LS, and 100 GL contains nine fuses. There may be additional fuses mounted on the right side of the fuse box. The windshield washer delayed action relay (a) the flasher unit (b) and the headlight relay (c) are mounted on the fuse box

Fuses

Units Protected	Fuse Amperage: Super 90	Fuse Amperage: 100, 100 LS, 100 GL
Turn signals	8	8
Windshield washer, engine fan, horn, temperature gauge, fuel gauge, oil pressure light, backup light	16	16
Wipers, stop light, license plate light, instrument lights, glove compartment light, lighter, clock, interior light	16	16
Right parking and tail light	8	8
Left high beam	16	8
Right high beam, high beam indicator	16	8
Left low beam	8	8
Right low beam	8	8
Left parking and tail light	8	8
Rear window defogger	——	8

Always replace blown (melted) fuses with new ones of the correct amperage. Otherwise, electrical overloads and possible wiring damage may result.

1R. Headlight, right
1L. Headlight, left
2R. Indicator light, right
2L. Indicator light, left
3. Oil pressure switch
4. Horn
5. Regulator
6. Alternator
7. Starter
8. Ignition coil
9. Distributor
10. Series resistor, ignition coil
11. Spark plugs
12. Battery 12 volt
13. Backup light switch
15. Combination relay
16. Connection, left indicator light
17. Fan motor
18. Regulating resistor, fan motor
18a. Connector, fan motor
19. Combination instrument
a Instrument illumination
b Oil warning light
c Alternator warning light
20. Windshield wiper motor
21. Speedometer
a Instrument illumination
d Indicator warning light
e High beam warning light
22. Windshield wiper motor switch
23. Indicator—dimmer switch
24. Clock
a Instrument illumination
25. Cigarette lighter
25a. Glove compartment light
26. Horn contact ring
27. Resistor, instrument illumination
28. Light switch
29. Steering—ignition lock
30. Connector, steering—ignition lock
31. Connector, tail light harness
32. Door contact, right
33. Door contact, left
34. Courtesy light
35. Tank fuel gauge
36R. Tail light, right
36L. Tail light, left
h Indicator light
i Tail light
k Brake light
l Backup light
37. License plate illumination
38. Indicator unit
39. Contact breaker
40. Trunk light

OPTIONAL ACCESSORIES

41. Fog lamp switch
42. Relay
43. Fog lamps
44. Radio
45. Horn changeover switch
46. Relay, two-tone horn
47. Two-tone horn

COLOR CODES

ws white
sw black
ge yellow
br brown
gr grey
gn green
rt red
li lilac
hbl light blue

Wiring Diagrams

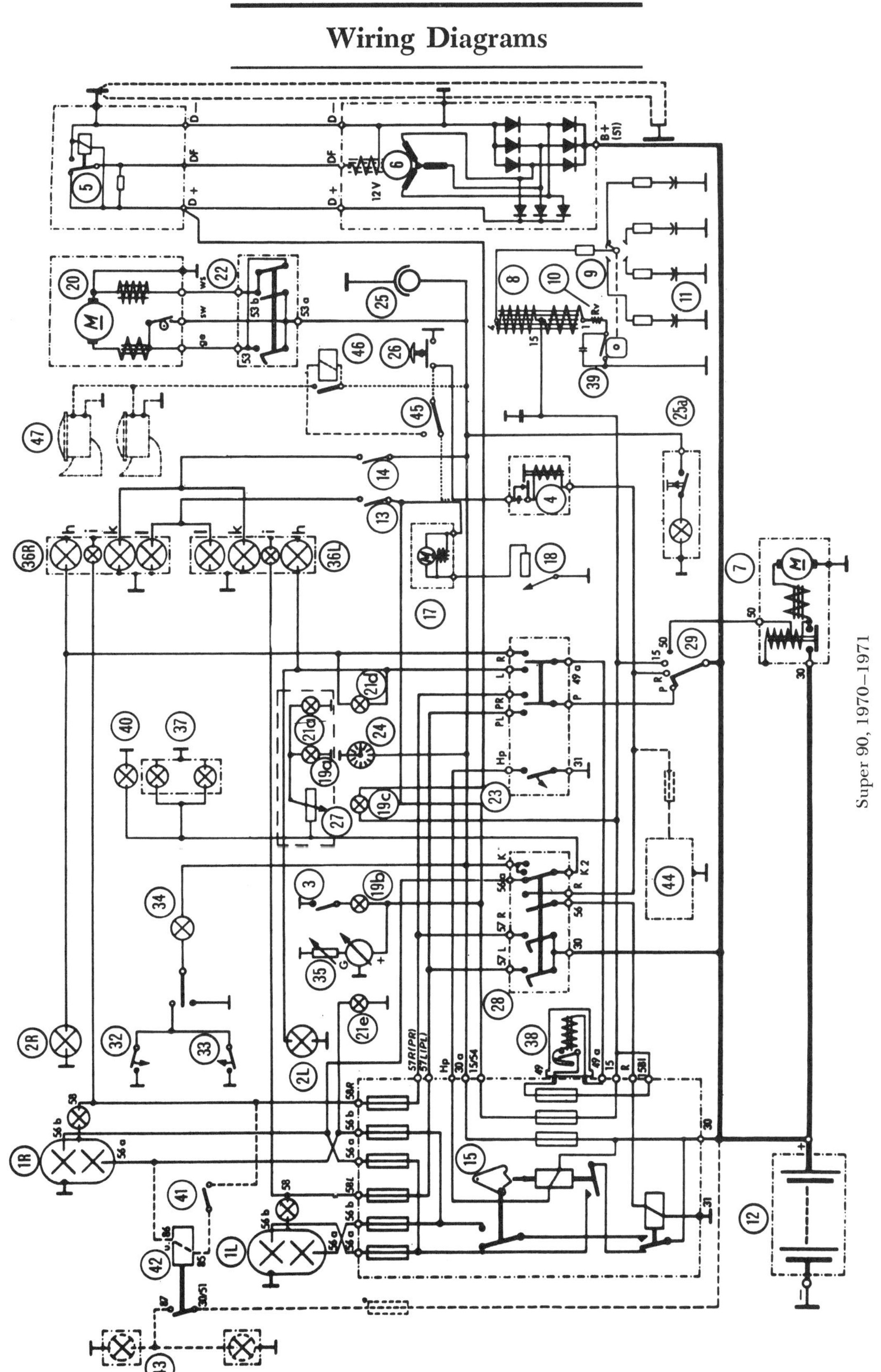

Super 90, 1970–1971

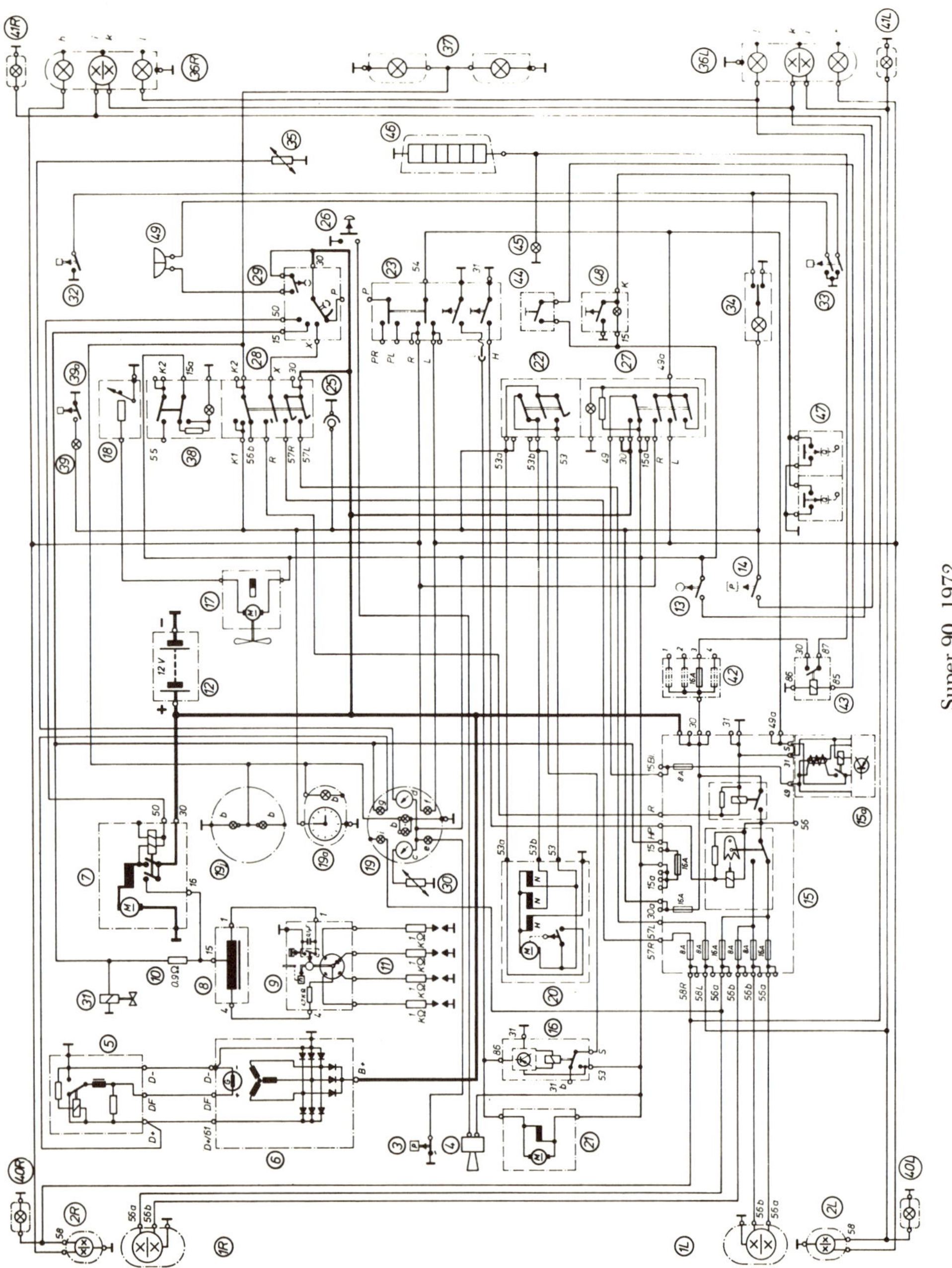

Super 90, 1972

1R. Right headlight
1L. Left headlight
2R. Right turn signal/parking light
2L. Left turn signal/parking light
3. Oil pressure switch
4. Horn
5. Regulator
6. Alternator
7. Starter
8. Ignition coil
9. Distributor and contact breaker points
10. Resistor for item 8
11. Sparkplug
12. Battery
13. Backup light switch
14. Brake light switch
15. Combination relay
15a. Flasher relay
16. Relay for windshield washer
17. Fan meter
18. Resistor for item 17
19. Combination gauge
19a. Clock
19b. Instrument illumination
19c. Temperature gauge
19d. Fuel gauge
19e. Oil pressure warning light
19f. Turn signal indicator light
19g. Alternator charge indicator light
19h.
19i. High beam indicator light
19j. Odometer
20. Wipermotor
21. Washermotor
22. Wiper switch
23. Flasher/headlight dimmer/ windshield washer switch
24.
25. Cigarette lighter/socket
26. Horn button
27. Emergency flasher switch
28. Light switch
29. Ignition/Steering lock
30. Engine temperature sending unit
31. Electromagnetic valve
32. Front right door contact switch
33. Front left door/buzzer contact switch
34. Interior light and switch
35. Fuel gauge sending unit
36R. Right tail light
36L. Left tail light
36h. Turn signal light
i Tail light
k Brake warning light
l Backup light
37. License plate lights
38. Auxiliary switch
39. Glove compartment light
39a. Glove compartment light switch
40R. Right front side marker light
40L. Left front side marker light
41R. Right rear side marker light
41L. Left rear side marker light
42. Auxiliary fuse box
43. Relay for item 46
44. Relay for item 46
45. Indicator light for item 46
46. Rear window defogger
47. Dual circuit brake control system
48. Switch and control light for item 47
49. Buzzer

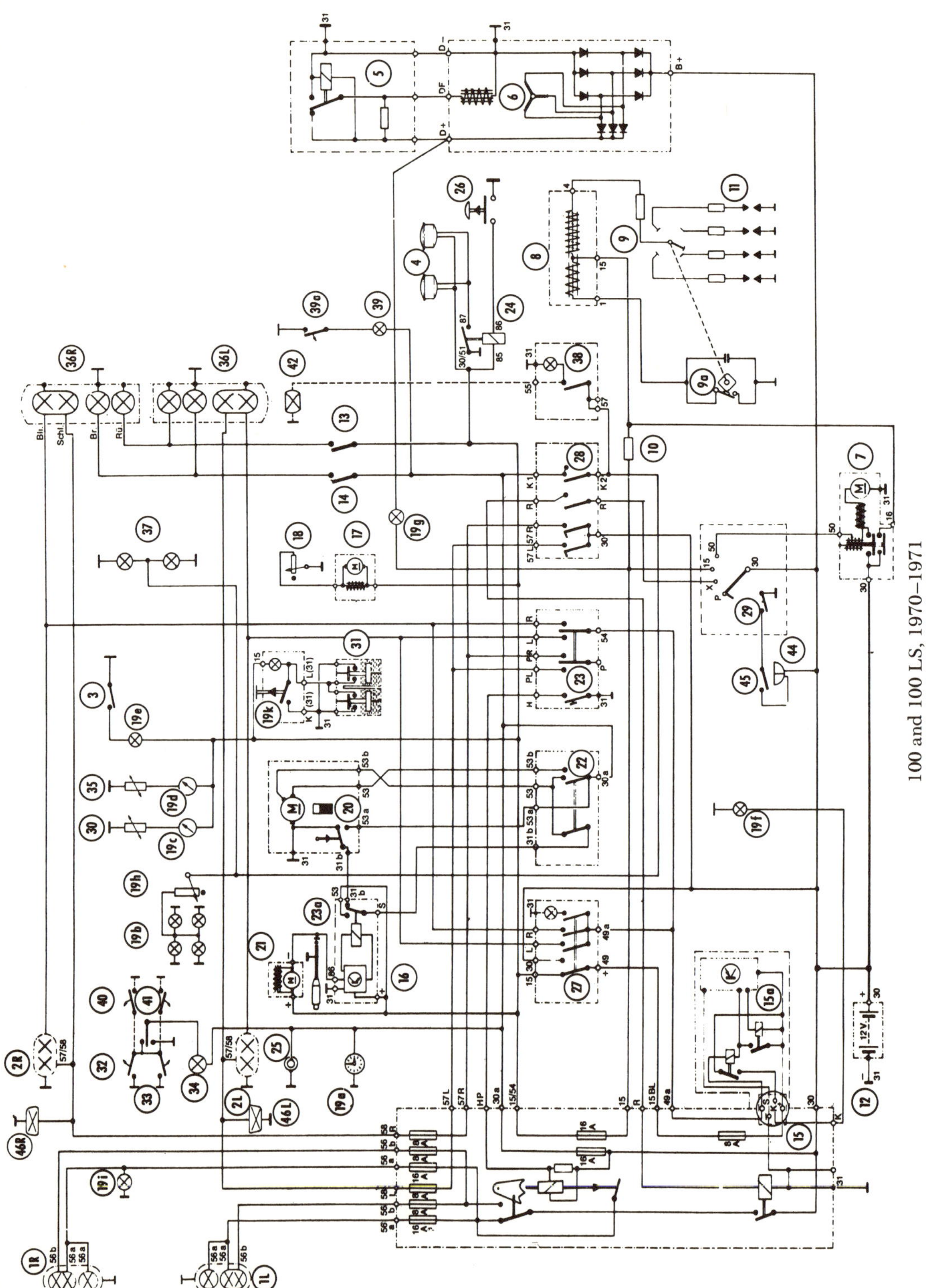

100 and 100 LS, 1970–1971

1R. Headlight, right
1L. Headlight, left
2R. Turn signal, right
2L. Turn signal, left
3. Oil pressure switch
4. Horn
5. Governor
6. Alternator
7. Starter
8. Ignition coil
9. Distributor
9a. Contact breaker
10. Series resistor for item 8
11. Spark plugs
12. Battery
13. Backup light switch
14. Brake light switch
15. Combination relay
15a. Flasher unit
16. Relay, windshield washer
17. Blower motor
18. Series resistor for item 17
19a. Clock
19b. Instrument illumination
19c. Temperature gauge
19d. Fuel gauge
19e. Oil warning lamp
19f. Turn signal warning lamp
19g. Battery warning lamp
19h. Regulating resistor for item 19b
19i. High beam warning lamp
20. Wiper motor
21. Washer motor
22. Wiper switch
23. Turn signal—dimmer switch
23a. Washer impulse tracer
24. Multi-connector
25. Cigarette lighter
26. Horn button
27. Emergency warning light switch
28. Light switch
29. Steering-ignition lock
30. Temperature transmitter
32. Door contact switch, front, right
33. Door contact switch, front, left
34. Interior light and switch
35. Fuel tank gauge
36R. Tail light, right
36L. Tail light, left
37. License plate light
38. Switch, tail fog light
39. Glove compartment light
39a. Switch for item 39
40. Door contact switch, rear, right
41. Door contact switch, rear, left
42. Tail fog light (optional extra)
19k. Twin-circuit brake warning lamp
24. Switching relay for position 4
31. Twin-circuit braking system
44. Audible buzzer
45. Door contact switch for item 44
46R., 46L. Side marker lights

COLOR CODES

ws	white
sw	black
ge	yellow
br	brown
gr	gray
gn	green
rt	red
li	lilac
bl	blue
hllbl	light blue

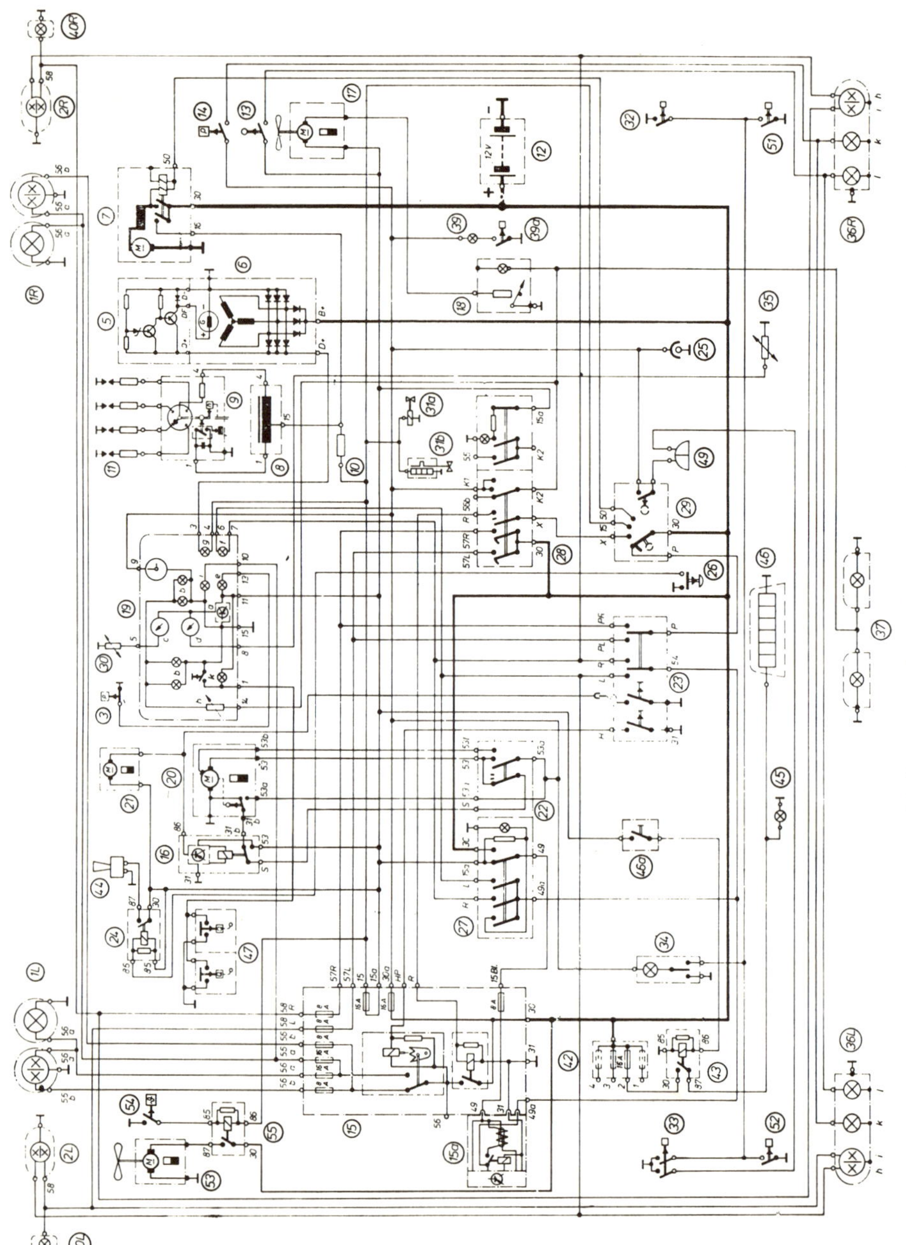

100, 100 LS, and 100 GL, 1972–1973

1R. Right headlight
1L. Left headlight
2R. Right turn signal/parking light
2L. Left turn signal/parking light
3. Oil pressure switch
5. Regulator
6. Alternator
7. Starter
8. Ignition coil
9. Distributor with contact breaker
10. Resistor, item 8
11. Spark plugs
12. Battery
13. Backup light switch
14. Stop light switch
15. Combination relay
15a. Flasher relay
16. Windshield washer relay
17. Fan motor for heater and fresh air
18. Resistor, item 17
19. Combination gauge
19a. Electronic voltage compensator
19b. Instrument illumination
19c. Temperature gauge
19d. Fuel gauge
19e. Oil pressure warning light
19f. Turn signal indicator light
19g. Alternator charge warning light
19h. Resistor for item 19b
19i. High beam indicator light
19j. Clock
19k. Dual circuit brake warning light and control button
20. Wiper motor
21. Washer motor
22. Wiper switch
23. Turn signal and headlight dimmer switch with windshield washer button
24. Relay (horn)
25. Cigarette lighter
26. Horn button
27. Emergency flasher
28. Light switch
29. Ignition/steering lock
30. Engine temperature sending unit
31a. Idle cut-off valve
31b. Mixture control valve
32. Front right door contact switch
33. Front left door contact switch
34. Interior light and switch
35. Fuel gauge sending unit
36R. Right rear lights
36L. Left rear lights
36h. Turn signal
36i. Tail light
36k. Stop light
36l. Back-up light
37. License plate lights
39. Glove compartment light
39a. Switch, item 39
40R. Right side marker
40L. Left side marker
42. Fuse box
43. Relay for item 46
44. Horn signal
45. Indicator light for item 46
46. Rear window defogger
46a. Switch for item 46
47. Dual circuit brake control system
49. Buzzer
51. Rear door contact switch, right
52. Rear door contact switch, left
53. Fan motor (radiator)
54. Thermal starting valve
55. Relay for item 53

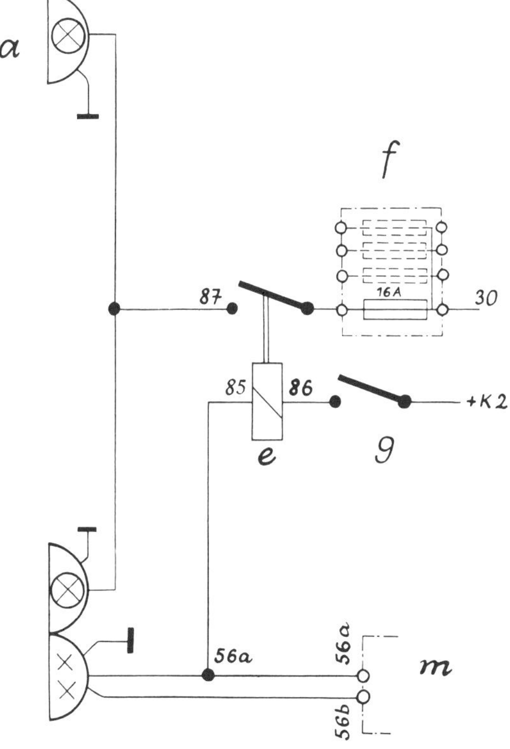

Wiring for fog or driving light installation. In this installation, the extra lights are available only when the high beams are on

a Fog or driving lights
f 16 amp fuse
g Fog or driving light switch
m Headlight relay
e Relay for fog or driving lights
K2 Terminal K2 on light switch

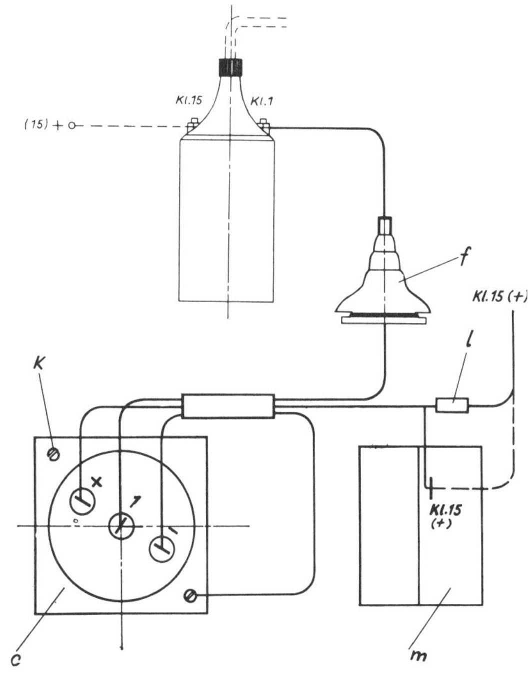

Wiring for 100, 100 LS, and 100 GL tachometer

c Tachometer
f Rubber grommet
K Tachometer mounting screw
l Wire connector
m Emergency warning light switch

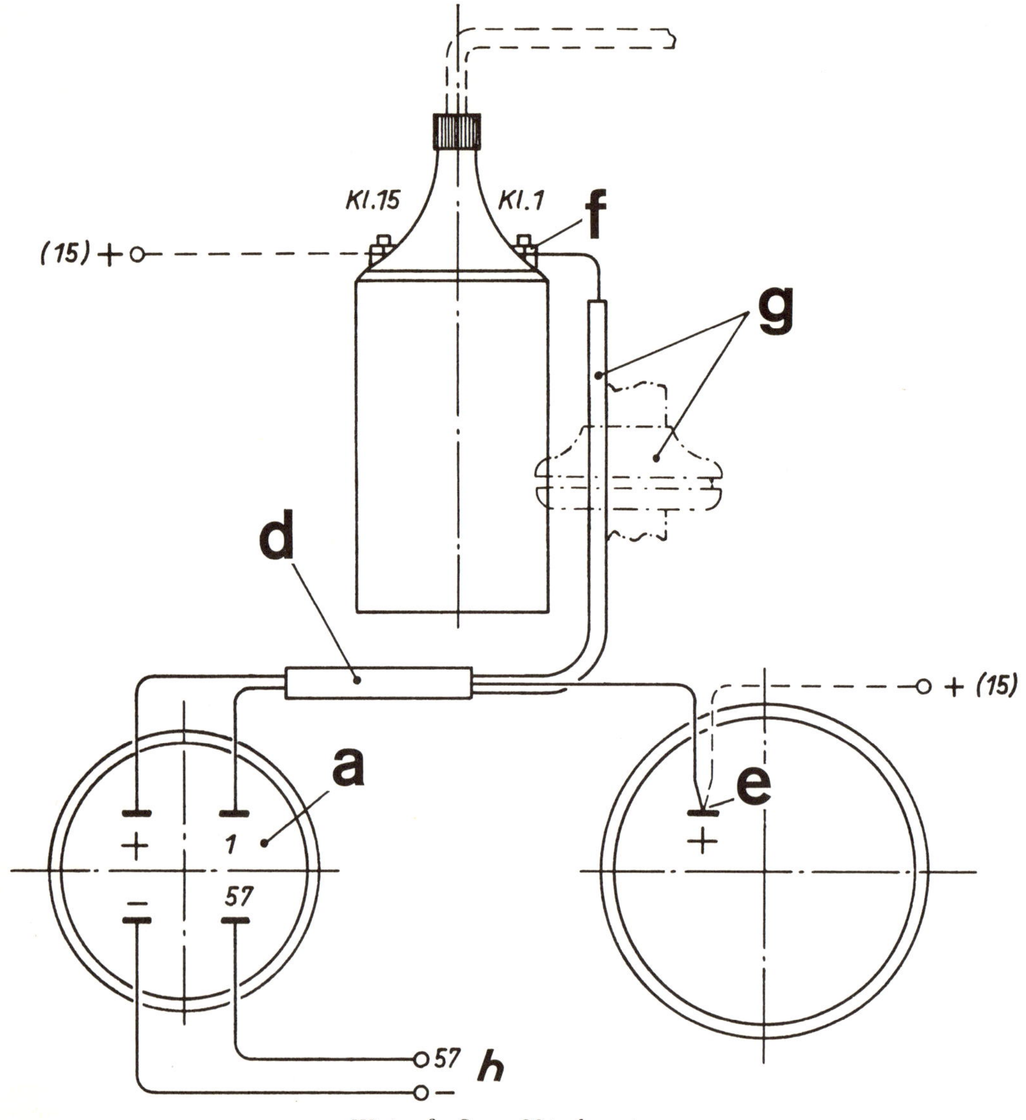

Wiring for Super 90 tachometer

a Tachometer
d Wire harness
e Fuel gauge
f Connection at terminal 1 of the ignition coil
g Rubber grommet
h Clock connections

Chapter Six

Clutch and Transmission

Manual Transmission

The transmission is combined with the differential in a transaxle. Fourth gear is an overdrive ratio. Due to the complexity of this unit and the extensive specialized equipment required, no overhaul procedures will be covered in this book.

Manual Transmission Gear Ratios

1	3.40
2	1.94
3	1.36
4	0.97 *
R	3.10

* 0.93 on Super 90

Removal and Installation

The engine/transaxle unit must be removed from the car as explained under "Engine Removal and Installation." Then the transmission can simply be unbolted from the engine and slid back. On replacement, tighten the bolts to 54, 33, and 18 ft lbs, respectively, for the three sizes of bolts.

NOTE: *It is possible to remove just the transaxle on the Super 90, but this procedure is as difficult as removing the whole powertrain unit. It requires moving the engine and transaxle about in the chassis while supporting them with some rather elaborate lifting and supporting brackets. The front crossmember must also be removed. Therefore, it would be simpler to remove the engine and transaxle together.*

Linkage Adjustment

1. Slide the seats all the way back and set the handbrake.
2. Remove the six sheet-metal screws which attach the console. Unscrew the shift knob and lift off the console.
3. The shift lever bracket has a spring-loaded ball which should engage the groove in the long shift rod when the transmission is in Neutral.
4. To adjust it, loosen the four bolts which hold the shift lever bracket to the floor and move the bracket to the front or rear. Tighten the bolts and recheck the adjustment.
5. If the long shift rod has a rubber damper apparatus in the middle, make sure

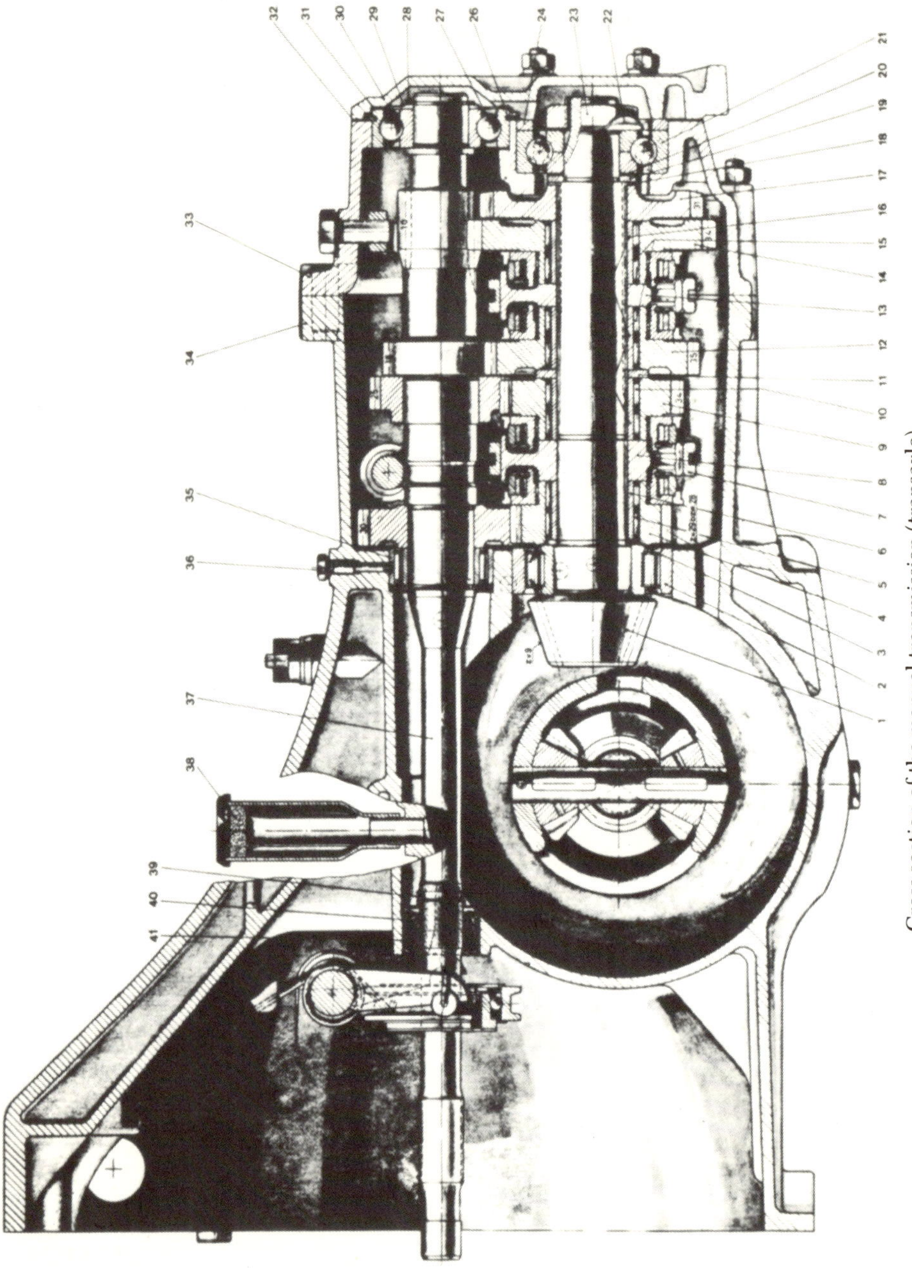
Cross section of the manual transmission (transaxle)

1. Drive pinion
2. Roller bearing
3. Spacer
4. Sliding gear, 4th gear
5. Needle bearing
6. Needle bearing inner race
7. Operating sleeve
8. Guide sleeve
9. Sliding gear, 3rd gear
10. Needle bearing
11. Thrust washer
12. Sliding gear, 2nd gear
13. Guide sleeve
14. Sliding gear, 1st gear
15. Needle bearing
16. Needle bearing, inner race
17. Reverse gear
18. Shim
19. Shim
20. Shim
21. Four point bearing
22. Lock plate
23. Hex nut
24. Shim
25. Reverse gear ass. (not illustrated)
26. Snap-ring
27. Grooved ball bearing
28. Circlip
29. Support disc
30. End cover
31. Shim
32. Gasket, end cover
33. Transmission cover
34. Transmission case
35. Needle bearing
36. Hex head screw
37. Main shaft
38. Breather valve
39. Oil slinger
40. Shaft seal
41. Bushing

that it is in good condition and not causing any unnecessary play.

6. Grease the moving parts lightly.
7. Replace the console and the shift knob.

When adjusting the floorshift linkage, the spring loaded ball should engage the slot (N) in the shift rod (33) with the transmission in Neutral. If it does not, loosen bolts (8) and move the bracket

Clutch

The clutch is a diaphragm spring type and cable actuated. Periodic adjustment is required to maintain the proper pedal free-play.

Removal and Installation

1. Remove the engine and transaxle as a unit.
2. Separate the engine and transaxle.
3. Mark the relationship of the pressure plate to the flywheel.
4. Unbolt the pressure plate from the flywheel, loosening the bolts alternately a little bit at a time to prevent warpage.

Before removing the pressure plate bolts (a) mark the pressure plate (b) and the flywheel as shown at the arrow. The dummy shaft (d) is used to center the driven plate (clutch disc) on reinstallation

5. Inspect all parts. Make sure that the flywheel and pressure plate are not scored. A scored pressure plate should be replaced. A scored flywheel can often be resurfaced by machining. Minor roughness can be cleaned up with fine emery cloth. If the driven plate has oil on it, check for engine or transmission leakage.
6. To install the clutch, place the driven plate on the pressure plate, making sure that it is facing the right way.
7. Hold the clutch assembly against the flywheel, aligning the marks made in Step 3, and insert a dummy shaft through the pressure plate and the driven plate into the crankshaft pilot bearing. A dummy shaft is simply a shaft of the same diameter as the hole in the driven plate.
8. Install the pressure plate bolts finger tight. Then tighten the bolts evenly, in rotation, to avoid distortion. Torque the bolts to 24–27 ft lbs. Remove the dummy shaft.
9. The clutch release bearing in the front of the transmission housing should be checked before reassembly. It is retained by two springs.
10. Bolt the transaxle back to the engine. It may be necessary to turn the transmission shaft slightly to align the driven plate splines. Bolt torque is 54, 33, and 18 ft lbs, respectively, for the three sizes of bolts.
11. Replace the engine/transaxle unit in the car. Check the clutch adjustment.

The clutch release bearing can easily be removed by disengaging the two springs

Pedal Free-Play Adjustment

The pedal free-play is adjusted at the clutch end of the cable. Free-play is the distance that the pedal travels from the released position to the point at which clutch spring pressure can be felt. This can be measured by placing a yardstick alongside the clutch pedal. Play should be 0.6–0.8 in.

1. On the 100, 100 LS, and 100 GL, loosen the upper cable nut. Turn both nuts clockwise to reduce play, and counterclockwise to increase. After the adjustment is made, tighten the upper nut to lock the cable in place.

Clutch adjustment point on the 100, 100 LS, and 100 GL. (a) is the clutch cable, (b) is the clutch lever, (c) and (d) are the adjusting nuts

2. On the Super 90, turn the adjusting nut at the end of the inner cable clockwise to increase play, and counterclockwise to reduce. Make sure that the toggle is seated in the notch on the clutch arm.

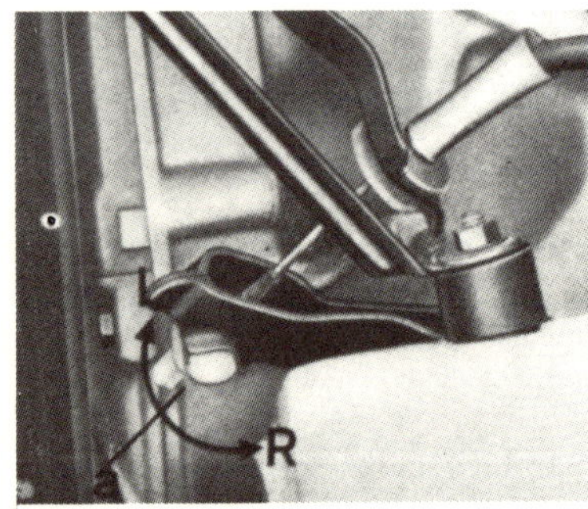

Super 90 clutch adjustment nut (a). (L) and (R) indicate left and right

3. The total pedal travel should be at least 6.1 in. If it is not adequate, the pedal pivot can be loosened and moved up.

CLUTCH CABLE

Removal and Installation

1. Loosen the adjustment.
2. Disengage the cable from the clutch arm.
3. Unhook the cable from the pedal. Remove the threaded eye from the pedal end of the cable. Remove the adjustment nut(s).
4. Remove the C-clip which holds the outer cable at the adjustment point. Remove all the washers and bushings, first noting their locations.
5. Pull the cable out of the firewall toward the engine compartment side.
6. Install and connect the new cable. Adjust the pedal free-play.

Automatic Transmission

The automatic transmission is a hydraulically operated three-speed unit with a torque converter. No automatic transmission overhaul procedures are given in this book, as this work requires numerous specialized tools and procedures.

Removal and Installation

The automatic transmission can be disconnected from the engine and removed with the engine in the car. The engine must be mounted to the frame in some manner or supported on a jack or lift to prevent if from falling when the mounts are disconnected.

1. Drain the transmission. Remove the grille and the apron under the bumper.

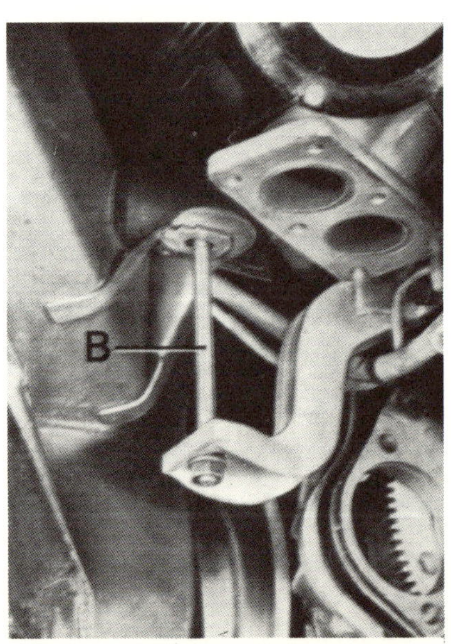

Insert bolts (B) through each engine mount to support the engine. Note that the starter has been removed for access to the torque converter bolts

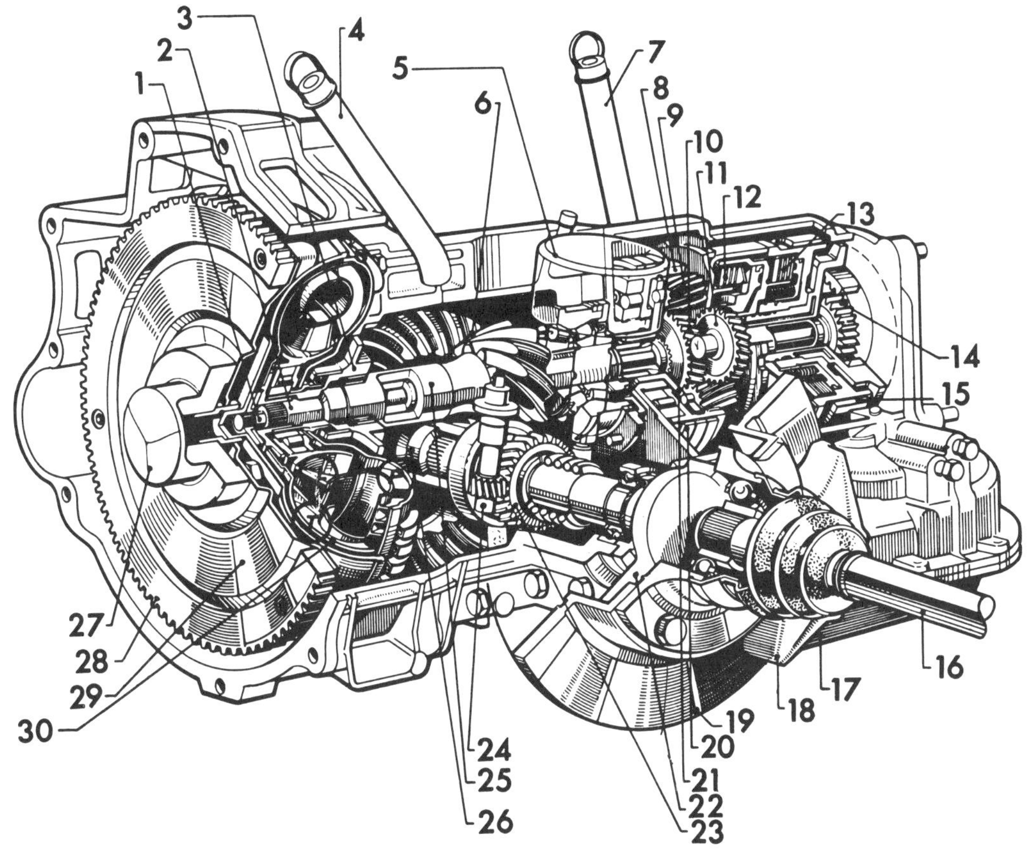

Cross section of the automatic transmission (transaxle)

1. Pump shaft
2. Turbine shaft
3. Stator support
4. Oil filler tube, differential
5. Governor
6. Drive pinion
7. Filler tube, planetary gear
8. Annulus
9. Small planetary gear
10. Large sun gear
11. Large planetary pinion
12. Forward clutch
13. Direct and reverse clutch
14. Oil pump
15. 2nd gear brake band
16. Driveshaft
17. Oil pan
18. Brake caliper
19. Brake disc
20. 1st gear and reverse brake band
21. Planetary gear carrier
22. Stub axle
23. Impeller, governor and speedometer drive
24. Speedometer pinion shaft
25. Drive pinion shaft
26. Differential
27. Crankshaft, engine
28. Gear ring
29. Drive plate
30. Torque converter

P Impeller
L Stator
T Turbine

2. Disconnect the brake lines from the brake hoses and plug the ends of the hoses.

3. Disconnect the acclerator linkage.

4. Remove the front exhaust pipe.

5. Remove the oil filter and starter.

6. Disconnect both driveshafts and suspend them from the upper wishbones. Disconnect the stabilizer bar at both lower wishbones.

7. Unbolt the shift linkage selector cable holder at the transmission. Remove the selector cable from the lever. Remove the selector cable holder.

8. Disconnect the crossmember at the engine mounts and at the support. Place a jack or other support under the transmission.

9. Remove the guard and disconnect the left and right engine mounts. Be careful not to change the adjustment of the left mount, which is held by locknuts.

10. Insert a 3/8 x 8 in. bolt through each side in place of the engine mounts. Lower the power plant until it is supported by the bolts.

11. Disconnect the transmission vacuum modulator hose.

12. Unbolt the torque converter by working through the hole for the starter.

13. Unbolt the engine from the transmission and remove the transmission to the

rear. Fasten the torque converter in the transmission housing with a strap, so it doesn't fall out.

14. To install the transmission, reverse the removal procedure. Lift the transmission into place and bolt it to the engine. Transmission to engine bolt torque is 54, 33, and 18 ft lbs, respectively, for the three bolt sizes. Torque converter bolt torque is 22 ft lbs.

15. Lift both the engine and transmission and install the selector lever holder.

16. When installing the engine mounts, make sure that the projection engages the groove in the mount.

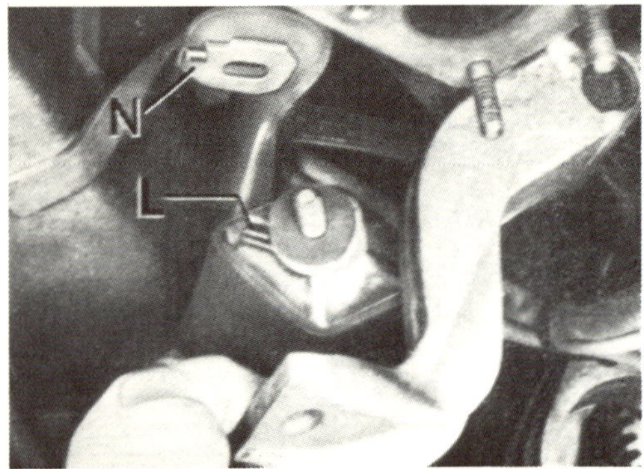

Be sure that the projection (N) engages the groove (L) of the engine mount

17. After installing the engine/transmission assembly, check the alignment of the unit. Refer to "Engine Installation" for details.

18. Refill the transmission. Refer to Chapter One for details.

Pan Removal and Installation

See "Automatic Transmission Fluid Change" in Chapter One for details on this operation.

Kickdown Switch

The kickdown switch is mounted behind the accelerator pedal. With the ignition switch on, the switch should make an audible click when the pedal is pressed all the way down.

The transmission should downshift when the accelerator is depressed to the wide open throttle position at speeds between 39 and 65 mph for second gear, and 16 and 36 mph for first gear.

Neutral Safety Switch Adjustment

The neutral safety switch prevents the engine from being started with the transmission in any position other than Park or Neutral. It also activates the backup lights. The switch is at the base of the shift lever, inside the floorshift console.

To replace or adjust the switch:

1. Remove the four screws which hold the console to the floor.

2. Shift into Neutral. Remove the two screws which hold the shift position indicator plate to the console. Remove the shift knob and the console.

3. Disconnect the switch electrical leads. These are: red/black—neutral safety, black—backup lights, blue/red—backup lights. The backup light wires are at the front.

4. Remove the two switch retaining screws. Remove the switch.

5. Install the new switch so that the neutral safety switch contacts are together.

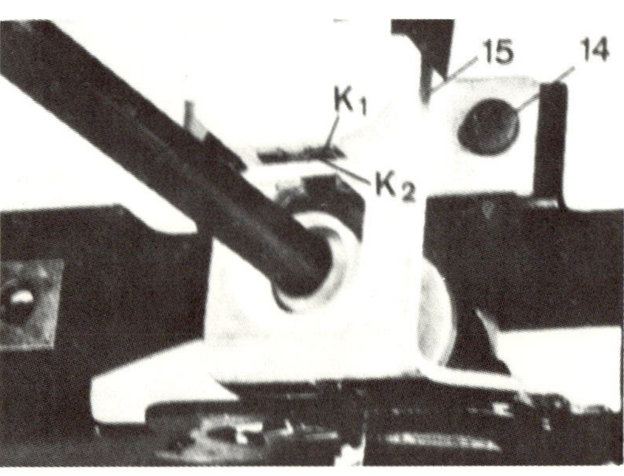

When installing the neutral safety/backup light switch (15) contacts (K1) and (K2) must be together with the shift lever in Neutral. (14) is one of the mounting screws

6. Install the electrical connectors. Hold the footbrake while making sure that the engine will start only in Neutral and Park. Make sure that the backup lights operate only in Reverse. If the switch does not operate properly, it may have to be moved on its slotted mounting bracket.

7. Replace the console cover.

Shift Linkage Adjustment

The function of this adjustment is to make sure that the transmission is fully engaged in each shift position. If this is not done, the transmission may be only partially engaged in a range position. This would result in severe damage due to slippage.

1. Place the selector lever in Park.

2. Loosen the cable clamping nut at the transmission end.

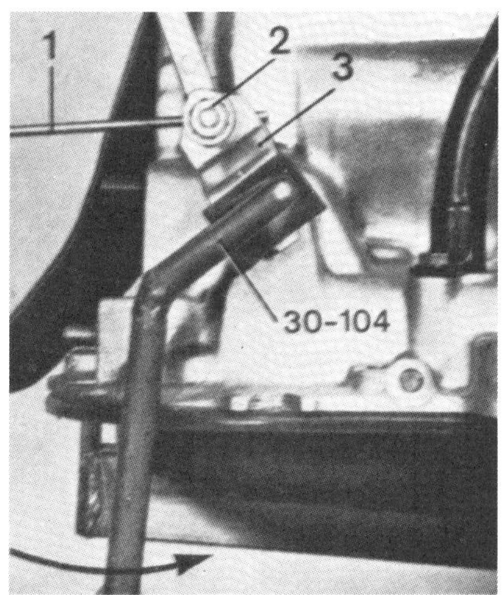

When adjusting the automatic transmission linkage, the selector lever (3) should be pushed back to the stop with the clamping nut (2) loose so that the cable (1) is free to move. 30–104 is a special tool used to push the selector lever back; it is not necessary

3. Press the selector lever on the transmission back to the stop.
4. Tighten the clamping nut.
5. Start the engine and move the selector lever toward Drive. The engine speed must decrease before the lever reaches Drive. Move the selector lever toward Reverse. The engine speed must also fall off before the lever reaches Reverse.
6. If the lever is adjusted correctly, the distance from Neutral to Drive and from Neutral to Reverse must be equal. If the distances vary, repeat the adjustment.

Vacuum Modulator Adjustment

The vacuum modulator, on the rear of the transmission, regulates the firmness and timing of shifts in relation to speed and throttle opening. A leaking modulator will result in transmission fluid being sucked into the engine through the vacuum modulator and burned. This will produce a smoky exhaust and a continually low transmission fluid level. The modulator must be adjusted any time it, or it's seal, has been replaced. This adjustment is also necessary if the shift timing is incorrect.

NOTE: *It is recommended that this job be entrusted to a skilled automatic transmission specialist or to a dealer's shop. The result of a careless or wrong adjustment could be very expensive.*

1. Disconnect and plug the vacuum hose at the modulator.

The two (Bs) show where the test gauge is to be connected. The vacuum modulator is the cylindrical unit to the left of the test plug.

2. Remove the test plug from the right side of the transmission. Connect a pressure gauge with a scale up to 150 psi.
3. Place the selector lever in Neutral and idle the engine at 1,000 rpm. Adjust the modulator until the gauge shows 48.4 psi. Stop the engine.
4. Remove the gauge and replace the plug and vacuum line.
5. The transmission should upshift with wide-open throttle from first to second gear at 19–21 mph, and from second to third at 54–58 mph.

Band Adjustments

NOTE: *It is recommended that this job be entrusted to a skilled automatic transmission specialist or to a dealer's shop. The result of a careless or wrong adjustment could be very expensive.*

Second gear brake band adjusting screw and locknut (66) and (67). First gear brake band adjusting screw and locknut (60) and (67)

SECOND GEAR BAND

1. Loosen the locknut.
2. Tighten the adjusting screw to 87 in. lbs.
3. Loosen the adjusting screw and retighten to 44 in. lbs.
4. Turn the adjusting screw out 1¾–2 turns.
5. Tighten the locknut.

FIRST GEAR BAND

1. Loosen the locknut.
2. Tighten the adjusting screw to 87 in. lbs.
3. Loosen the adjusting screw and retighten to 44 in. lbs.
4. Turn the adjusting screw out 3¼–3¾ turns.
5. Tighten the locknut.

Transaxle

The transmission and differential are combined in a transaxle. On manual transmission models, the transmission and differential share a common lubricant supply. No transaxle overhaul procedures are given here due to the specialized tools, knowledge, and procedures required. The final drive ratio is 3.89:1 (3.91 with automatic). All 1973 models have a 4.11 ratio. With the overdrive Fourth gear used, the actual final drive ratio in Fourth gear is 3.63 for the Super 90 and 3.76 (3.99 in 1973) for the 100, 100 LS, and 100 GL.

Removal and Installation

The transaxle is removed from the car in unit with the engine. See "Engine Removal and Installation" for details. On the automatic, it is possible to remove the transaxle only, leaving the engine in place. See "Automatic Transmission Removal and Installation" for details.

Drive Axles

The front wheel drive axle shafts have two Rzeppa constant velocity joints each. These joints can handle lateral movement caused by suspension travel, as well as being able to transmit power at the angles required by steering movements.

DRIVESHAFTS

Removal and Installation

The steering knuckles must be removed along with the shafts.

1. Support the vehicle and remove the wheels. Let the front suspension hang free.
2. Have an assistant hold the brakes for this step. Unbolt the driveshaft from the transmission stub axle and brake disc. There should be an insulator between the driveshaft and brake disc.
3. Remove the cotter pin and the castellated nut from the tie-rod end. Press out the tie-rod end from the steering knuckle arm. A small puller or press is required to free the tie-rod end.

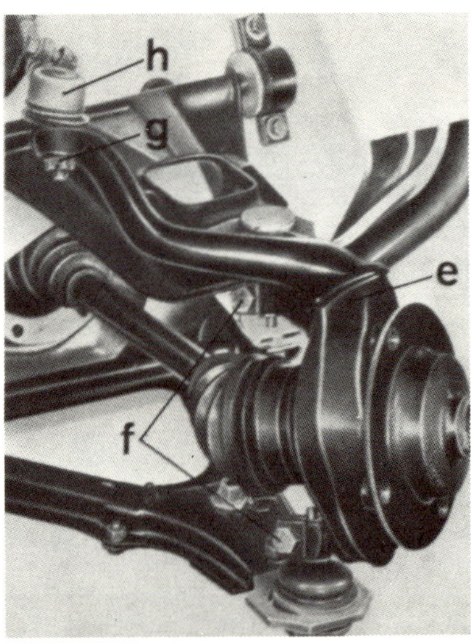

The castellated nut (g) and the cotter pin must be removed before pulling out the tie-rod end (h) from the steering knuckle (e). (f) indicates the steering knuckle mounting bolts

4. Remove the two steering knuckle mounting bolts.
5. Remove the steering knuckle and driveshaft assembly.
6. Reverse the procedure for installation. Torques are:

Fastener	*Torque (ft lbs)*
Driveshaft to stub axle	77
Steering knuckle mounting bolts	34
Tie-Rod end	26

7. Check the wheel alignment.

Disassembly

This operation is necessary to replace the rubber boots. It requires use of a press or puller setup.

1. Clamp the steering knuckle in a vise.
2. Remove the cotter pin. Unscrew the castellated nut and reverse it on the threads to protect them from damage.
3. Press the driveshaft from the steering knuckle. Steps 4–8 cover steering knuckle service.
4. Press out the wheel hub from the steering knuckle.
5. Remove the spacer, Nilos ring, and ball bearing inner race.
6. Drive the outer ball bearing race from the knuckle. Remove the internal snap-rings, using snap-ring pliers, and press out the second ball bearing outer race.
7. Replace the snap-rings. Press in the outer races. Fill the space between the races with high melting point wheel bearing grease.
8. Place the spacer and Nilos ring in the wheel hub. Press on the ball bearing inner race and install a new spacer bushing. Place the hub in the steering knuckle and press in the second ball bearing inner race.
9. Remove both rubber boot clamps and slide the boots off the joints.
10. Clamp the inner driveshaft in a vise. Spread the snap-ring in the joint and have an assistant hit the outer end of the shaft with a soft hammer. A powerful blow is required.

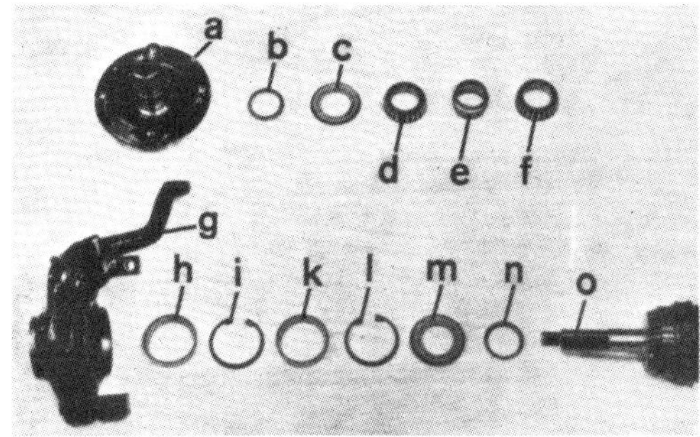

Steering knuckle and wheel hub assembly

a	Wheel hub	h	Ball bearing outer race
b	Spacer	i	Snap-ring
c	Nilos ring	k	Outer ball bearing race
d	Ball bearing inner race	l	Snap-ring
e	Spacer bushing	m	Nilos ring
f	Ball bearing inner race	n	Spacer
g	Right steering knuckle	o	Driveshaft

11. Drive the joint housing off the inner shaft, using the soft hammer.
12. Pull off the rubber boots.
13. Clean the joint with alcohol and air-dry.
14. Install new rubber boots.

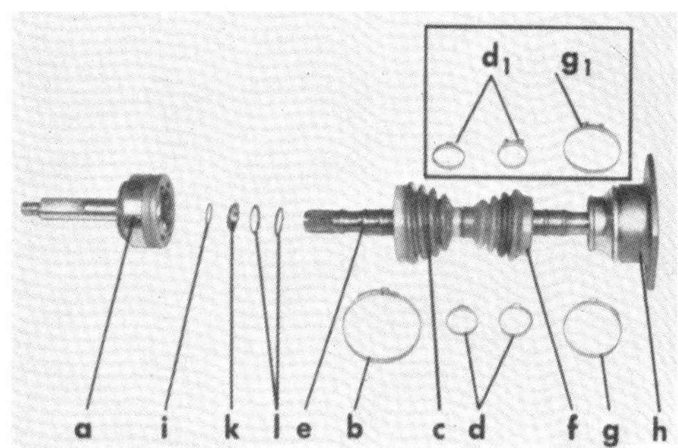

Driveshaft assembly

a	Outer driveshaft with Rzeppa joint	f	Rubber boot
b	Clamp	g	Clamp
c	Rubber boot	g1	Clamp
d	Clamps	h	Rzeppa joint with flange
d1	Clamps	i	Snap-ring
e	Inner driveshaft	k	Pressure ring
		l	Disc springs

15. Place two new disc springs on the inner shaft with their concave side out. Install a pressure ring with the convex side out.

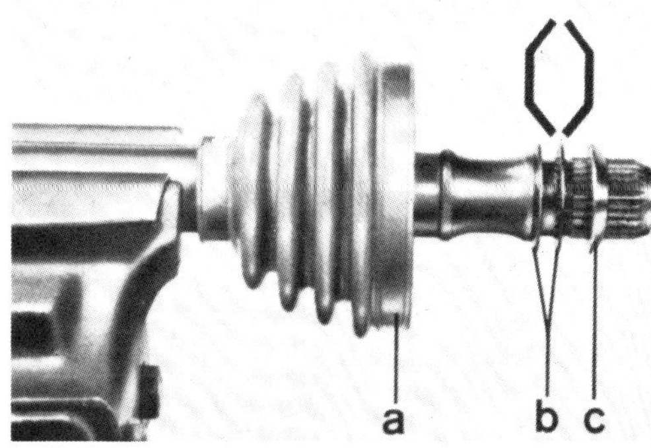

Installation of disc springs and pressure ring on inner drive shaft

a Outer rubber boot
b Disc springs
c Pressure ring

16. Place a new snap-ring in the joint. Place the ends in the machined groove.
17. Slide the joint on the inner shaft, so that the snap-ring begins to go into place. Drive the joint into place, hitting the outer end of the driveshaft with a soft hammer. The snap-ring should snap into place. The outer end of the shaft may also be pounded on a wooden block.

18. Fill each joint with 60 cc of molybdenum disulfide base grease.

19. Put the rubber boots in place. Install the boot clamps, making sure that the free ends trail in the normal direction of rotation.

20. Grease and install the spacer and Nilos ring. Press the driveshaft into the wheel hub. Adjust the hub nut so that there is 0.002–0.003 in. wheel bearing play, measured with a dial indicator at the outer edge of the wheel hub.

Rear Suspension

The rear axle and suspension assembly is attached to the body as a unit. The rear axle is attached to two suspension arms and the torsion bar springs are located in a fully sealed cross tube. A stabilizer (Panhard rod) is attached to the rear axle tube and the cross tube. The rear axle may be removed for repairs with or without the cross tube.

NOTE: *A jack must never be placed under the axle tube; it can be placed under the cross tube safely.*

REAR AXLE

Removal and Installation

WITHOUT CROSS TUBE

1. Depress the brake pedal about 1.2 in. and fasten the pedal in this position to close the compensating bore in the master cylinder.
2. Remove both shock absorbers.
3. Raise and support the vehicle and remove the rear wheels. Support the axle tube.
4. Disconnect the handbrake cable. Push out the protective sleeve on either side of the cable. Remove the rubber boot and pull the handbrake cable out. Pull the cable down through the slot in the bracket.

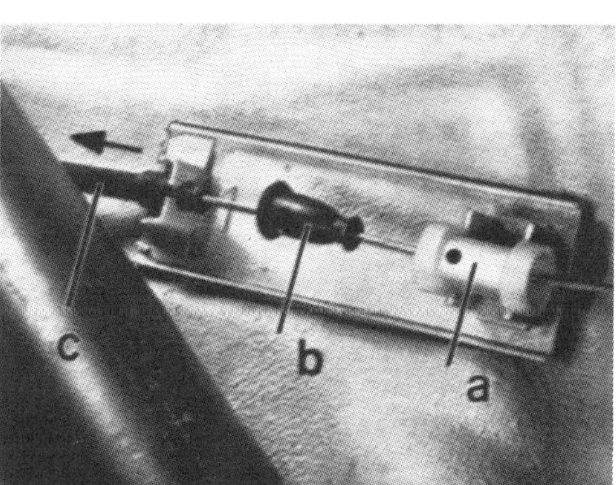

Handbrake cable attachment. The protective sleeve (a) must be pulled out and the rubber boot (b) pulled back, so that the cable (c) can be pulled out in the direction of the arrow

5. Disconnect and plug the brake lines.
6. Remove the handbrake cable from the suspension arms by bending the retaining clamps open.
7. Remove the transverse stabilizer bar.
8. Unbolt the right and left suspension arms.
9. Lift the rear axle from the suspension arms.
10. Installation is the reverse of removal. Torques are:

Rear suspension components

a Brake drum and wheel hub
b Brake assembly
c Stop pad
d Shock absorber
e Suspension arm
f Handbrake cable
g Brake line
h Transverse panhard rod
i Axle tube
k Stabilizer
l Cross tube
m Torsion bar
n Mounting tube
o Torsion bar
p Handbrake adjustment
r Stop pad
s Shock absorber
t Rubber bearing
u Wheel cylinder
v Rear axle, outer
w Brake drum and wheel hub
x Grease cap
y Mounting bolt
z Mounting bolt

Fastener	*Torque (ft lbs)*
Suspension arms to axle	27–34
Stabilizer to axle	27–34

With Cross Tube

It is not advisable to remove the rear cross tube or complete rear axle assembly, since a special centering gauge is required for proper installation of the cross tube.

WHEEL BEARINGS AND STUB AXLES

Removal and Installation

1. Depress the brake pedal about 1.2 in. and fasten the pedal in this position to hold closed the compensating bore in the master cylinder.
2. Detach and plug the brake lines on both sides.
3. Pry off the grease cap and remove the cotter pin, castellated nut, nut, and washer. Remove the wheel and brake drum.
4. Remove the bearing inner race from the brake drum.
5. Carefully (it may fly out) pry out the brake shoe retaining spring. Remove the brake shoes, complete with pressure rod and spring, bottom bracket first. Disconnect the handbrake cable.
6. Unbolt the stub axle and brake backing plate.
7. Pry out the shaft seal (it should always be replaced) and remove the inner race of the roller bearing.
8. Drive the roller bearing outer race from the brake drum. Remove the snap-ring and drive the outer roller bearing race from the drum.
9. Replace the snap-ring and drive in the outer race of the outer roller bearing.
10. Press in the outer race of the inner roller bearing.
11. Lightly coat the inner race of the inner roller bearing with wheel bearing grease and push it into the outer race.
12. Drive a new shaft seal into position with the open end facing the roller bearing. Fill the space between the two roller bearings with about 10 oz of wheel bearing grease.

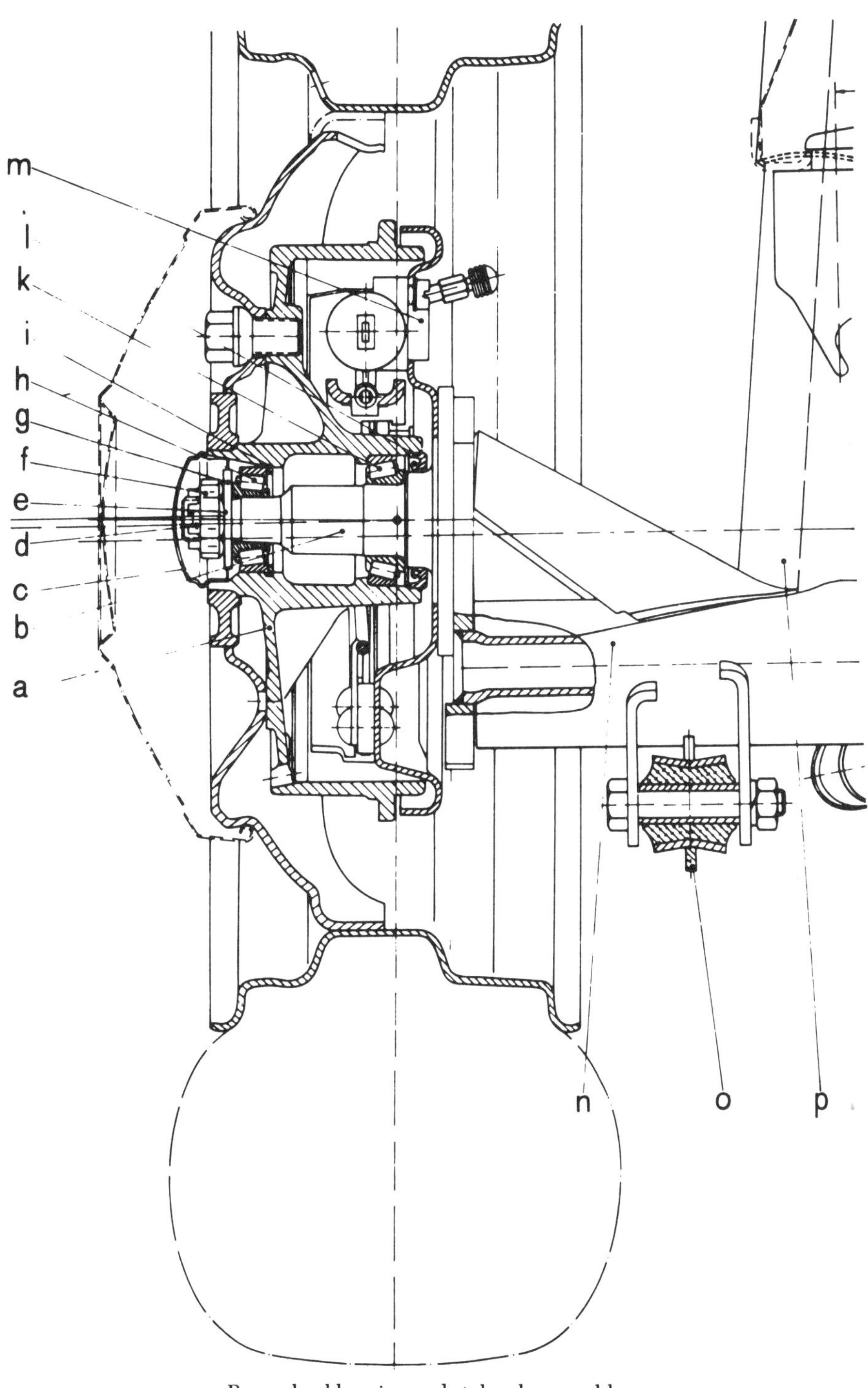

Rear wheel bearing and stub axle assembly

a Brake drum
b Rear stub axle
c Cap
d Cotter pin
e Nut
f Castellated nut
g Washer
h Roller bearing
i Snap-ring
k Roller bearing
l Shaft seal
m Brake assembly
n Rear axle
o Suspension arm
p Shock absorber

13. Coat the inner race of the outer roller bearing with grease and install the inner race.

14. Replace the stub axle and brake backing plate with the groove in the stub axle up. Bolt torque is 14–15 ft lbs for 8G bolts and 22 ft lbs for 10K bolts.

15. Assemble the brake shoes, connect the handbrake cable, and insert the brake shoes on the bottom bracket first, then at the wheel cylinder. Replace the retaining spring.

16. Replace the brake drum and wheel, special washer, nut, castellated nut, and cotter pin. Wheel bearing play should be 0.001–0.002 in., measured with a dial indicator. If the play is not correct, readjust the castellated nut. Fill the grease cap with about 10 oz of wheel bearing grease and replace it.

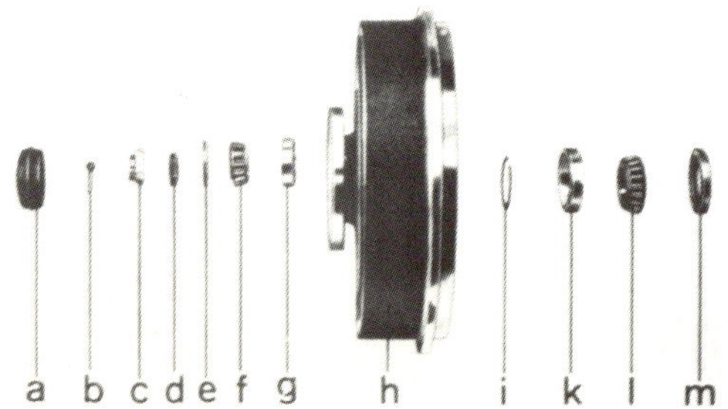

Rear brake drum and wheel bearing components

a Cap
b Cotter pin
c Castellated nut
d Nut
e Washer
f Inner race roller bearing
g Outer race roller bearing
h Brake drum
i Snap-ring
k Outer race roller bearing
l Inner race roller bearing
m Shaft seal

SHOCK ABSORBERS

Testing

To test the shock absorbers, bounce the rear of the car up and down by hand a few times. When released, the car should return to its normal ride height and stop bouncing immediately. If the shocks are worn, they should be replaced in pairs to provide equal damping.

Removal and Installation

1. Raise and support the car. Support the weight of the axle tube.

2. Remove the Panhard rod.

3. Unbolt the bottom of the shock absorber.

4. Hold the flats on the top of the shock absorber rod with a wrench and remove the nuts, disc, and rubber pad.

5. Remove the shock absorber.

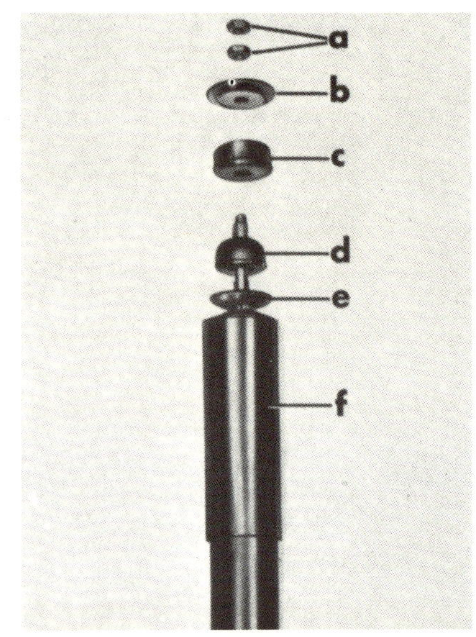

Details of the upper end of the rear shock absorbers, parts (a–c) are installed inside the trunk

a Nuts
b Disc, edge up
c Rubber pad, curved side up
d Rubber pad, curved side up
e Disc, part of shock absorber
f Shock absorber

6. Install the rubber bumper, rounded side up, on top of the new shock absorber rod.

7. Install the shock absorber through the floor pan.

8. Inside the trunk, install a rubber pad with the curved side up, a disc with the edge up, and the nuts. Use the second nut to lock the first.

9. Bolt the bottom of the shock absorber in place. Replace the Panhard rod. Torques are:

Fastener	*Bolt Torque (ft lbs)*
Upper shock absorber nut	18
Lower shock absorber mounting	32
Panhard rod	27–34

Front Suspension

The Super 90 front suspension uses torsion bars, while the 100, 100 LS, and 100 GL use strut type spring and shock absorber units. Otherwise the two front suspension systems are quite similar, being arms (wishbones) and having a cross-chassis stabilizer bar connecting the two lower control arms.

NOTE: *Exercise extreme caution when working with the front suspension. Coil springs and torsion bars are under great tension and can cause severe injury if released suddenly.*

SHOCK ABSORBERS

Testing

To test the shock absorbers, bounce the front of the car up and down by hand a few times. When released, the car should return to its normal ride height and stop bouncing immediately. If the shocks are worn, they should be replaced in pairs to provide equal damping.

Removal and Installation—Super 90

This operation is best performed with the vehicle resting on its wheels.

1. Unbolt the shock absorber from the lower control arm.

Details of Super 90 front suspension

1. Steering column
2. Hardy disc
3. Steering gear
4. Bracket
5. Rack
6. Rzeppa joint, inner
7. Boot, inner
8. Tie-rod
9. Shock absorber
10. Drive shaft
11. Boot, outer
12. Rzeppa joint, outer
13. Springs
14. Wishbone joint
15. Fit ring
16. Snap-ring
17. Steering knuckle
18. Outer drive joint
19. Spacer
20. Hub
21. Pressure piece
22. Hex. head screw
23. Adjustment level
24. Strut bearing assembly
25. Rubber bearing
26. Stabilizer
27. Front spring
28. Stabilizer strut
29. Wishbone
30. Support joint assembly

a Wishbone bearing, upper
b Stabilizer strut bearing

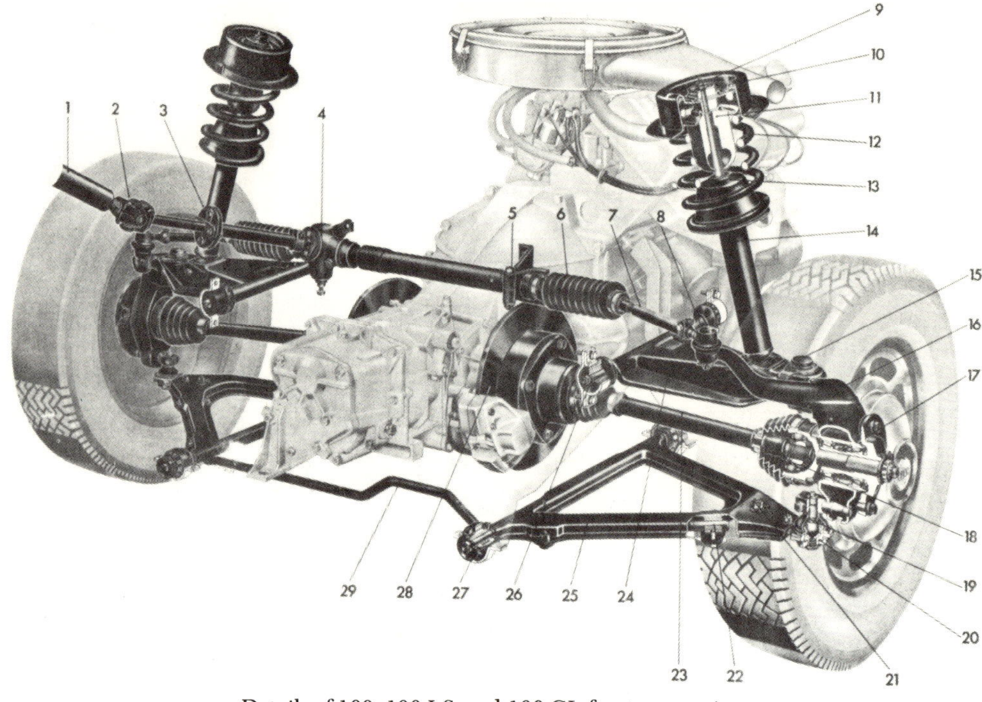

Details of 100, 100 LS, and 100 GL front suspension

1. Steering column and outer tube
2. Steering joint
3. Hardy disc
4. Steering gear
5. Mount
6. Boot
7. Tie-rod
8. Front ball and socket joint
9. Spring retainer, upper
10. Rubber ring
11. Stop pad
12. Spring
13. Spring retainer, .lower
14. Shock absorber
15. Support joint
16. Steering knuckle and tie-rod arm
17. Wheel hub
18. Rzeppa joint
19. Wishbone joint
20. Caster adjustment
21. Camber adjustment
22. Stabilizer bearing
23. Driveshaft
24. Wishbone, upper
25. Wishbone, lower
26. Wishbone bearing, upper
27. Wishbone bearing, lower
28. Brake disc
29. Stabilizer

2. Inside the engine compartment, hold the flats on top of the shock absorber rod with a wrench. Remove the locknut and nut. Remove the disc and upper mounting pad.

3. Remove the shock absorber.

4. Install the lower mounting pad (it has deep cavities on both sides) and disc on the new shock absorber rod.

5. Install the shock absorber from underneath.

6. Inside the engine compartment, install the upper mounting pad and disc. Install the nuts, torquing the first to 30 ft lbs, and using the second to lock the first.

7. Bolt the bottom of the shock absorber in place. Torque the bolt to 34 ft lbs.

STRUT

Removal and Installation—100, 100 LS, 100 GL

1. Support the vehicle and remove the wheels. Let the front suspension hang free.

2. Unbolt the strut unit from the upper control arm.

3. Inside the engine compartment, remove the three nuts which hold the top of the strut unit. Do not remove the nut and locknut in the center.

4. Pull the unit down and pull the top out through the wheel opening. It may be necessary to pull the steering knuckle down a bit for clearance.

This special tool is required to dismantle the front suspension strut unit (a)

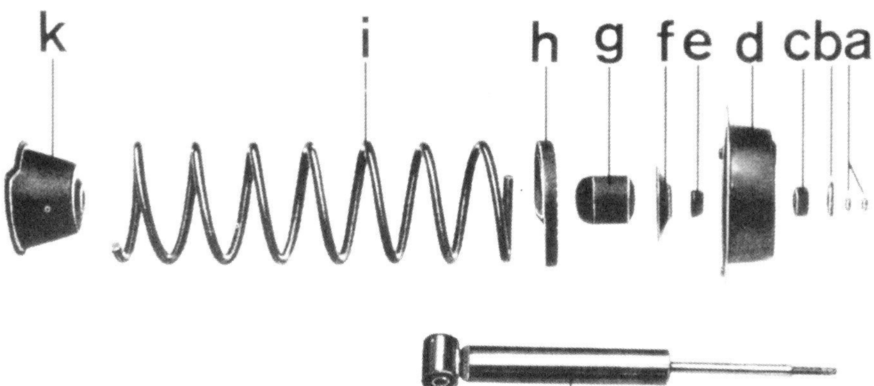

Exploded view of the front suspension strut unit

a Nut
b Plate
c Mounting pad, upper
d Spring retainer, upper
e Mounting pad, lower
f Plate
g Stop pad
h Ring
i Spring
k Spring retainer, lower
l Shock absorber

5. It is not recommended that the strut unit be disassembled unless the necessary special tools to do this safely are available. The units should be serviced in pairs to maintain equal shock absorbing qualities and ride height. Spacers are available to correct ride height. The strut unit must be disassembled to install these. The proper ride height with standard size tires is 8.2–8.7 in., measured from the floor to the 0.32 in. diameter hole in the front bearing shell of the lower control arm inner pivot.

6. When replacing the strut unit, torque the three bolts and nuts (which hold the upper end of the strut to the body) to 13–15 ft lbs and the lower end to 62–69 ft lbs. The torque for the shock absorber-to-spring retaining nut is 18–26 ft lbs.

7. Check the wheel alignment.

UPPER CONTROL ARM

Removal and Installation

SUPER 90

1. Raise the vehicle and let the front suspension hang free. Remove the wheels.

2. Remove the upper control arm to steering knuckle bolt.

3. Pull the control arm up so that the control arm upper joint comes loose from the steering knuckle.

4. Remove the two nuts and bolts which hold the outer end of the control arm together.

5. Hold the long control arm inner pivot bolt in place and loosen the nut about three turns. Remove the control arm joint from the end of the control arm.

6. Remove the front crossmember. Remove the nuts from the pivot bracket bolts working inside the engine compartment.

7. Pull the pivot bracket away from the body. It is located by two pins.

8. Remove the bolts and take the control arm from around the shock absorber.

9. Reverse the procedure for installation. Make sure that the pivot bracket mounting bolts are in position. Torques are:

Fastener	*Torque (ft lbs)*
Steering knuckle mounting bolt	34
Pivot bracket bolts	34
Control arm inner pivot bolt nut	54

10. Check the wheel alignment.

100, 100 LS, 100 GL

1. Remove the strut unit.

2. Remove the upper control arm to steering knuckle bolt.

3. Pull the control arm up so that the control arm upper joint comes loose from the steering knuckle.

4. Remove the four mounting bolts and the control arm.

5. Reverse the procedure for installation. Torques are:

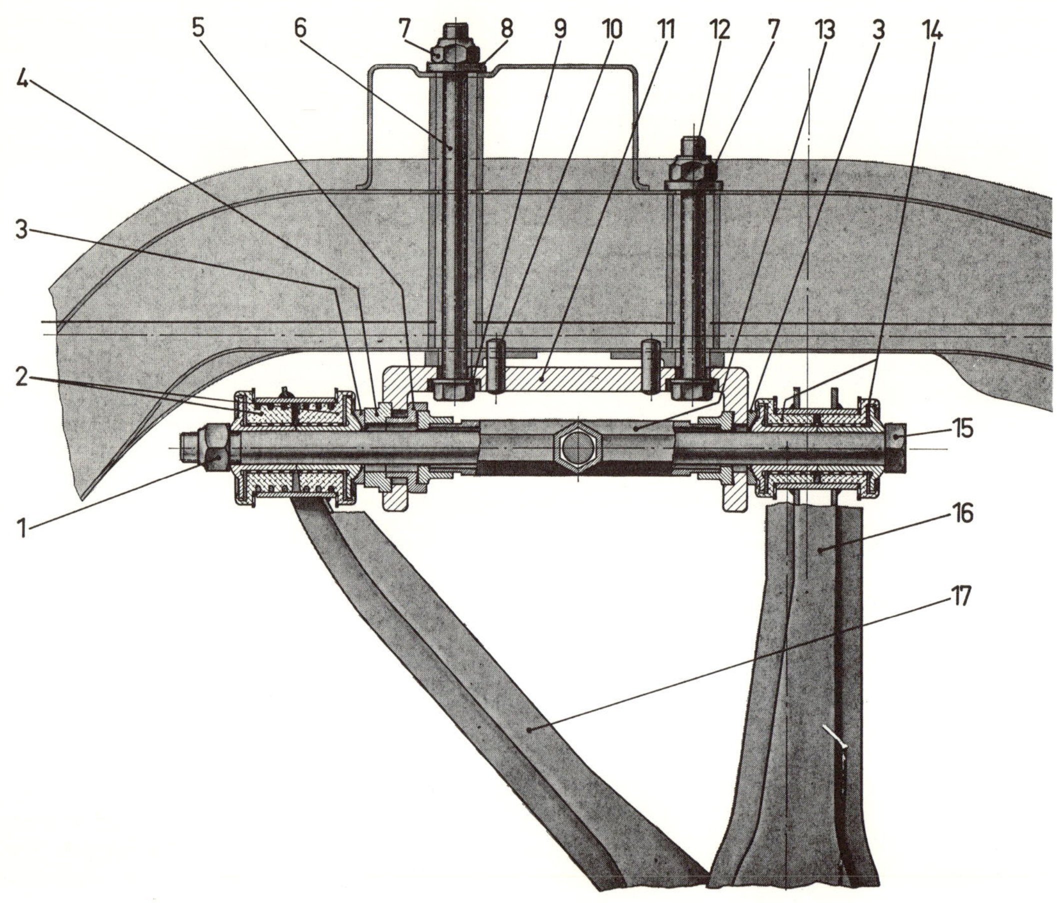

Overhead view of the Super 90 upper control arm

1. Lock nut
2. Upper bearing
3. Ball cup
4. Eccentric for caster adjustment
5. Guide
6. Hex head screw
7. Lock nut
8. Washer
9. Washer
10. Key pin
11. Mounting bracket
12. Hex head screw
13. Adjustment tube for camber adjustment
14. Upper control arm bearing for wishbone
15. Set screw
16. Upper control arm, left/right
17. Upper control arm support, left/right

Fastener	*Torque (ft lbs)*
Steering knuckle mounting bolt	34
Control arm to body	14–18

6. Check the wheel alignment.

LOWER CONTROL ARM

Removal and Installation

SUPER 90

1. Disconnect the steering knuckle as described in Steps 1–5 of "Driveshaft Removal and Installation" in Chapter Six.
2. Remove the stabilizer bar.
3. Detach the bottom of the shock absorber. This is easier if the spring load is temporarily taken off the lower control arm by prying upward. Let the suspension hang free after this is done.
4. Loosen the bolt at the front of the torsion bar until only 4–5 threads are still engaged. This can be seen by lifting the floor covering above the crossmember.
5. Remove the bolt which holds the two parts of the control arm together.
6. Remove the bolt at the front of the torsion bar.
7. Pull the front of the control arm off the front of the torsion bar after unbolting the bearing.
8. Unbolt the rear bearing and pull the rear of the control arm off to the front.

9. Reverse the procedure for installation. Torques are:

Fastener	*Torque (ft lbs)*
Shock absorber lower mount	34
Front control arm bearing	18
Control arm connecting bolt	26
Torsion bar front bolt	22
Torsion bar front bolt locknut	29
Rear control arm bearing	18
Stabilizer bar ends	26

10. Check the wheel alignment.

Super 90 lower control arm

a Torsion bar front bolt locknut
b Torsion bar front bolt
c Reinforcement bracket
d Torsion bar
e Control arm connecting bolt
f Front control arm bearing

100, 100 LS, 100 GL

1. Raise the vehicle and let the suspension hang free. Remove the wheels.
2. Remove the stabilizer bar. It may be necessary to move the exhaust pipe.
3. Support the lower control arm. Remove the lower control arm to steering knuckle bolt. Let the arm down to pull the joint loose from the steering knuckle.
4. Unbolt the bearing bolts and remove the control arm.
5. Reverse the procedure for installation. Torques are:

Fastener	*Torque (ft lbs)*
Stabilizer	14–18
Steering knuckle mounting bolt	34
Control arm pivot bearings, front	26–34
Control arm pivot bearings, rear	14–18

6. Check the wheel alignment.

ADJUSTMENTS

Ride Height

Super 90

Rear ride height is not readily adjustable. Front ride height is measured from the floor to the underside of the lower control arm inner bearing. With standard size tires it should be 6.9–8.3 in. for the sedan and 6.2–7.6 in. for the station wagon. The car should be bounced and settled before making the measurement. To adjust the ride height turn the rear torsion bar adjusting bolt. The measurements on both sides should be alike, or different by no more than 0.4 in.

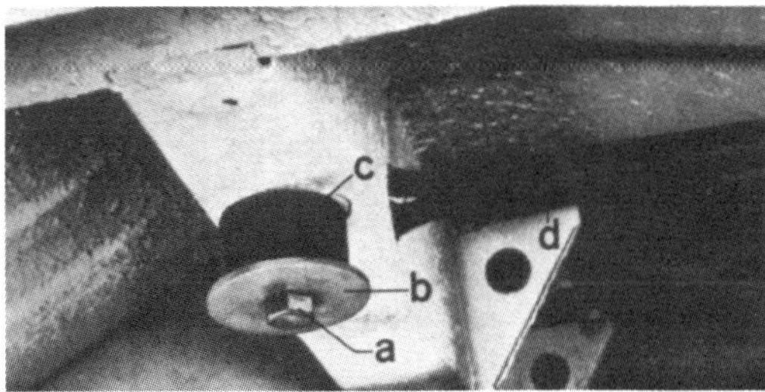

To adjust Super 90 ride height, the torsion bar adjusting bolt (a) must be turned

b Washer
c Rubber block
d Torsion bar

100, 100 LS, 100 GL

The suspension strut units must be removed and disassembled and new springs or spacers installed to adjust ride height on these models. It is not recommended that the strut unit be disassembled unless the necessary special tools to do this safely are available. The proper front ride height with standard size tires is 8.2–8.7 in., measured from the floor to the 0.32 in. diameter hole in the front bearing shell of the lower control arm inner pivot. The measurements on both sides should be alike, or different by no more than 0.3 in. The car should be bounced and settled before making the measurement. Rear ride height is not readily adjustable.

100, 100 LS, and 100 GL ride height is adjusted by inserting spacers (D) on the strut unit (A). (S) is the special strut compressor

WHEEL ALIGNMENT

Before checking wheel alignment, tire pressures should be brought up to specifications and the front ride height checked. The car should be bounced and settled before each alignment check or adjustment. The adjustments should be made in this order: caster, camber, toe-out.

Caster

Caster is the backward or forward tilt (from vertical) of the steering knuckle centerline at the top and it is measured in degrees. A steering knuckle centerline tilted backward at the top has positive (+) caster, while one tilted forward has negative (−) caster.

NOTE: *This adjustment cannot be made accurately without special alignment equipment.*

SUPER 90

1. Loosen the front nut on the upper control arm inner pivot bolt.
2. Using a thin wrench in front of the upper control arm mounting bracket, adjust the caster angle.
3. Leave the nut loose for the camber adjustment. Otherwise, tighten it to 54 ft lbs while holding the bolt head.

Super 90 caster adjustment is made by loosening nut (b) and turning eccentric (a) with a thin wrench, SW32

100, 100 LS, 100 GL

1. Loosen the large locknut at the bottom of the outer end of the lower control arm.
2. Turn the eccentric bolt, which passes through the locknut, to adjust caster.

100, 100 LS, and 100 GL caster and camber adjustment points

a Camber adjustment
b Nut
c Bolt
d Locknut
e Caster adjustment

Camber

Camber is the inward or outward tilt, measured in degrees, of the wheel at the top. A wheel tilted outward at the top has positive (+) camber. A wheel tilted inward has negative (−) camber.

NOTE: *This adjustment cannot be made accurately without special alignment equipment.*

SUPER 90

1. Loosen the front nut on the upper control arm inner pivot bolt.
2. Turn the adjustment tube in the center of the upper control arm mounting bracket to adjust camber.
3. Hold the bolt head and tighten the nut to 54 ft lbs.

Super 90 camber adjustment is made by loosening nut (b) and turning the adjustment tube (a) with a wrench, SW19

100, 100 LS, 100 GL

1. Loosen the nut (on the top) on the bolt that passes through the outer end of the lower control arm.
2. Loosen the bolt (on the bottom) inboard of the nut loosened in Step 1.
3. Adjust camber by turning the large nut on top of the bolt loosened in Step 2.
4. Tighten the bolt and nut to 32 ft lbs.

Toe-Out

Audi front wheels are set with a slight toe-out, rather than toe-in as on conventional cars. Most front-wheel drive vehicles are set with toe-out to counteract the tendency of the driving wheels to toe-in excessively. Toe-out is the amount, measured in inches, that the wheels are closer together at the rear than at the front. Toe-out is checked with the wheels straight ahead.

NOTE: *This adjustment can be made accurately without special alignment equipment.*

1. Toe-out can be determined by measuring and comparing the distance between the center of the tire tread, front and rear, or by measuring and comparing the distance between the inside edges of the wheel rims, front and rear. If the wheel rims are used as the basis of measurement, the car should be rolled forward slightly and a second set of measurements taken. This avoids any error induced by bent wheels. If at all possible a toe-in gauge should be used; it will give a much more accurate measurement.
2. Toe-out is adjusted at the steering tie-rods at either end of the steering rack. Loosen the clamp. Loosen the clip for the rubber boot at the end of the rack and slide the boot back.

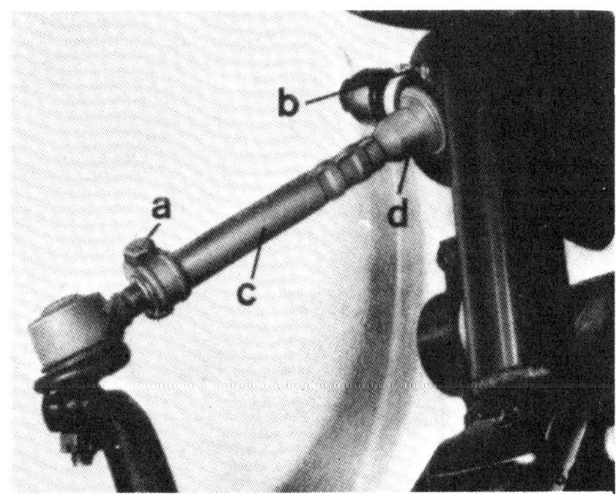

Toe-out is adjusted by loosening nut (a) on each steering tie-rod (c) and pushing back the rubber boot and clamp (b) in order to use a wrench on the flats (d)

Wheel Alignment

	CASTER		*CAMBER*			*WHEEL PIVOT RATIO (deg)*	
Model	*Range (deg)*	*Pref Setting (deg)*	*Range (deg)*	*Pref Setting (deg)*	*Toe-Out (in.)*	*Inner Wheel*	*Outer Wheel*
Super 90	0°10′N–0°30′P	0°10′P	0°5′N–0°35′P	0°15′P	0.00–0.08	20	18°50′–19°30′
100, 100 LS, 100 GL	0°14′N–0°26′P	0°6′P	0°9′N–0°31′P	0°11′P	0.00–0.08	20	18°30′–19°30′

N—Negative
P—Positive

3. Turn both rods to lengthen or shorten them an equal amount. If the tie-rods are not adjusted equally, the steering wheel will be crooked and the turning arcs of the front wheels will be changed.

4. Tighten the clamps and replace the boots.

Steering

Audi uses rack and pinion type steering. The steering geometry is designed to give a variable ratio effect, giving faster steering response as the steering wheel is turned toward either right or left lock. The steering column and linkage is arranged so as to break away and telescope safely in an accident, rather than penetrating into the passenger compartment. No service operations involving removal or disassembly of the steering column are given here. It is recommended that such critical and delicate operations be entrusted to qualified service personnel.

STEERING WHEEL

Removal and Installation

1. Center the wheel.

2. Pry off the wheel pad (horn button). The Super 90 has two small holes in the back of the wheel. A small screwdriver may be inserted to push the pad off.

3. Unbolt and remove the wheel. A steering wheel puller should not be necessary.

4. On installation, torque the bolt to 36 ft lbs. Do not pound on the wheel, as the collapsible column may be damaged.

Turn Signal and Headlight Dimmer Switch Replacement

1. Remove the steering wheel.

2. Disconnect the battery ground cable.

3. Remove the wire from the horn contact ring. Remove the two screws and the horn contact ring.

4. Remove the screws which hold the column casing at the top and just below the instrument panel. The Super 90 has an additional screw in the top edge of the casing. It may be necessary, for access, to remove the padding from the underside of the instrument panel.

5. Remove the casing. Be careful to note the arrangement of any springs and washers removed from the top of the column.

6. The switch may now be disconnected, unscrewed, and removed. The wires are color coded for ease of replacement.

IGNITION AND STEERING LOCK SWITCH

Removal and Installation

To perform this operation, proceed with Steps 1–5 of "Turn Signal and Headlight Dimmer Switch Replacement." The lock switch is clamped to the steering column with special bolts whose heads shear off on installation. These must be drilled out in order to remove the switch. When replacing the unit, make sure that the lock tang is aligned with the slot in the steering column.

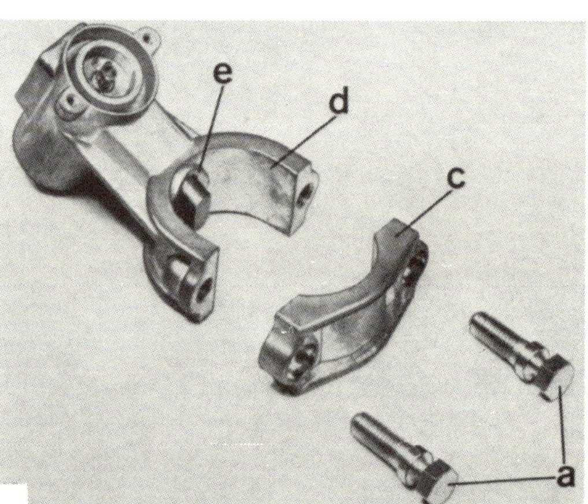

The ignition and steering lock switch is held in place by two bolts (a) whose heads shear on installation to deter theft

c Lower housing
d Upper housing
e Steering lock tang

STEERING GEAR

Removal and Installation

SUPER 90

1. Point the front wheels straight ahead. Loosen the bolt and open the clamp at the bottom of the steering column, inside the car.

2. Remove the four bolts and slide up the plate at the base of the steering column.

3. Bend open the lockplate and remove the coupling bolts.

4. Disconnect the ends of the steering tie-rods by removing the cotter pins and nuts and pressing out the tie-rod ends. A small puller or press is required to free the tie-rod ends.
5. Unbolt the support brackets from below.
6. Pry the brackets loose from inside the engine compartment.
7. Pull the steering gear out to the left, after turning the coupling down.
8. On installation, center the steering gear and the steering wheel. Torques are:

Fastener	*Torque (ft lbs)*
Coupling bolts	11–15
Steering gear bracket bolts	13
Tie-rod ends	26

100, 100 LS, 100 GL

1. Point the front wheels straight ahead. Disconnect the steering column from the firewall.
2. Disconnect the steering shaft from the steering gear.
3. Disconnect the ends of the steering tie-rods from the steering knuckles by removing the cotter pins and nuts and pressing out the tie-rod ends. A small puller or press is required to free the tie-rod ends.
4. Unbolt the steering gear from the firewall. Slide the unit toward the right and pull it up and out through the engine compartment.
5. On installation, center the steering gear and the steering wheel. Torques are:

Fastener	*Torque (ft lbs)*
Steering gear to firewall	25
Tie-rod ends	26
Steering shaft to steering gear	18
Steering column to firewall	18

STEERING LINKAGE

Tie-Rod Removal and Installation

1. Jack up the car and remove the wheel.
2. Disconnect the end of the steering tie-rod from the steering knuckle by removing the cotter pin and nut and pressing out the tie-rod end. A small puller or press is required to free the tie-rod end.
3. The steering gear boots can be replaced with no further disassembly at this point.
4. Loosen the clamp and slide the rubber boot as far back as possible.
5. Turn the steering all the way to the side being worked on. Do not force it against the stops.
6. Bend open the lockplate behind the knurled cylinder on the tie-rod. Unscrew the tie rod.

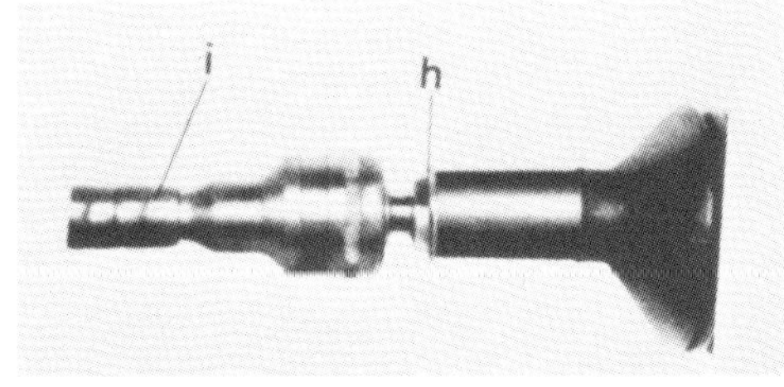

Nut (h) is loosened to remove the tie-rod (i) from the steering gear

7. Reverse the procedure for installation. Adjust the new tie-rod to the same length as the old one. Torque the tie-rod to 51 ft lbs, then set the lockplate. Tie-rod outer end torque is 26 ft lbs.
8. Check the toe-out.

Chapter Eight

Brakes

Brake System

All models have dual circuit hydraulic brakes with front disc brakes and rear drum brakes. A vacuum operated power assist is standard equipment. On the 100, 100 LS, and 100 GL, some 1972, and all 1973, models have cooling air directed to the brake discs from the electric radiator fan. The fan is switched on by a thermal switch in the right brake caliper. 1973 models also have a pad lining wear indicator light.

ADJUSTMENT

The front disc brakes are self-adjusting. The rear drum brakes must be adjusted periodically, or whenever free travel is one third or more of the total pedal travel.

1. Raise the rear of the car. Do not place a jack under the rear axle tube.
2. Block the front wheels and release the parking brake. Step on the brake pedal hard to center the linings.
3. Turn the front adjusting nut on the brake backing plate until the wheel can't be rotated forward by hand.
4. Loosen the adjusting nut until the wheel can be turned freely without drag.
5. Repeat Steps 3 and 4 for the rear adjusting nut.

When adjusting the rear brakes, turn the adjusting nuts (A) toward (a) to tighten and (b) to loosen

6. Repeat Steps 3, 4, and 5 for the other rear wheel.
7. Step on the brake pedal hard, release it and make sure that the wheels still rotate without drag.

Hydraulic System

MASTER CYLINDER

Removal and Installation

1. Have an assistant hold the brake pedal down about 1½ in. Disconnect the brake line nearest the firewall.
2. Hold a container under the fitting

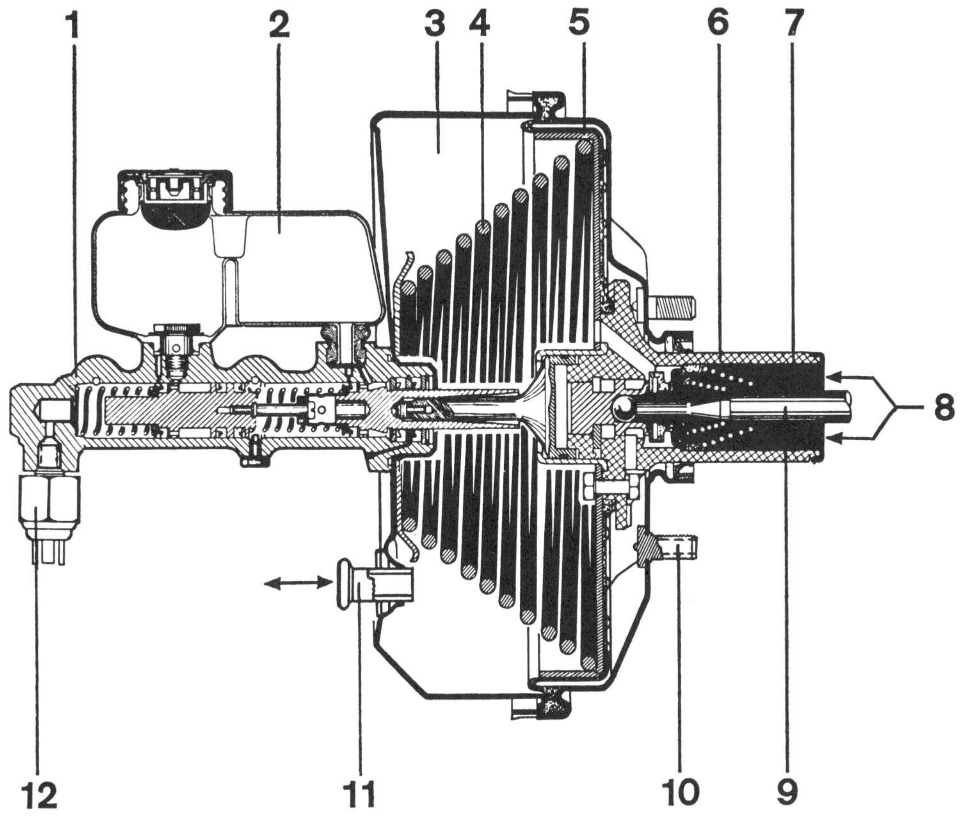

Cross section of brake master cylinder and vacuum brake booster

1. Master cylinder
2. Brake fluid container
3. Vacuum cylinder
4. Spring
5. Diaphragm
6. Timing housing
7. Filter
8. Air intake
9. Pressure rod
10. Mounting bolts
11. Vacuum connection
12. Brake light switch

disconnected in Step 1 and have the assistant release the pedal. The contents of the reservoir will drain into the container. Discard the used fluid.

3. Disconnect the other brake line.

4. Disconnect the stoplight switch wiring from the master cylinder.

5. Unbolt and remove the master cylinder from the power brake unit. Be careful not to lose the sealing ring between the two units.

6. Installation is the reverse of removal. Master cylinder bolt torque is 17 ft lbs. Fill and bleed the system. There should be a pedal free-play of 0.2 in. It can be adjusted on the linkage, inside the car.

Overhaul

If the master cylinder leaks externally, or if the pedal sinks while being held down, the master cylinder is worn. It must be removed and rebuilt or replaced.

1. Clean the outside of the master cylinder.

2. Remove the brake fluid reservoir, unscrew the brake light switch, remove the snap-ring and dismantle the unit. It will be necessary to partially unscrew the stop screw to remove the secondary piston.

3. All parts must be thoroughly cleaned in alcohol or clean brake fluid. Dry the parts with compressed air and be sure that the compensating port is not plugged.

4. Visually inspect all components. Replace any that are suspect. Rubber boots and reservoir plugs should always be replaced.

5. On assembly, lubricate all internal metal parts with clean brake fluid.

6. Assemble and install the piston.

7. Check the pistons for ease of operation. If they do not readily return to the stop screw or disc, dismantle the master cylinder and lightly polish the cylinder

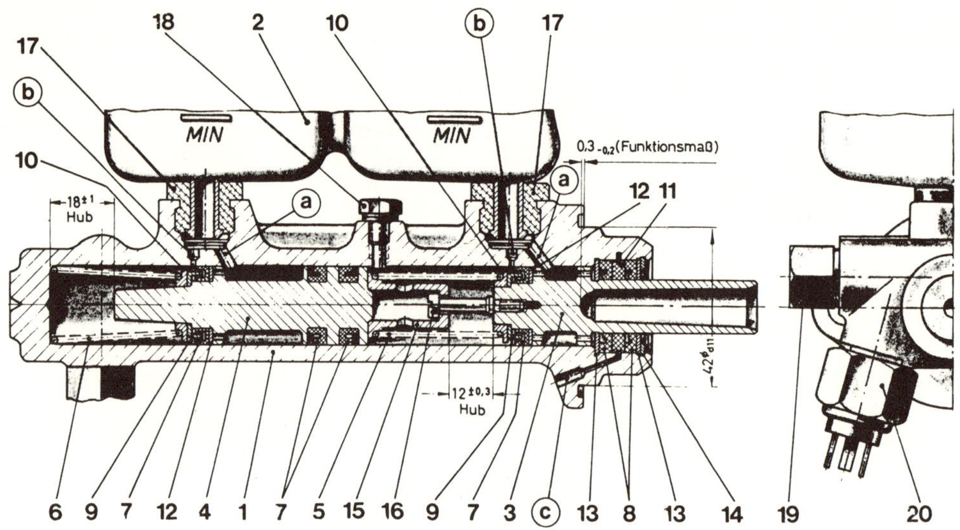

Cross section of brake master cylinder

1. Master cylinder
2. Brake fluid container
3. Primary piston
4. Secondary piston
5. Primary spring
6. Secondary spring
7. Primary boot
8. Secondary boot
9. Support ring
10. Spring retainer
11. Intermediate ring
12. Filler disc
13. Stop disc
14. Snap-ring
15. Stop sleeve
16. Inner stop screw
17. Container plug
18. Outer stop screw
19. Pressure valve
20. Brake light switch

a Filling bore
b Compensation bore
c Air compensating bore

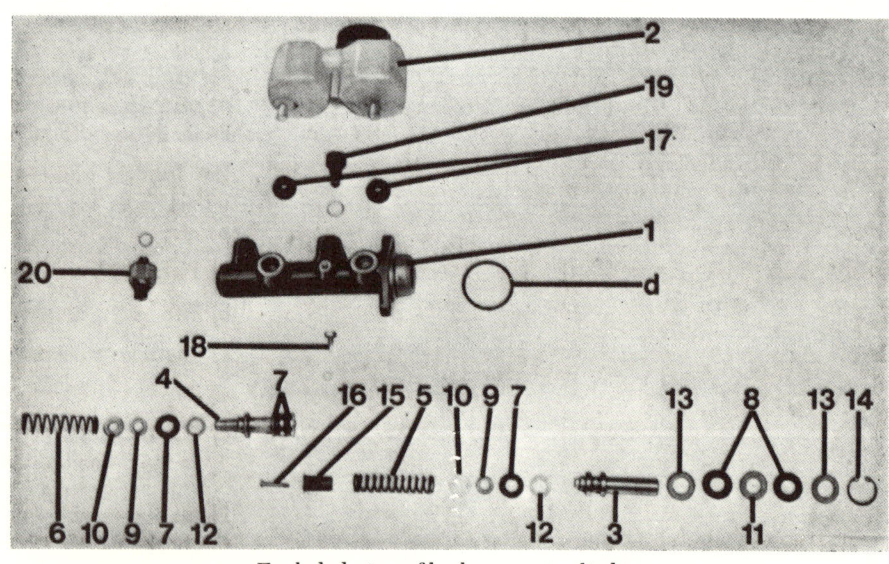

Exploded view of brake master cylinder

1. Master cylinder
2. Brake fluid container
3. Primary piston
4. Secondary piston
5. Primary spring
6. Secondary spring
7. Primary boot
8. Secondary boot
9. Support ring
10. Spring retainer
11. Intermediate ring
12. Filler disc
13. Stop disc
14. Snap-ring
15. Stop sleeve
16. Inner stop screw
17. Container plug
18. Outer stop screw
19. Pressure valve
20. Brake light switch

d Ring

surface. Do this by revolving the cylinder around a piece of crocus cloth held on your finger. Do not polish in a lengthwise direction. Clean the cylinder again after polishing.

8. Be sure that the boots are installed correctly and not damaged.

9. The remainder of the assembly procedure is the reverse of disassembly. Grease should not be used on the pushrod, as it will swell the rubber boots.

SYSTEM BLEEDING

The hydraulic system must be bled whenever the pedal feels spongy which indicates that compressible air has entered the system. The system must also be bled whenever any component has been disconnected or there has been a leak.

1. Clean off the top of the master cylinder. Make sure that the fluid level is between the marks.

2. Attach a hose to the bleeder valve at the first wheel to be bled. A rubber cap may have to be removed first. Mechanics usually start at the wheel farthest from the master cylinder and work closer. Pour a few inches of brake fluid into a clear container and stick the end of the tube below the surface.

NOTE: *The tube and container of brake fluid are not absolutely necessary, but this is a very sloppy job without them.*

3. Open the bleeder valve about ½ turn. Have an assistant slowly depress the pedal. Close the valve just before the pedal reaches the end of its travel. Have the assistant let the pedal back up.

4. Check the fluid level. If the reservoir runs low enough to allow air to enter, the procedure will have to be restarted.

5. Repeat Step 3 until no more bubbles come out of the hose.

6. Repeat the bleeding operation, Steps 3–5, at the other three wheels. Some cars with automatic transmission have three bleeder screws on each front brake caliper. On these cars, the bleeding sequence should be: upper right front, upper left front, lower outer right front, lower inner right front, lower outer left front, lower inner left front, left rear, and right rear.

7. Check the master cylinder level again.

8. If repeated bleeding has no effect, there is an air leak, probably internally in the master cylinder or in one of the wheel cylinders.

Front Disc Brakes

All models use the same type of two piston front disc brakes, except for some 1972 automatic transmission models which use four piston brakes. These four piston units can easily be identified by the presence of three bleeder screws instead of the usual one. Procedures for the two piston brakes may be adapted to the four piston units.

DISC BRAKE PADS

Removal and Installation

Although the four front brake pads may wear unevenly, they may not be switched around to equalize wear. They must always be replaced in sets of four. Minimum permissible friction pad thickness is 0.08 in.

NOTE: *This is the factory recommendation. State inspection laws may not allow this much wear.*

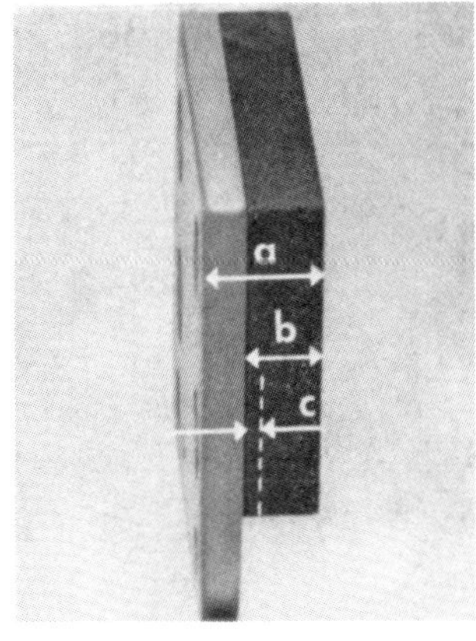

(a) is the thickness of the new pad and the backplate, (b) is the thickness of the new pad, and (c) is the minimum safe pad thickness, 0.08 in.

1. Pull out the lock clips and remove the retaining pins. While doing this, hold the cross springs in place.

2. Remove the cross springs and pull the pads from the calipers. On 1973 models, disconnect the pad lining wear indicator light leads.

3. To install new pads, drain off some of the brake fluid from the master cylinder,

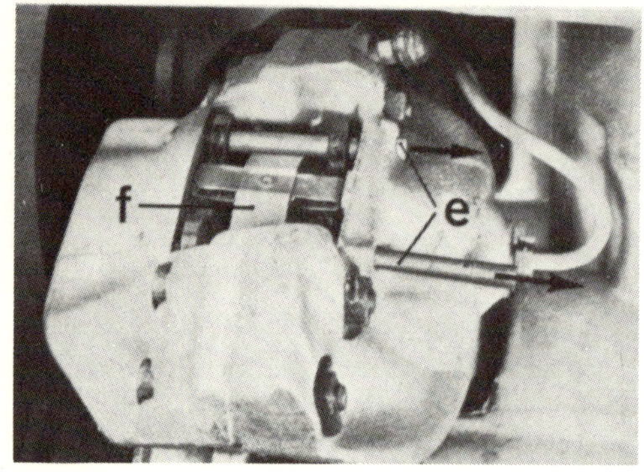

(e) is the pad retaining pins and (f) is the cross spring

since pressing the pistons back to install the pads will cause the brake fluid level to rise and probably overflow.

NOTE: *Brake fluid will destroy paint very quickly.*

4. Press the pistons completely into the cylinder and check their alignment. They should be at an angle of 20°; if not they must be rotated. A gauge can be made up to check this.

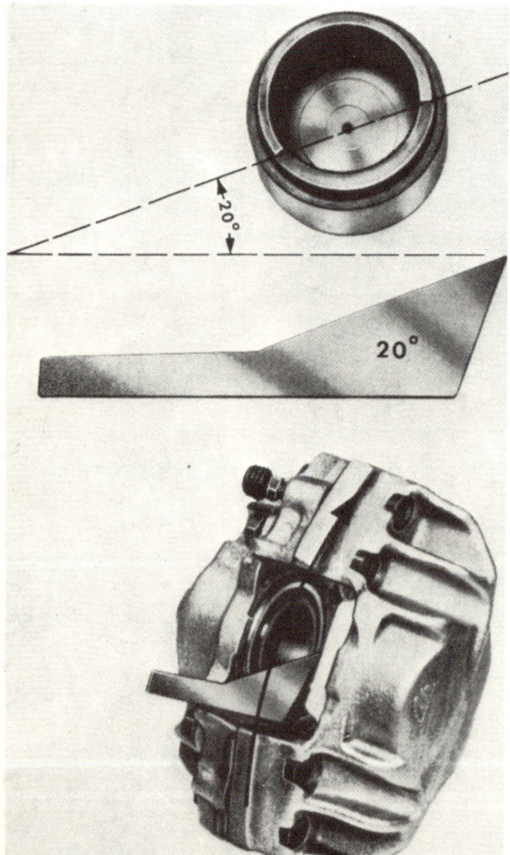

The pistons must be aligned at 20° in the caliper

5. Slide the pads into the caliper recess.
6. Replace the retaining spring and install the cross springs, retaining pins, and new lock clips.
7. Pump the brakes several times to position the pads.
8. Test the brakes, but do not make any panic stops. No hard stops should be made for approximately 100 miles if possible.

DISC BRAKE CALIPERS

Removal and Installation

The calipers are bolted to the transaxle housing.

Super 90

1. To remove the right caliper, disconnect and remove the battery.
2. Unscrew the upper caliper mounting nut.
3. Depress the brake pedal approximately 1½ in. and secure it in order to block the compensating port in the master cylinder and prevent fluid from running out.
4. Disconnect the brake line.
5. Remove the lower caliper mounting nut.
6. Installation is the reverse of removal. Note the following: The left and right calipers must not be interchanged, and should always be installed with the bleeder valve up. Install the calipers without the pads (install them later). Always use new lockwashers. Torque the mounting nuts to 69 ft lbs. Refill the master cylinder reservoir and bleed the system. Recheck the fluid level and test the brakes.

100, 100 LS, 100 GL

The caliper and brake disc must be removed together.

1. The front exhaust pipe must be removed for access to the right side.
2. Depress the brake pedal about 1½ in. and secure it there so that the master cylinder compensating port is closed. This prevents fluid from running out.
3. Remove the pads.
4. Disconnect the brake line at the caliper and plug the opening. On 1972–73 models, disconnect the electrical lead to the right caliper.
5. Remove the caliper nuts. Unbolt the driveshaft flange and slide it back and upward.

The caliper mounting nuts (a) on the 100, 100 LS, and 100 GL

6. Remove the disc and caliper, noting the insulating washer between the flange and disc.

7. Installation is the reverse of removal. Make sure that the calipers are not interchanged. On calipers with single bleeder screws, the screw must be at the top. On calipers with three bleeder screws, there should be one at the top. Torque the caliper mounting nuts to 69–76 ft lbs and the driveshaft flange bolts to 70–78 ft lbs. Refill the master cylinder reservoir and bleed the system. Recheck the fluid level and test the brakes.

Overhaul

NOTE: *The two halves of the caliper must not be separated, nor may the connecting bolts be loosened.*

1. Remove the pads.
2. Plug the brake line connection. Clean off the outside of the caliper unit, using hot water and a non-alkaline detergent.
3. Pry off the clamping ring from one cylinder, using a screwdriver.

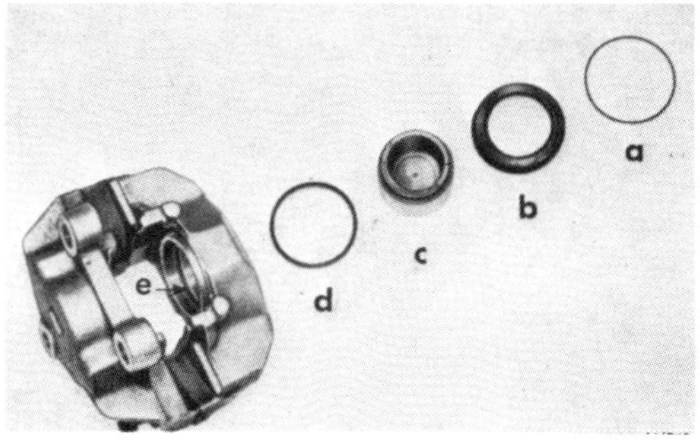

The caliper with one piston and cylinder assembly disassembled

a Clamping ring
b Cap
c Piston
d Seal
e Seal groove

4. Remove the cap from the same cylinder by hand.
5. Clamp an old pad in place on the cylinder opposite to the one being removed. Do not use a good pad; it will be ruined. Place a piece of wood across the center of the caliper to catch the piston. Apply air pressure to the brake line connection to force out the piston. Be careful, as the piston may be blown out of the caliper.

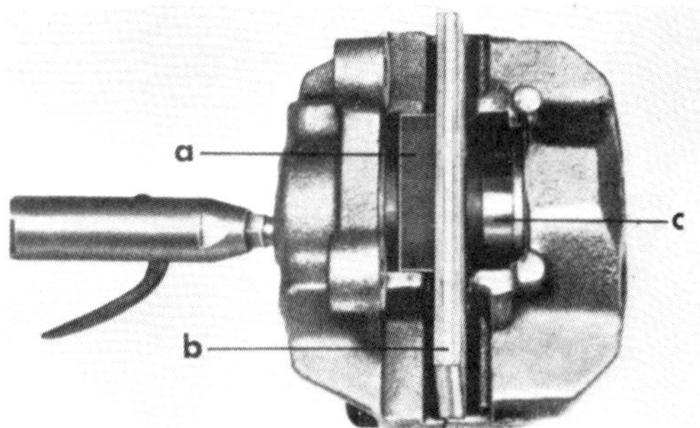

Air pressure is used to remove the piston (c) from the caliper. An old pad (a) and a piece of wood (b) are installed in the caliper

6. The seal can be removed from the cylinder groove with a plastic instrument. Do not use metal tools. Be extremely careful not to damage the cylinder finish.
7. The cylinder and the piston may not be resurfaced; they must be replaced when damaged. The piston and cylinder parts should be cleaned in alcohol.
8. Coat the cylinder and piston parts with clean brake fluid. Install the piston with a new seal, cap, and clamping ring. Make sure that the piston face is installed at a 20° angle, as discussed under "Brake Pad Replacement."
9. Steps 3–8 may now be repeated for the second piston.

BRAKE DISC

Removal and Installation

Super 90

1. Jack up the vehicle and remove the wheel.
2. Disconnect the steering knuckle from the upper wishbone. See "Upper Control Arm Removal and Installation" in Chapter Seven for details.
3. Unbolt the driveshaft flange and move it toward the outside.
4. Remove the disc downward, being careful not to drop it.

5. Installation is the reverse of removal. Torque the driveshaft flange bolts to 77 ft lbs.

100, 100 LS, 100 GL

Follow the procedure under "Caliper Removal and Installation." The caliper and disc must be removed together.

Inspection

Maximum permissible disc runout is 0.005 in. The disc may be reground but no more than 0.026 in. thickness may be removed from each side. Original disc thickness is 0.410 in. Maximum permissible thickness variation is 0.001 in.

FRONT WHEEL BEARINGS

Removal and Installation, Adjustment

Refer to "Driveshaft Disassembly" under "Transaxle" in chapter six for these procedures.

Rear Drum Brakes

BRAKE DRUMS

Removal and Installation

1. Jack up the car and remove the wheel. Do not use a jack under the rear axle tube. Release the parking brake.
2. Pry off the grease cap.
3. Remove the cotter pin and the nuts.
4. Pull off the brake drum by hand, making sure that the washer and roller bearing don't fall out. If the drum is held by the brakes, back off on the brake adjustment.
5. On reinstallation, tighten the nut to force the brake drum into place, then loosen it until there is 0.001–0.002 in. bearing play measured with a dial indicator.
6. Replace the castellated nut and install a new cotter pin.
7. Fill the grease cap with about 10 oz of wheel bearing grease.
8. Adjust the brakes if necessary.

BRAKE SHOES

Removal and Installation

1. Remove the brake drum.
2. Remove the big retaining spring at the bottom. Be careful it doesn't fly out.
3. Disconnect the parking brake cable and pull the shoes from the wheel cylinder.
4. Remove the shoes.
5. Reverse the procedure for installation, making sure that the front and rear shoes are not interchanged.

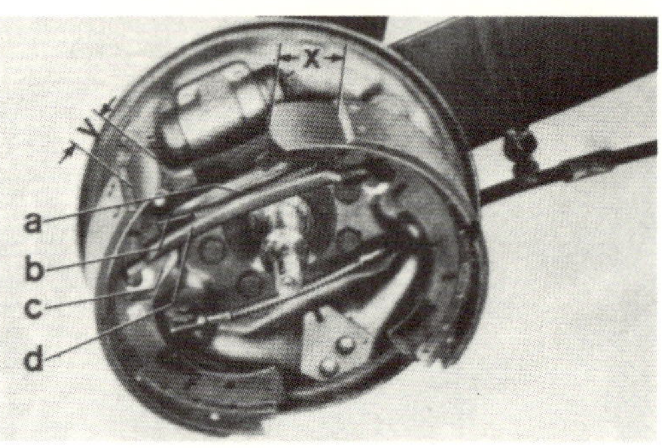

Details of the rear brakes with the bottom retaining spring removed. The measurement (x) for the front shoe is greater than (y) for the rear shoe

a Retaining clip
b Spring (long end at the rear)
c Handbrake lever
d Pressure rod

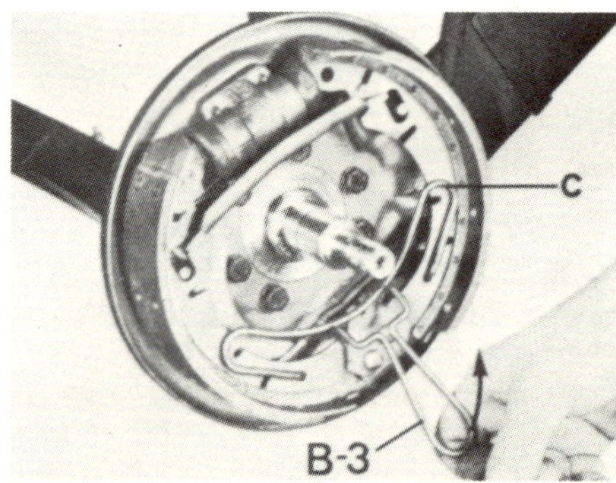

The bottom brake shoe retaining spring (c) is being replaced. Tool B-3 can be fabricated

WHEEL CYLINDERS

Removal and Installation

1. Remove the brake shoes.
2. Depress the brake pedal about 1.5 in. to block the master cylinder compensating port and prevent leakage. Secure the pedal in this position.
3. Disconnect the brake line and plug the opening.
4. Remove the two mounting screws from the backing plate.
5. Remove the cylinder.
6. Reverse the procedure for installation.

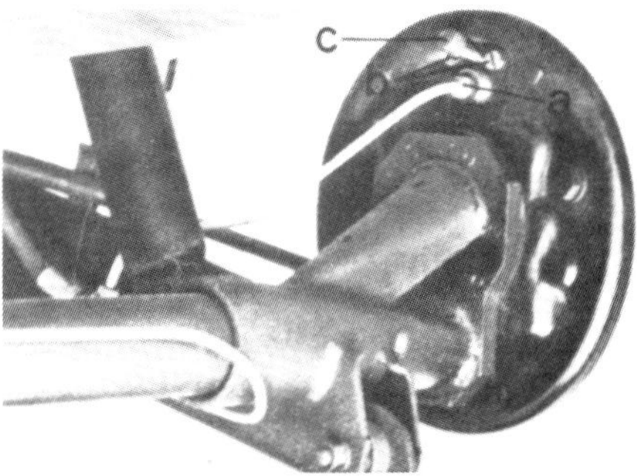

Wheel cylinder attachment details—(a) is the brake line fitting (b) is the two cylinder mounting screws (c) is the bleeder screw fitted with a cap

Overhaul

1. Clean the outside of the cylinder, using alcohol or clean brake fluid.
2. Remove the rubber boots and disassemble the cylinder.
3. Clean all parts in alcohol.
4. Air dry all parts.
5. If there are any pits or roughness inside the cylinder, it must be replaced.
6. Replace the piston if it is scratched or damaged in any way.
7. Lubricate all internal parts with clean brake fluid and reassemble the cylinder. Replace all rubber parts.

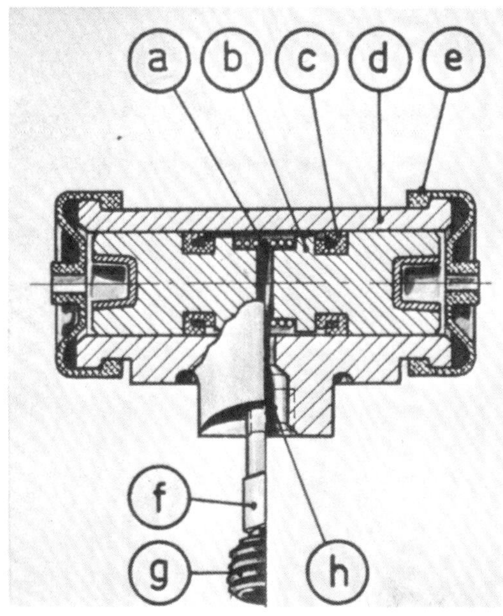

Cross-section of a rear wheel cylinder

a Spring
b Piston
c Grooved cup
d Cylinder
e Cap
f Bleeder valve
g Dust cap
h Brake line connection

8. Make sure the cylinders slide freely. If they do not, disassemble the cylinder and polish the inside of it lightly by revolving it around a piece of crocus cloth held by your finger. Do not polish the cylinder in a lengthwise direction. Clean the cylinder again after polishing. Air dry.
9. Replace the boots.
10. Replace the cylinder and tighten the bolts evenly. Bleed the system after it is reassembled.

REAR WHEEL BEARINGS

Removal and Installation, Adjustment

Refer to "Wheel Bearings and Stub Axle Removal and Installation" under "Rear Suspension" for these procedures.

Handbrake

ADJUSTMENT

The handbrake (parking brake) must be adjusted periodically to compensate for lining wear and cable stretching. The adjuster is at the cable junction, under the center of the car.

1. Block the front wheels. Raise and support the rear of the vehicle. Do not use a jack under the rear axle tube.
2. Pull the brake up to the first or second notch and put the transmission in Neutral.
3. If the wheels will not rotate freely, loosen the adjusting nut. Some early Super 90 models may have two wing nuts for ad-

Two-piece rear handbrake cable used on early Super 90—(a) indicates the two adjusting nuts

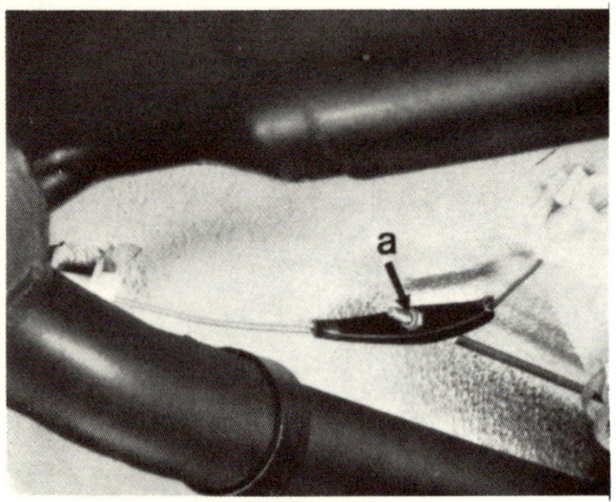

(a) indicates the adjusting point for one piece rear handbrake cables used on most models

justment; adjust them together for equal tension.

4. Tighten the adjusting nut until there is a light drag on the rear wheels.

5. Pull the handle up to the third or fourth notch; the wheels should lock.

6. Make sure that there is no drag when the handle is fully released.

CABLE

Removal and Installation

1. Jack up the rear of the car. Do not place a jack under the axle tube.

2. Block the front wheels and release the handbrake.

3. Remove the rear brake shoes.

4. Remove the cable adjusting nut(s) and detach the cable guides from the floor-pan.

5. Replace the cable and brake shoes. Check the parking brake adjustment.

Brake Specifications

(All measurements are given in in.)

Year	Model	Master Cylinder Bore	Rear Wheel Cylinder Piston Bore	Brake Disc or Drum Diameter		New Pad Lining Thickness	Minimum Safe Pad Lining Thickness
				Front Disc	Rear Drum		
1970–1972	Super 90	N.A.	0.625	11.02	7.87	0.39	0.08
1970–1972	100, 100 LS,	0.813	0.625	11.02①	7.87	0.39②	0.08
1973	100, 100 LS, 100 GL	0.874	0.688	11.5	7.87	0.49	0.08③

① 11.5 on later models with automatic transmission
② 0.41 on some later versions
③ Electrical wear indicators

Chapter Nine
Body

Doors

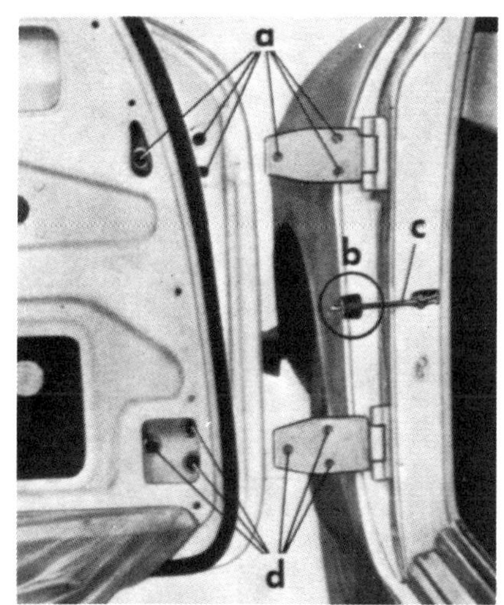

Super 90 door and hinge assembly

a Upper hinge bolts
b Cotter pin, washer, and rubber pad
c Door stay
d Lower hinge bolts

Removal and Installation

1. Remove the door panel.
2. Mark the position of the hinges on the door if it is to be reinstalled.
3. On the Super 90, detach the door stay from the door by reaching inside the door and removing the cotter pin, washer, and rubber pad.
4. On the 100, 100 LS, and 100 GL, detach the door stay from the body by prying off the snap-ring at the bottom and driving the pin out and upward.

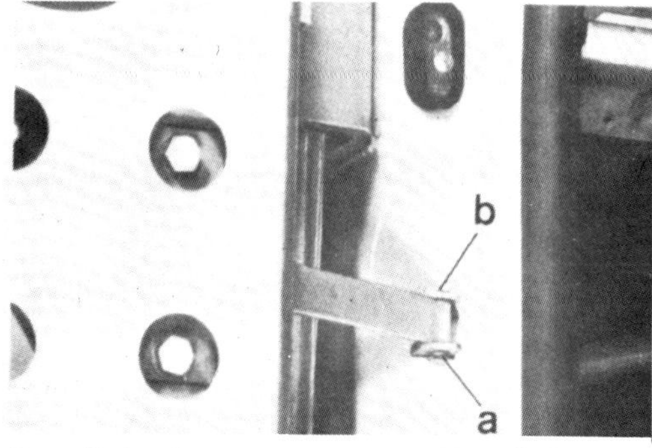

Pry off the door stay snap-ring (a) and drive the pin (b) out upward on the 100, 100 LS, and 100 GL

5. Support the door and remove the three bolts which hold the door to the hinge (two for rear doors).
6. Remove the door. The hinges may be unbolted from the body after removing the kick panel for access.
7. Reverse the procedure for installation.

DOOR PANELS

Removal and Installation

SUPER 90

1. Pry up the window crank covering and pull it off toward the pivot.

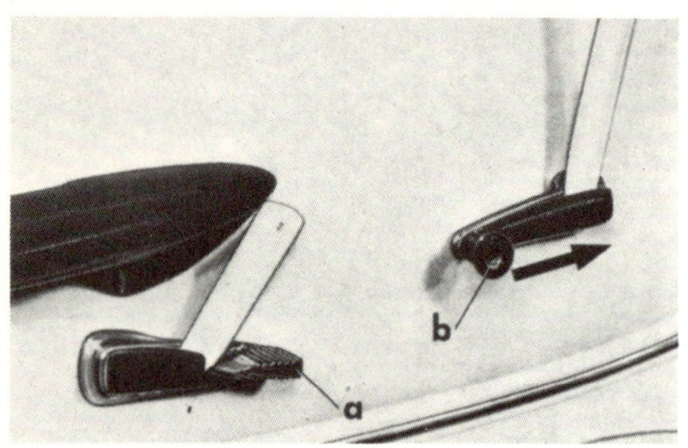

The covering on the window crank (b) is pried up and pulled off toward the arrow for access to the mounting screw. The covering on the door handle (a) must also be pried off

2. Pry off the inside door handle covering.
3. Remove the phillips head screw and the inside door handle. Remove the phillips head screw, the window crank, and the washers.
4. Unscrew and remove the armrest. Remove the vent window control by prying off the cap and unscrewing it. A hole is provided to aid in prying off the cap.

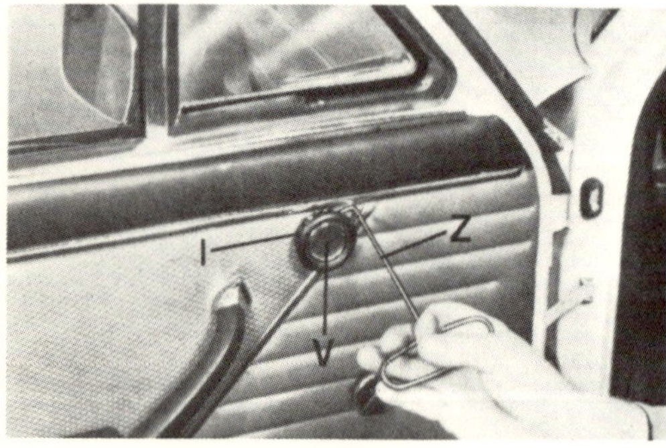

A hole is provided in the vent window knob (I) so that a hook (Z) can be used to remove the cap (V) for access to the mounting screw

5. Unscrew the door lock button.
6. Carefully pry off the door panel with a putty knife and remove it upward.
7. Remove the plastic sheeting from the door.
8. Reverse the procedure for installation, replacing the plastic sheeting.

100, 100 LS, 100 GL

1. On a front door, pry off the chrome cap at the front of the armrest. Unscrew and remove the armrest.

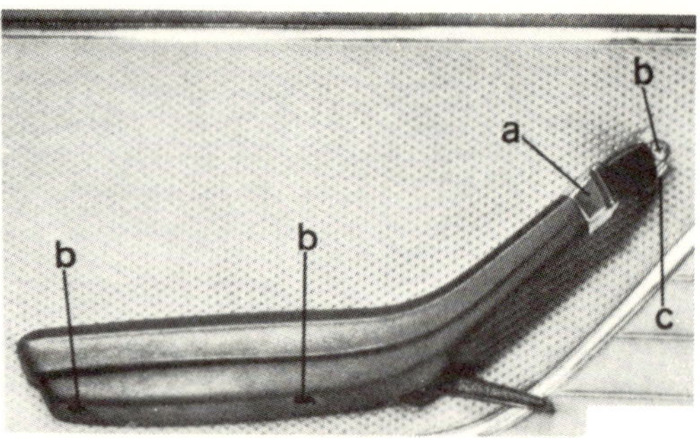

100, 100 LS, and 100 GL armrest details

a Chrome cap
b Phillips screws
c Mounting plate

2. On a rear door, unscrew and remove the armrest.
3. Unscrew and remove the inner door handle.
4. Pry the cover off the window crank, then unscrew and remove the crank. Remove the vent window control by prying off the cap and removing it. A hole is provided to aid in prying off the cap.
5. Carefully pry off the door panel with a putty knife and remove it.

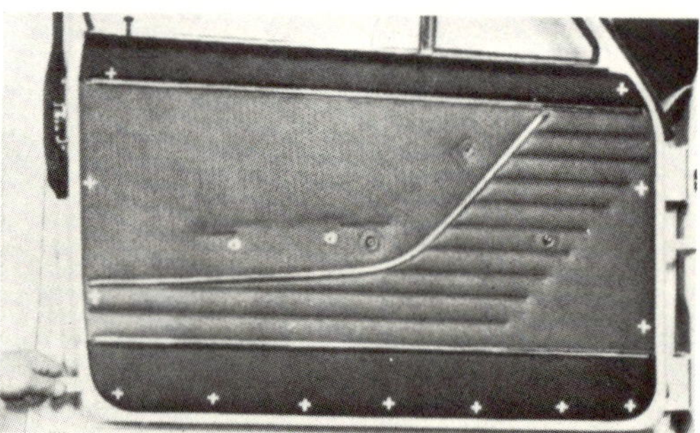

The crosses show the location of the door panel retaining clips

6. Remove the plastic sheeting from the door.
7. Reverse the procedure for installation, replacing the plastic sheeting.

DOOR WINDOWS

Removal and Installation

The window crank mechanism must be removed to remove the window glass.

SUPER 90

1. Remove the door panel.
2. Lower the window.
3. Remove the four bolts from around the window crank shaft.
4. Push the window up and tape it up.
5. Pull the crank mechanism to the rear and out.
6. Lower the window.
7. Pry back the rubber seal at the front and rear of the door in line with the bottom edge of the window opening. Remove the two trim nuts behind the seal, one at each end.
8. Pry out the chrome strip at the bottom of the outside of the window opening and slide the strip back about 0.08 in. to release it. Remove the strip. Turn the mounting clips for the strip 90° and remove them. Remove the rubber seal from the window slot in the window sill.
9. Remove the three mounting screws for the front window channel. One is under the rubber strip at the top of the door, another is inside at the window sill, and the third is inside the door. The window will have to be raised for access to the third screw.
10. If the car has opening vent windows (front door), pull the rubber seal for the vent window from the front window channel.

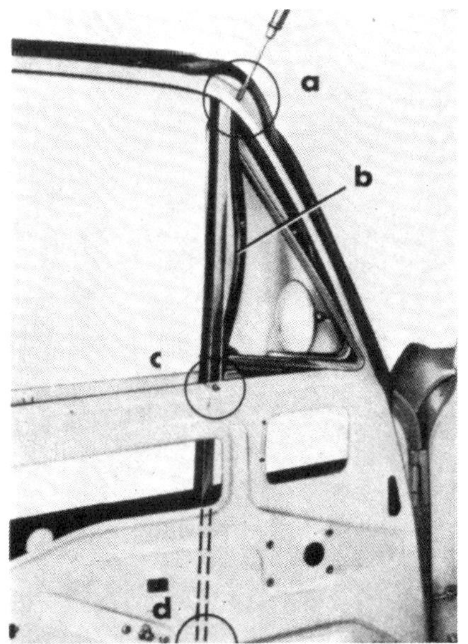

The Super 90 front window channel is retained by screws at (a), (c), and (d). (b) is the rubber seal for the vent window

11. Push the window nearly all the way up.
12. Press the channel down a bit, then pull it out through the window opening to the outside.
13. Pull the window up and out of the door.
14. Opening vent windows may be removed by removing the screw at the upper pivot (hidden behind the rubber molding at the top of the door) and the nuts at the lower pivot (accessible from inside).
15. Reverse the procedure for installation.

100, 100 LS, 100 GL

1. Remove the door panel.
2. Raise and tape up the window on four-door models. This should be done for either the front or rear door. Remove the four bolts from around the window crank shaft. Pull the crank mechanism arm out of the front of the guide rail at the bottom of the window. Remove the crank mechanism through the hole at the bottom of the door.

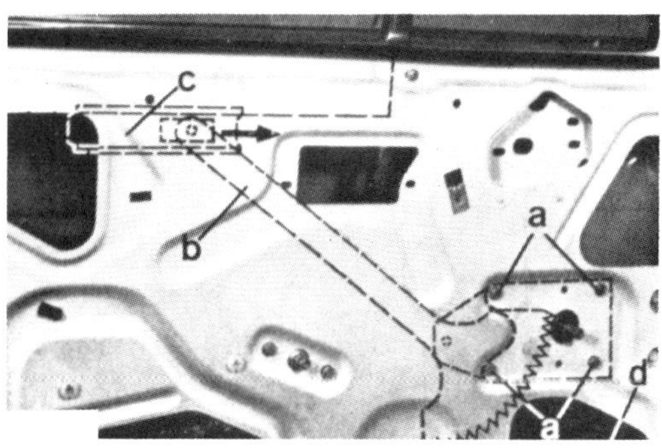

Window crank mechanism details on the 100, 100 LS, and 100 GL four-door models. (a) indicates the retaining bolts, (b) is the crank arm, (c) is the guide rail, and (d) is the access hole

3. On two-door models, lower the window. Remove the three bolts from around the window crank shaft. Pull the crank mechanism arm out of the rear of the guide rail at the bottom of the window. Raise the window and tape it in place. Remove the crank mechanism through the hole at the bottom of the door.
4. Unscrew the door lock button.
5. Lower the window.
6. Pry out the top of the seal in the front window channel. Remove the screw from behind the seal.
7. Remove the two screws which hold the lower part of the channel to the door.

Pull down the two slides that were held by the two screws just removed.

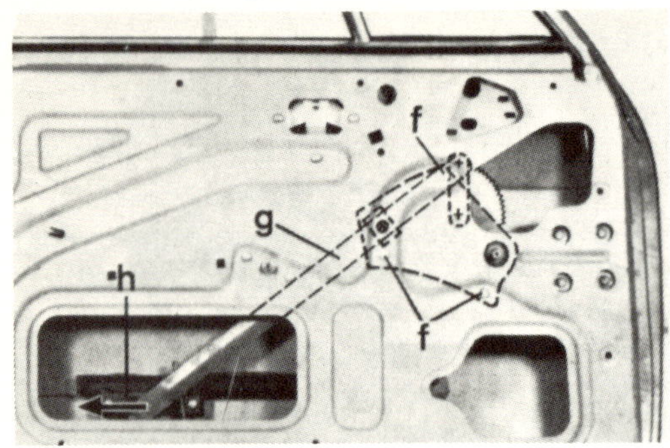

Window crank mechanism details on the 100, 100 LS, and 100 GL two-door models. (f) indicates the retaining bolts, (g) is the crank arm, and (h) is the guide rail.

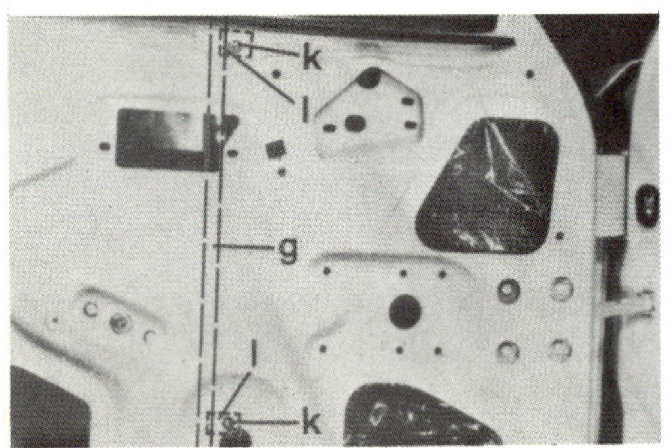

The 100, 100 LS, and 100 GL front window channel—(g) is retained by screws (k). (l) indicates the slides

8. Press the channel down a bit, then pull it out upward through the window opening to the outside.

9. Non-opening vent windows must now be pried out with the rubber frame. Opening vent windows can be removed, if necessary, by removing the screws which hold the upper pivot.

10. Remove the chrome strip inside the window sill by prying upward. Pry off the outer chrome strip.

11. On a two-door model, remove the two phillips screws which hold the cable to the window guide rail. Disconnect the cable inside the door.

12. Pull the window up and out of the door. Make note of the location of the guide rail before removing it from the window.

13. Reverse the procedure for installation, making sure that the guide rail is installed on the new window in the original location.

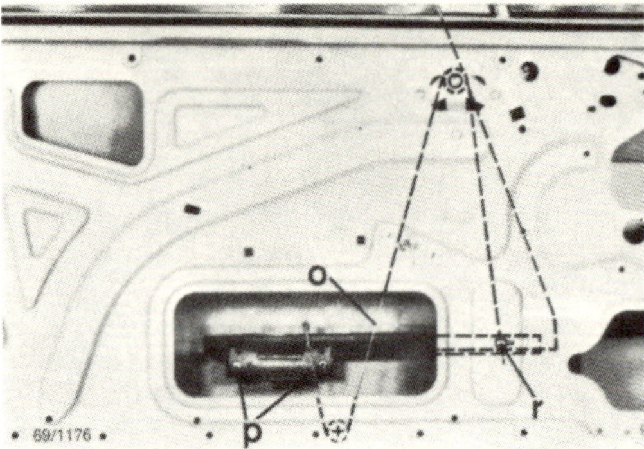

On two-door 100, 100 LS, and 100 GL models, the phillips screws (p) must be removed and the cable (o) disconnected at (r) before removing the window

SIDE WINDOWS

Side windows on two-door models can be removed by prying back the rubber seal on the inside and removing the four mounting screws for non-opening windows. Swing-out windows can be removed by removing the two screws behind the door post trim and the two at the rear latch. Removal of side (rear door) windows on four-door models is covered under "Door Windows."

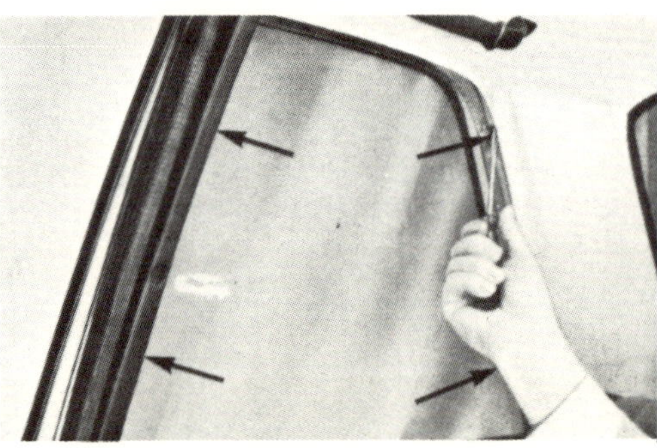

Location of the four screws which retain the non-opening side windows on two-door models

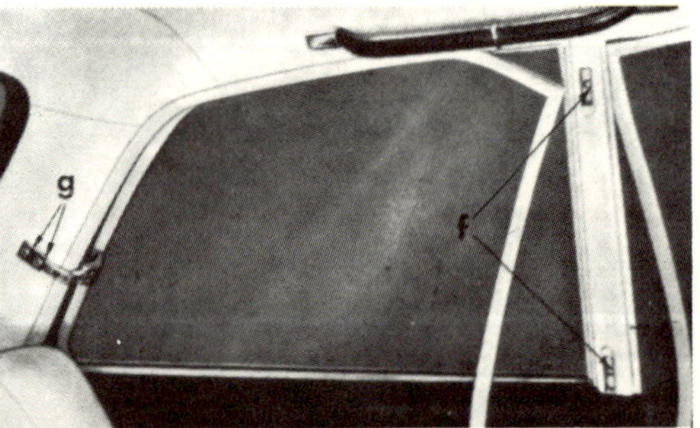

The screws which retain the opening side windows on two-door models are shown by (f) and (g)

LOCKS

The door locks are part of the door handles.

Removal and Installation

SUPER 90

1. Remove the door panel.
2. Close the window.
3. Remove the handle screw from the rear edge of the door. The front handle retaining nut may have to be removed from inside the door.

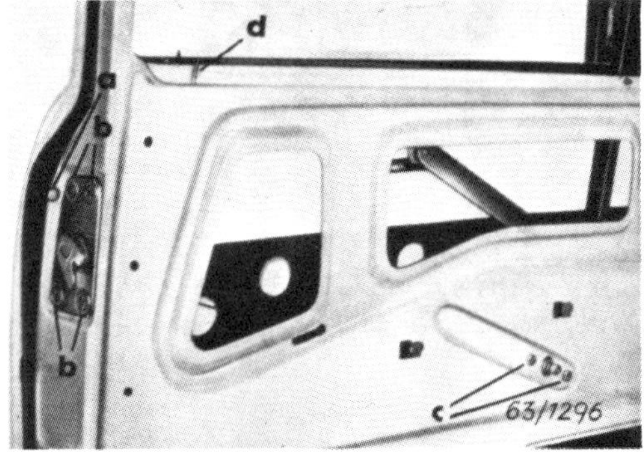

Super 90 door details

a Outside door handle screw
b Latch assembly bolts
c Door latch handle bolts
d Lock button

4. Drive the handle forward until it can be removed.
5. Remove the two bolts from around the inside door latch handle. Remove the four bolts from the latch assembly at the rear of the door.
6. Remove the entire mechanism from the door. Tilt the latch assembly slightly when removing to prevent jamming.
7. Reverse the procedure for installation, making sure that the lock button is in place and that the seals on the back of the handle are in place.

100, 100 LS, 100 GL

1. Remove the door panel.
2. Close the window.
3. Remove the handle screw from the rear of the door. It may be necessary to pull back the door gasket.
4. From inside the door, remove the nut which attaches the front of the handle.
5. Remove the handle.
6. On installation, make sure that the plastic seals are in place between the handle and the door.

Hood, Trunk, and Tailgate

Alignment

The hood and trunk can be aligned by loosening the hinge bolts in their slotted mounting holes and moving the hood or trunk lid as necessary. Most hoods have an adjustable rubber bumper to regulate height. The tailgate on the station wagon can be adjusted by loosening the hinge bolts in their slotted mounting holes and moving the tailgate on its hinges. The latch plate and latch striker at the bottom of the tailgate opening can be adjusted to prevent rattles. There also is an adjustable bumper at each side.

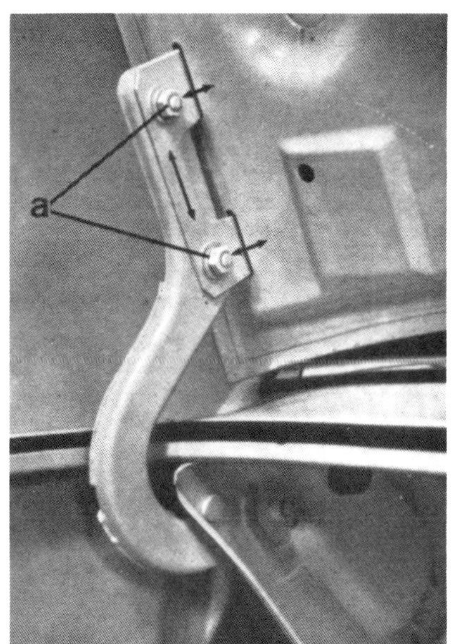

After loosening the trunk hinge bolts (a) the lid alignment can be adjusted

Fuel Tank

Removal and Installation

1. Remove the trunk floor mat. Disconnect the battery to prevent any possible sparks.

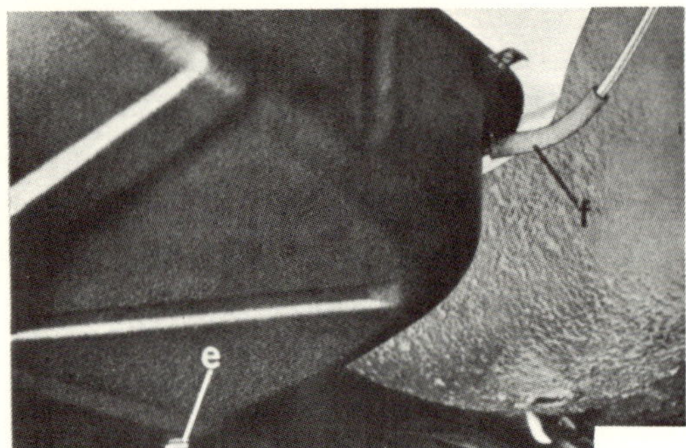

Underside of fuel tank. (e) is the drain plug and (f) is the fuel line

2. Drain the tank, using the plug at the bottom.
3. Disconnect the fuel line.
4. Detach the electrical connectors from the tank fuel gauge sending unit.
5. Detach the vent line from the corner of the tank. This may not be present on earlier cars.

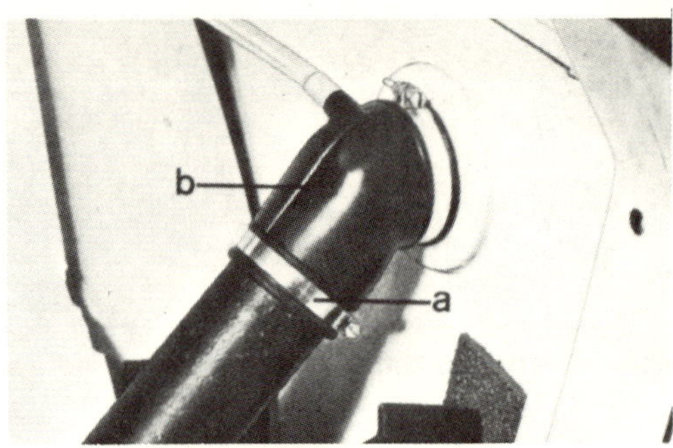

Loosen the hose clamp (a) to remove the filler tube (b) from the tank filler

6. Remove all the bolts which hold the tank to the trunk floor.
7. Detach the filler tube from the tank filler. On earlier cars, simply remove the gas cap and the rubber seal from the outside.
8. On installation, use sealant around the lower edge of the tank to prevent trunk water leaks.

Appendix

General Conversion Table

Multiply by	*To convert*	*To*	
2.54	Inches	Centimeters	.3937
30.48	Feet	Centimeters	.0328
.914	Yards	Meters	1.094
1.609	Miles	Kilometers	.621
.645	Square inches	Square cm.	.155
.836	Square yards	Square meters	1.196
16.39	Cubic inches	Cubic cm.	.061
28.3	Cubic feet	Liters	.0353
.4536	Pounds	Kilograms	2.2045
4.546	Gallons	Liters	.22
.068	Lbs./sq. in. (psi)	Atmospheres	14.7
.138	Foot pounds	Kg. m.	7.23
1.014	H.P. (DIN)	H.P. (SAE)	.9861
——	To obtain	From	Multiply by

Note: 1 cm. equals 10 mm.; 1 mm. equals .0394″.

Conversion—Common Fractions to Decimals and Millimeters

Inches			Inches			Inches		
Common Fractions	*Decimal Fractions*	*Millimeters (approx.)*	*Common Fractions*	*Decimal Fractions*	*Millimeters (approx.)*	*Common Fractions*	*Decimal Fractions*	*Millimeters (approx.)*
1/128	.008	0.20	11/32	.344	8.73	43/64	.672	17.07
1/64	.016	0.40	23/64	.359	9.13	11/16	.688	17.46
1/32	.031	0.79	3/8	.375	9.53	45/64	.703	17.86
3/64	.047	1.19	25/64	.391	9.92	23/32	.719	18.26
1/16	.063	1.59	13/32	.406	10.32	47/64	.734	18.65
5/64	.078	1.98	27/64	.422	10.72	3/4	.750	19.05
3/32	.094	2.38	7/16	.438	11.11	49/64	.766	19.45
7/64	.109	2.78	29/64	.453	11.51	25/32	.781	19.84
1/8	.125	3.18	15/32	.469	11.91	51/64	.797	20.24
9/64	.141	3.57	31/64	.484	12.30	13/16	.813	20.64
5/32	.156	3.97	1/2	.500	12.70	53/64	.828	21.03
11/64	.172	4.37	33/64	.516	13.10	27/32	.844	21.43
3/16	.188	4.76	17/32	.531	13.49	55/64	.859	21.83
13/64	.203	5.16	35/64	.547	13.89	7/8	.875	22.23
7/32	.219	5.56	9/16	.563	14.29	57/64	.891	22.62
15/64	.234	5.95	37/64	.578	14.68	29/32	.906	23.02
1/4	.250	6.35	19/32	.594	15.08	59/64	.922	23.42
17/64	.266	6.75	39/64	.609	15.48	15/16	.938	23.81
9/32	.281	7.14	5/8	.625	15.88	61/64	.953	24.21
19/64	.297	7.54	41/64	.641	16.27	31/32	.969	24.61
5/16	.313	7.94	21/32	.656	16.67	63/64	.984	25.00
21/64	.328	8.33						

Conversion—Millimeters to Decimal Inches

mm	inches	mm	inches	mm	inches	mm	inches	mm	inches
1	.039 370	31	1.220 470	61	2.401 570	91	3.582 670	210	8.267 700
2	.078 740	32	1.259 840	62	2.440 940	92	3.622 040	220	8.661 400
3	.118 110	33	1.299 210	63	2.480 310	93	3.661 410	230	9.055 100
4	.157 480	34	1.338 580	64	2.519 680	94	3.700 780	240	9.448 800
5	.196 850	35	1.377 949	65	2.559 050	95	3.740 150	250	9.842 500
6	.236 220	36	1.417 319	66	2.598 420	96	3.779 520	260	10.236 200
7	.275 590	37	1.456 689	67	2.637 790	97	3.818 890	270	10.629 900
8	.314 960	38	1.496 050	68	2.677 160	98	3.858 260	280	11.032 600
9	.354 330	39	1.535 430	69	2.716 530	99	3.897 630	290	11.417 300
10	.393 700	40	1.574 800	70	2.755 900	100	3.937 000	300	11.811 000
11	.433 070	41	1.614 170	71	2.795 270	105	4.133 848	310	12.204 700
12	.472 440	42	1.653 540	72	2.834 640	110	4.330 700	320	12.598 400
13	.511 810	43	1.692 910	73	2.874 010	115	4.527 550	330	12.992 100
14	.551 180	44	1.732 280	74	2.913 380	120	4.724 400	340	13.385 800
15	.590 550	45	1.771 650	75	2.952 750	125	4.921 250	350	13.779 500
16	.629 920	46	1.811 020	76	2.992 120	130	5.118 100	360	14.173 200
17	.669 290	47	1.850 390	77	3.031 490	135	5.314 950	370	14.566 900
18	.708 660	48	1.889 760	78	3.070 860	140	5.511 800	380	14.960 600
19	.748 030	49	1.929 130	79	3.110 230	145	5.708 650	390	15.354 300
20	.787 400	50	1.968 500	80	3.149 600	150	5.905 500	400	15.748 000
21	.826 770	51	2.007 870	81	3.188 970	155	6.102 350	500	19.685 000
22	.866 140	52	2.047 240	82	3.228 340	160	6.299 200	600	23.622 000
23	.905 510	53	2.086 610	83	3.267 710	165	6.496 050	700	27.559 000
24	.944 880	54	2.125 980	84	3.307 080	170	6.692 900	800	31.496 000
25	.984 250	55	2.165 350	85	3.346 450	175	6.889 750	900	35.433 000
26	1.023 620	56	2.204 720	86	3.385 820	180	7.086 600	1000	39.370 000
27	1.062 990	57	2.244 090	87	3.425 190	185	7.283 450	2000	78.740 000
28	1.102 360	58	2.283 460	88	3.464 560	190	7.480 300	3000	118.110 000
29	1.141 730	59	2.322 830	89	3.503 903	195	7.677 150	4000	157.480 000
30	1.181 100	60	2.362 200	90	3.543 300	200	7.874 000	5000	196.850 000

To change decimal millimeters to decimal inches, position the decimal point where desired on either side of the millimeter measurement shown and reset the inches decimal by the same number of digits in the same direction. For example, to convert .001 mm into decimal inches, reset the decimal behind the 1 mm (shown on the chart) to .001; change the decimal inch equivalent (.039″ shown) to .00039″).

Tap Drill Sizes

Screw & Tap Size	National Fine or S.A.E. Threads Per Inch	Use Drill Number
No. 5	44	37
No. 6	40	33
No. 8	36	29
No. 10	32	21
No. 12	28	15
1/4	28	3
5/16	24	1
3/8	24	Q
7/16	20	W
1/2	20	29/64
9/16	18	33/64
5/8	18	37/64
3/4	16	11/16
7/8	14	13/16
1 1/8	12	1 3/64
1 1/4	12	1 11/64
1 1/2	12	1 27/64

Screw & Tap Size	National Coarse or U.S.S. Threads Per Inch	Use Drill Number
No. 5	40	39
No. 6	32	36
No. 8	32	29
No. 10	24	25
No. 12	24	17
1/4	20	8
5/16	18	F
3/8	16	5/16
7/16	14	U
1/2	13	27/64
9/16	12	31/64
5/8	11	17/32
3/4	10	21/32
7/8	9	49/64
1	8	7/8
1 1/8	7	63/64
1 1/4	7	1 7/64
1 1/2	6	1 11/32

Decimal Equivalent Size of the Number Drills

Drill No.	Decimal Equivalent	Drill No.	Decimal Equivalent	Drill No.	Decimal Equivalent
80	.0135	53	.0595	26	.1470
79	.0145	52	.0635	25	.1495
78	.0160	51	.0670	24	.1520
77	.0180	50	.0700	23	.1540
76	.0200	49	.0730	22	.1570
75	.0210	48	.0760	21	.1590
74	.0225	47	.0785	20	.1610
73	.0240	46	.0810	19	.1660
72	.0250	45	.0820	18	.1695
71	.0260	44	.0860	17	.1730
70	.0280	43	.0890	16	.1770
69	.0292	42	.0935	15	.1800
68	.0310	41	.0960	14	.1820
67	.0320	40	.0980	13	.1850
66	.0330	39	.0995	12	.1890
65	.0350	38	.1015	11	.1910
64	.0360	37	.1040	10	.1935
63	.0370	36	.1065	9	.1960
62	.0380	35	.1100	8	.1990
61	.0390	34	.1110	7	.2010
60	.0400	33	.1130	6	.2040
59	.0410	32	.1160	5	.2055
58	.0420	31	.1200	4	.2090
57	.0430	30	.1285	3	.2130
56	.0465	29	.1360	2	.2210
55	.0520	28	.1405	1	.2280
54	.0550	27	.1440		

Decimal Equivalent Size of the Letter Drills

Letter Drill	Decimal Equivalent	Letter Drill	Decimal Equivalent	Letter Drill	Decimal Equivalent
A	.234	J	.277	S	.348
B	.238	K	.281	T	.358
C	.242	L	.290	U	.368
D	.246	M	.295	V	.377
E	.250	N	.302	W	.386
F	.257	O	.316	X	.397
G	.261	P	.323	Y	.404
H	.266	Q	.332	Z	.413
I	.272	R	.339		

ANTI-FREEZE INFORMATION

Freezing and Boiling Points of Solutions According to Percentage of Alcohol or Ethylene Glycol

Freezing Point of Solution	Alcohol Volume %	Alcohol Solution Boils at	Ethylene Glycol Volume %	Ethylene Glycol Solution Boils at
20°F.	12	196°F.	16	216°F.
10°F.	20	189°F.	25	218°F.
0°F.	27	184°F.	33	220°F.
–10°F.	32	181°F.	39	222°F.
–20°F.	38	178°F.	44	224°F.
–30°F.	42	176°F.	48	225°F.

Note: above boiling points are at sea level. For every 1,000 feet of altitude, boiling points are approximately 2°F. lower than those shown. For every pound of pressure exerted by the pressure cap, the boiling points are approximately 3°F. higher than those shown.

To Increase the Freezing Protection of Anti-Freeze Solutions Already Installed

Cooling System Capacity Quarts	Number of Quarts of **ALCOHOL** Anti-Freeze Required to Increase Protection													
	From +20°F. to					From +10°F. to					From 0°F. to			
	0°	−10°	−20°	−30°	−40°	0°	−10°	−20°	−30°	−40°	−10°	−20°	−30°	−40°
10	2	2¾	3½	4	4½	1	2	2⅓	3¼	3¾	1	1¾	2½	3
12	2½	3¼	4	4¾	5¼	1¼	2¼	3	3¾	4½	1¼	2	2¾	3½
14	3	4	4¾	5½	6	1½	2½	3½	4½	5	1¼	2½	3¼	4
16	3¼	4½	5½	6¼	7	1¾	3	4	5	5¾	1½	2¾	3¾	4¾
18	3¾	5	6	7	7¾	2	3¼	4½	5¾	6½	1¾	3	4¼	5¼
20	4	5½	6¾	7¾	8¾	2	3¼	5	6¼	7¼	1¾	3½	4¾	5¾
22	4½	6	7½	8½	9½	2¼	4	5½	6¾	8	2	3¾	5¼	6½
24	5	6¾	8	9¼	10½	2½	4½	6	7½	8¾	2¼	4	5½	7
26	5¼	7¼	8¾	10	11¼	2¾	4¾	6½	8	9½	2½	4½	6	7½
28	5¾	7¾	9½	11	12	3	5¼	7	8¾	10¼	2½	4¾	6½	8
30	6	8¼	10	11¾	13	3	5½	7½	9¼	10¾	2¾	5	7	8¾

Test radiator solution with proper tester. Determine from the table the number of quarts of solution to be drawn off from a full cooling system and replace with concentrated anti-freeze, to give the desired increased protection. For example, to increase protection of a 22-quart cooling system containing Alcohol anti-freeze, from +10°F. to −20°F. will require the replacement of 5½ quarts of solution with concentrated anti-freeze.

Cooling System Capacity Quarts	Number of Quarts of **ETHYLENE GLYCOL** Anti-Freeze Required to Increase Protection													
	From +20°F. to					From +10°F. to					From 0°F. to			
	0°	−10°	−20°	−30°	−40°	0°	−10°	−20°	−30°	−40°	−10°	−20°	−30°	−40°
10	1¾	2¼	3	3½	3¾	¾	1½	2¼	2¾	3¼	¾	1½	2	2½
12	2	2¾	3½	4	4½	1	1¾	2½	3¼	3¾	1	1¾	2½	3¼
14	2¼	3¼	4	4¾	5½	1¼	2	3	3¾	4½	1	2	3	3½
16	2½	3½	4½	5¼	6	1¼	2½	3½	4¼	5¼	1¼	2¼	3¼	4
18	3	4	5	6	7	1½	2¾	4	5	5¾	1½	2½	3¾	4¾
20	3¼	4½	5¾	6¾	7½	1¾	3	4¼	5½	6½	1½	2¾	4¼	5¼
22	3½	5	6¼	7¼	8¼	1¾	3¼	4¾	6	7¼	1¾	3¼	4½	5½
24	4	5½	7	8	9	2	3½	5	6½	7½	1¾	3½	5	6
26	4¼	6	7½	8¾	10	2	4	5½	7	8¼	2	3¾	5½	6¾
28	4½	6¼	8	9½	10½	2¼	4¼	6	7½	9	2	4	5¾	7¼
30	5	6¾	8½	10	11½	2½	4½	6½	8	9½	2¼	4¼	6¼	7¾

Test radiator solution with proper hydrometer. Determine from the table the number of quarts of solution to be drawn off from a full cooling system and replace with undiluted anti-freeze, to give the desired increased protection. For example, to increase protection of a 22-quart cooling system containing Ethylene Glycol (permanent type) anti-freeze, from +20°F. to −20°F. will require the replacement of 6¼ quarts of solution with undiluted anti-freeze.

ANTI-FREEZE CHART

Temperatures Shown in Degrees Fahrenheit
+32 is Freezing

Cooling System Capacity Quarts	Quarts of **ALCOHOL** Needed for Protection to Temperatures Shown Below												
	1	2	3	4	5	6	7	8	9	10	11	12	13
10	+23°	+11°	− 5°	−27°									
11	+25	+13	0	−18	−40°								
12		+15	+ 3	−12	−31								
13		+17	+ 7	− 7	−23								
14		+19	+ 9	− 3	−17	−34°							
15		+20	+11	+ 1	−12	−27							
16		+21	+13	+ 3	− 8	−21	−36°						
17		+22	+16	+ 6	− 4	−16	−29						
18		+23	+17	+ 8	− 1	−12	−25	−38°					
19		+24	+17	+ 9	+ 2	− 8	−21	−32					
20			+18	+11	+ 4	− 5	−16	−27	−39°				
21			+19	+12	+ 5	− 3	−12	−22	−34				
22			+20	+14	+ 7	0	− 9	−18	−29	−40°			
23			+21	+15	+ 8	+ 2	− 7	−15	−25	−36°			
24			+21	+16	+10	+ 4	− 4	−12	−21	−31			
25			+22	+17	+11	+ 6	− 2	− 9	−18	−27	−37°		
26			+22	+17	+12	+ 7	+ 1	− 7	−14	−23	−32		
27			+23	+18	+13	+ 8	+ 3	− 5	−12	−20	−28	−39°	
28			+23	+19	+14	+ 9	+ 4	− 3	− 9	−17	−25	−34	
29			+24	+19	+15	+10	+ 6	− 1	− 7	−15	−22	−30	−39°
30			+24	+20	+16	+11	+ 7	+ 1	− 5	−12	−19	−27	−35

+ Figures are above Zero, but below Freezing.

− Figures are below Zero. Also below Freezing.

Cooling System Capacity Quarts	Quarts of **ETHYLENE GLYCOL** Needed for Protection to Temperatures Shown Below													
	1	2	3	4	5	6	7	8	9	10	11	12	13	14
10	+24°	+16°	+ 4°	−12°	−34°	−62°								
11	+25	+18	+ 8	− 6	−23	−47								
12	+26	+19	+10	0	−15	−34	−57°							
13	+27	+21	+13	+ 3	− 9	−25	−45							
14			+15	+ 6	− 5	−18	−34							
15			+16	+ 8	0	−12	−26							
16			+17	+10	+ 2	− 8	−19	−34	−52°					
17			+18	+12	+ 5	− 4	−14	−27	−42					
18			+19	+14	+ 7	0	−10	−21	−34	−50°				
19			+20	+15	+ 9	+ 2	− 7	−16	−28	−42				
20				+16	+10	+ 4	− 3	−12	−22	−34	−48°			
21				+17	+12	+ 6	0	− 9	−17	−28	−41			
22				+18	+13	+ 8	+ 2	− 6	−14	−23	−34	−47°		
23				+19	+14	+ 9	+ 4	− 3	−10	−19	−29	−40		
24				+19	+15	+10	+ 5	0	− 8	−15	−23	−34	−46°	
25				+20	+16	+12	+ 7	+ 1	− 5	−12	−20	−29	−40	−50°
26					+17	+13	+ 8	+ 3	− 3	− 9	−16	−25	−34	−44
27					+18	+14	+ 9	+ 5	− 1	− 7	−13	−21	−29	−39
28					+18	+15	+10	+ 6	+ 1	− 5	−11	−18	−25	−34
29					+19	+16	+12	+ 7	+ 2	− 3	− 8	−15	−22	−29
30					+20	+17	+13	+ 8	+ 4	− 1	− 6	−12	−18	−25

For capacities over 30 quarts divide true capacity by 3. Find quarts Anti-Freeze for the ⅓ and multiply by 3 for quarts to add.

For capacities under 10 quarts multiply true capacity by 3. Find quarts Anti-Freeze for the tripled volume and divide by 3 for quarts to add.

Area Distributors

Maine
Massachusetts
New Hampshire
Rhode Island
Vermont

Volkswagen Northeastern Distributor, Inc.
Porsche Audi Division
100 Fordham Road
Wilmington, Massachusetts 01887
(617) 658—6700

Illinois
Iowa
Minnesota
North Dakota
South Dakota

Volkswagen North Central Distributor, Inc.
Porsche Audi Division
287 Northfield Road
Northfield, Illinois 60093
(312) 446—8890

Kentucky
Ohio

Midvo, Incorporated
Porsche Audi Division
5000 Post Road
Dublin, Ohio 43017
(614) 889—2911

Indiana
Michigan

Import Motors Ltd., Inc.
Porsche Audi Division
P.O. Box 2008
(2660 28th Street, S. E.)
Grand Rapids, Michigan 49501
(616) 949—7788

Florida
Georgia
South Carolina

Volkswagen Southeastern Distributor, Inc.
Porsche Audi Division
155 East 21st Street
Jacksonville, Florida 32203
(904) 355—1684

Delaware
Pennsylvania

Volkswagen Atlantic, Inc.
Porsche Audi Division
1001 South Trooper Road
Valley Forge, Pennsylvania 19481
(215) 666—7500

Alabama
Louisiana
Mississippi
Tennessee (West)

International Auto Sales & Service, Inc.
Porsche Audi Division
P.O. Box 29127, Michoud Station
4200 Michoud Boulevard
New Orleans, Louisiana 70129
(504) 254—1500

Connecticut
New Jersey
New York

Porsche Audi Eastern, a Division of World-Wide Volkswagen Corporation
Greenbush Road
Orangeburg, New York 10962
(914) 359—5000

Maryland
North Carolina
Tennessee (East)
Virginia
West Virginia
Washington, D.C.

Volkswagen South Atlantic Distributor, Inc.
Porsche Audi Division
9300 George Palmer Highway
Lanham, Maryland 20801
(301) 577—2600

Arizona
California (South)
Nevada (South)
Hawaii

Volkswagen Pacific, Inc.
11300 Playa Street
Culver City, California 90230
(213) 390—6226
or 870—3381

Alaska
Idaho
Montana
Oregon
Washington

Porsche Audi Northwest, Inc.
10350 S. W. Fifth Street
Beaverton, Oregon 97005
(503) 646—3111

Arkansas
Kansas
Missouri

Volkswagen Mid-America, Inc.
Porsche Audi Division
8825 Page Boulevard
St. Louis, Missouri 63114
(314) 429—2141

Colorado
New Mexico
Oklahoma
Texas
Wyoming

Volkswagen South Central Distributor, Inc.
Porsche Audi Division
P.O. Box 2207
San Antonio, Texas 78206
(512) 341—8881

California (North)
Nevada (North)
Utah

Porsche Audi West
7100 Johnson Industrial Drive
Pleasanton, California 94566
(415) 828—6700

Nebraska

Nebraska Porsche Audi, Inc.
8825 Page Boulevard
St. Louis, Missouri 63114
(314) 429—2141

Wisconsin

Volkswagen North Central Distributor, Inc.
Porsche Audi Division
287 Northfield Road
Northfield, Illinois 60093
(312) 446—8890